Praise for *God on Broadway*

God on Broadway dares to ask about God in the shining light and bright song and glittering tears of American musical theater. With moving and winsome prose, Gillespie overturns disciplinary boundaries while holding on to the heart of theology. He proves the sense and the use of Hans Urs von Balthasar's grand experiment in theological dramatics while moving it into a plaintive, popular register. But *God on Broadway* is also something more than all that. It is a theology that asks its readers to brave the stage of their own being and doing, a theology that dares us to meet the divine heart already and always rising to meet us at the very center of the action.

—Anne M. Carpenter, Danforth Chair in Theological Studies, Saint Louis University; author of *Nothing Gained Is Eternal: A Theology of Tradition*

God on Broadway offers that delicious sort of theology that looks for god in the silly and profane and finds god there, singing, dancing, and playing. The book does not end with this discovery, since it sees that divinity, if it is divine, must reveal art, and not the other way around. Gillespie's theodramaturgy draws us to the divine encounter that always exceeds Broadway's evergreen yearning to put god on stage.

—David V. Mason, editor, *Ecumenica: Performance and Religion*; author of *The Performative Ground of Religion and Theatre*

Gillespie's book is an exciting mix of performance studies with the power of theological aesthetics. He describes in detail how some form of divine presence is revealed in every theatrical spectacle. Drama as a mediation of God's grace? Sure! And Gillespie shows how every performance, and the community created by that immediate event, gives us "an opportunity to recognize God's possibility anew in the ordinary space between human beings." Take and read!—and be inspired.

—Anthony J. Godzieba, professor emeritus of fundamental, systematic, and philosophical theology, Villanova University

If the theatre (*theatrum*) is indeed a "place of seeing," Charles A. Gillespie's visionary *God on Broadway* is the theatrical flash which irradiates the theological potential of dramatic spectacle. With his characteristic *joie de vivre*, good humor, and intellectual hospitality, Gillespie invites his readers to return anew to classic and emerging classics in contemporary drama with an eye toward their theological interpretation. Under his thoughtful direction—in dialogue with Saint Augustine and Hans Urs von Balthasar, the unofficial "saint" of all theological dramatics—Broadway is unveiled to be a living site of theophany, recollection, apocalyptic, witness, and gift.

—Jennifer Newsome Martin, John J. Cavanaugh Associate Professor of the Humanities in the Program of Liberal Studies and associate professor in the department of theology, University of Notre Dame

GOD

on

BROADWAY

GOD

on

BROADWAY

Revealing the **Sacred** in the **Spectacle**

Charles A. Gillespie

FORTRESS PRESS
MINNEAPOLIS

GOD ON BROADWAY
Revealing the Sacred in the Spectacle

Copyright © 2025 Fortress Press. All rights reserved. Except for brief quotations in critical articles or reviews, no part of this book may be reproduced in any manner without prior written permission from the publisher. Email copyright@fortresspress.com or write to Permissions, Fortress Press, PO Box 1209, Minneapolis, MN 55440-1209.

Library of Congress Control Number: 2025009650 (print)

Cover image: Studio spotlight background with smoke, from Rattanachai Singtrangarn via Getty Images
Cover design: Kris E. Miller

Print ISBN: 978-1-5064-8185-2
eBook ISBN: 978-1-5064-8186-9

For Tara Powers

Contents

Introduction ... 1
    Sitting in the House ... 2
    Preshow Announcements and the LuPone Paradigm ... 4
    Inspirations: Theatrical Theology and *Theo-Drama* ... 7
    On *And* and *On* ... 12
    Broadway Seasons of God's Love: 2015–2016 ... 14

1. Broadway's Commercial Theology ... 19
    Broadway and Commercial Theology ... 23
    Platonic Hangovers and Patristic Performance Anxieties ... 25
    Confessions of a Theatre Kid ... 29
    Let's Go On with the Show ... 33

2. Paying Attention to Spectacle and Revelation ... 39
    Interpreting Theology, Spectacle, and Revelation ... 40
    Dramatic Revelations ... 46
    Attending and Attention That Must Be Paid ... 50
    God's Show Business ... 55

3. Playing with Dangerous Memories ... 57
    Memories of Happiness and Light ... 57

CONTENTS

	Dangerous Memory Play: Live!	61
	Staging a Theological Memory Play	65
	We've Got Gods in the House Tonight	69
	Back to Life: Theatrical Revivals	73
	God Is Love in a Time of COVID-19	75
In-One: On Instrumentalizing		83
4. Tradition and Traditions		89
	"How Do We Keep Our Balance?"	90
	"It's a Public Thing"	101
	Staging the Truth	105
	Benedictions	113
In-One: On Blasphemy		118
5. Angels and America and Apocalypse		127
	Revelation and Theodramatic Time	128
	Advent: *Millennium Approaches*	134
	Christmas: "Today 4 U"	139
	A Winter's Ball: Angelica's Rewind	143
	Epiphany: Eliza's Gasp	145
6. Staging Sacramental Spectacles		151
	Revivals, Translations, and Transubstantiations	151
	Creeds and Communions	155
	Theatrical Sacraments	157
	Hushed Wonder	161
7. Variations on a Theme		167
	"You Will Be Found"	170

Finale Ultimo	174
Acknowledgments: Curtain Call	177
Bibliography	183
Notes	191
Index	217

Introduction

What has Broadway to do with Jerusalem? Histories that link contemporary Broadway shows to the spring festivals of ancient Athens, through lush medieval pageants and liturgies, and the American vaudeville theatre are not the whole story. *God on Broadway* explores the theological questions cracked open by commercial theatre.[1] It shows how the Great White Way—that apex of tourist consumerism and a synonym for the business of spectacle—can be a place for revelations, speculative theophany, and critical theological reflection. God is ready to be part of the show. God takes the stage as the clowning Jesus Christ of *Godspell*. God seems to overhear Tevye's soliloquy prayers from the balcony. Backstage traditions and superstitions invoke God. The booming voice of a director calls cues and prophesies via "god mic." Actors religiously perform mystifying rules about a Scottish king's name. Broadway remembers God "waiting in the wings," watching, and taking part in the action.

Broadway shows operate in wider culture as a secular catechist. They instruct us about God outside the walls of an institutional church. High school drama clubs teach lighthearted and "performative" accounts of religious belonging. Original cast recordings, from *Oklahoma!* and *Les Misérables* to *Wicked* and *Hamilton*, redefine civic and theological landscapes with their distinctly popular hymnody. *God on Broadway* sits out in the house—where an audience of paying customers and strangers transform into co-players—and shows how God can be revealed in the small choices of a playwright and the flashy song-and-dance numbers of musicals.

This book is not an investigation of the many ways religious themes and symbols or biblical characters and situations have appeared on the stage. This book is also not a general theory of religion in plays or in the history of theatre. Rather, looking for God "on Broadway" is a way of *doing* Christian theology, a method for interpreting and talking about God *for* and *with* a mixed and public audience. Theology performs on Broadway. This book invites theatre lovers and theologians to play along.

SITTING IN THE HOUSE

Theatre mirrors life; like any mirror, what theatre shows depends on the angle of the viewer.[2] All writers and their books express a finite perspective too. A writer can only compose words from a particular standpoint and a particular human experience. With the aid of imagination and study, a writer can find words that reflect experiences different from their own. But those words will be nonetheless shaped by perspective. The writer of this book is a lover of Broadway and avant-garde experimental theatre and low-budget community theatre and is a Roman Catholic Christian who teaches Catholic studies. It would probably be a different book if its author despised commercial entertainment as gaudy and believed only in the truth of the Flying Spaghetti Monster. At the same time, the writer of this book did doctoral training in religious studies at a public university and wrote a dissertation about Hans Urs von Balthasar while living in and around New York City. It would probably be a different book if its author once worked professionally on Broadway as an actor or a designer or an usher and wrote as a theatre critic for a newspaper.

The ideas at play in this book have been necessarily shaped by many of the same conditions that contour its author's life: whiteness, economic and housing stability, US citizenship, a particular body with its own limitations and wonders, parenthood, fulfilling work, access to services both essential and luxurious, elite educational opportunities both academic and religious. The sense of "God" and the "Broadway" in this book emerge from the finite experience of its writer. Over time, the sense of "God" and "Broadway" in this book have evolved thanks to the darkening of Broadway stages by the COVID-19 pandemic and teaching multiple iterations of an undergraduate course with the same title.

In many ways, perspective is the point. Looking for God on Broadway reveals anew how all theology interprets the living God from a *particular* position. Theology is a human endeavor, and humans are finite creatures. Finite creatures experience the same phenomena of the world in differing ways. The image of a Broadway theater can thus be quite instructive for theologians and anyone else interested in making sense of the claims about God that give meaning, dimension, and value to human lives. There are *different* vantage points available "in the house," yet everyone sees "the same" show. This idea may require a little illumination by way of a thought experiment and example. Consider what was one of the most famous tourist attractions on Broadway for many years, itself a victim of the COVID-19 pandemic: *Phantom of the Opera* and its chandelier. An experience of that falling chandelier is *necessarily* different for those seated in the orchestra section, who *look up* to see the chandelier fall, from those seated at the top of the balcony *looking down*. Only those lucky enough to sit in the "cheap seats" get the added thrill of watching the crowd below cower in fear at the Phantom's revenge; only those lucky enough to sit "down in front" get the added jolt of adrenaline as they worry for their safety because of mega-musical spectacle.

But which of these two different experiences—that of the orchestra VIPs looking up or that of the balcony exiles looking down—saw the "real" show? An economic logic would look to pricing: surely the more expensive tickets (the orchestra) had a better position to view the action on stage. The higher price of the ticket signals the value in being so close to the magic of actors and their craft. Those in orchestra seats *experience* part of the story as unwitting, but certainly delighted, participants in the Phantom's attack. For a moment, those patrons are both on Broadway and at the Paris Opera. Yet the plot of *Phantom* raises some questions about what audiences and scholarly critics should value. Those sitting in the balcony, paradoxically, see the events that unfold in the theater in solidarity with the Phantom himself. Those seated in the balcony had the unique opportunity to watch the special effect of the chandelier transform fellow audience members, just for a brief moment, into players in the great masquerade of the show. The fictional world of the play (we remain in New York or London, not Paris) spills out beyond the apron to overwhelm the first few rows of paying audience members who perform terror or amusement or glee. Only those banished to the margins of the nosebleeds get to watch the audience become part of the meaning of the spectacle.

Already, a familiar "inside/outsider" dialectic that haunts religious studies and other academic disciplines arrives to confound the simplest of questions: Who *actually* saw the "real" show? Indulging such a question invites all sorts of arbitrary distinctions between the knowledge of the play attained by watching from row A or row Z; from partially obstructed views, boxes, standing room, or special seats up on the stage; from watching the show as one of its actors in its company or a stagehand or as an usher or as a paying member of the audience. It invites questions about *particular* performances and the random nights where things go wrong or incredibly right.

Does it matter if a great Broadway show was witnessed in its original production or with a replacement cast? Does it matter, even, if that show went on tour or became part of a middle school repertoire? There are *differences* in how a show's various audiences encounter the story performed on stage. Rather than debate the minutiae of perception, this book simply joins in the plural and public possibilities of a seat in what theatre people call the "house": that part of the theater space that welcomes strangers to become guests of the show. *God on Broadway* sits "in the house" with the audience. This is not an "insider" account of the way that Broadway religion understands its God. At the same time, it is not an "outsider" analysis of the material cultures and lived religions of Broadway companies or fans. Instead, this book offers a theological interpretation of the symbol of God as revealed on the Broadway stage and beyond from the midst of the action. This midpoint—at once insider-participant and outsider-observer—is theology's dramatic mode.[3]

PRESHOW ANNOUNCEMENTS AND THE LUPONE PARADIGM

God on Broadway proposes a method that learns from overlapping fields: ritual and performance studies, religious and theatre studies, and theology and drama. Each of these fields privileges different materials and deploys varying interpretive techniques. Promising a book with a title like *God on Broadway* creates an immediate discipline problem. What methods and dispositions could ever make popular entertainment appropriate for Christian theological interpretation? Doesn't the entire project threaten to both ruin the fun of a Broadway show *and* sully the seriousness of its properly divine subject matter? Which sorts of techniques, disciplines, rules, approaches, and methods are necessary to find God on Broadway? Perhaps there is a need for something to set the scene, to establish a theatrically theological mood.

The conundrum is not unlike one of the great ethical maxims of contemporary Broadway: Silence those phones and electronic devices![4] I am particularly fond of the occasional reminder to "unwrap candy before the start of the performance." The goal seems fair enough. These rules are about creating the environment for shivers of excitement, wonder, and applause. It can be hard to get lost in the world of a play while hearing the crinkle of a chocolate wrapper. The hush that falls over the auditorium makes way for the big revelation: a curtain rising, a swelling orchestral overture, a celebrity in the spotlight. Plays and musicals call for the same quiet audience behaviors as opera, symphony, or even an art museum gallery. Lydia Goehr points out that this attentive quiet emerges from a historical development in the nineteenth century to revere (perhaps even worship) the genius of the artist. Most audiences in the United States have been trained to consume theatre according to naturalistic expectations and their social norms: Remain seated and silently witness the illuminated spectacle on stage. Consciously violating these norms may be considered rude, threatening, amateurish, disrespectful, or trite. In musicological terms, Goehr calls this the "Beethoven Paradigm."[5]

Broadway's version of the Beethoven paradigm might just as well be named for the actress Patti LuPone. The sound of a phone call or the light emitted by a rogue text message midway through a performance can rupture what LuPone calls the "theatrical experience." Indeed, LuPone enforced that rule by snatching a texting patron's cell phone as she left the stage during a 2015 performance.[6] Earlier, during a 2009 performance of *Gypsy*, LuPone demonstrated—quite literally—how technology ruins the theatrical experience during her showstopping number "Rose's Turn." She stopped singing in order to break character and reprimand an audience member for taking flash photos: "You heard the announcement at the beginning; you heard the announcement at intermission. Who do you think you are?"[7] The preshow announcement creates a community with moral obligations to keep performers safe from harm while creating the conditions for a theatrical experience.

A theatrical experience might well also be a religious one. The "LuPone paradigm" flags how ringing cell phones and glowing electronics can threaten to profane the sacred space of a Broadway theater. Anthropologist Mary Douglas's theory of danger and taboo has been literalized.[8] Flash photography poses a direct physical danger: Unpredictable flashes threaten to distract performers who must execute highly technical choreography. Sound and light pollute the purity of the quiet and the dark, hence, the taboo of singing along with the cast at a musical or chatting with your seatmates about the costumes or plans for after-theatre drinks. Electronic devices *doubly* pollute because they crash the outside world back into the performance space.

Even three rows in front of me, illuminated electronic devices can distract from the artistic world projected by narrative, music, stagecraft, and acting. The LuPone paradigm ensures that *all* of the audience enjoys a "theatrical experience" where they might be immersed in the world of the play. But this requires collective obedience to the (divine) command of the preshow announcement delivered by a booming, disembodied voice and reinforced by the flesh and blood prophetess on stage.

Work that crosses lines of disciplinary obedience might also raise LuPone's question "Who do you think you are?" A preshow announcement will be necessary to make clear my goals in looking for, at, and with God on Broadway. This book argues that a theatrical experience is a *theological* experience. But religion has also been a rich category for correlating gods and stages. My interpretation of the LuPone paradigm by way of a classic text in the anthropology of religion highlights the immediacy between studying God and studying Broadway. The categories of performance and ritual work as well for theatrical phenomena as they do for religious phenomena.

The lesson can just as easily be taught in a classroom demonstration. I love to ask students to name the similarities and differences between the main chapel in the center of our campus and our big center for the performing arts. Both have large audience capacities, microphones, lighting, stages, props, set pieces, and changeable scenery. Both enforce the expectations of the LuPone paradigm on attendees. One is a place for theatrical revelation; the other is a place for religious entertainment. As Cia Sautter explores in *The Performance of Religion,* "We are always performing our religion, and that performance simply is amplified on stage as a crucible of reality."[9] The conversation always becomes great fun once I point out that one of our smaller performance spaces (appropriately called the Little Theatre) occupies a room that was formerly the school's Catholic chapel. Indeed, to borrow David V. Mason's title, there is a "performative ground" shared by both religion and theatre.[10]

The LuPone paradigm requires an event, but Broadway *includes* the afterlife of commercial plays and musicals as written texts that can be read, studied, and restaged by professionals and amateurs. When thinking about a drama as a literary medium, it can be easy to assume that God can be best noticed on Broadway only by means of explicit religious citations or through the work of a religious semiotics. This approach recalls one of the strategies in the field of religion and literature: Find something unavoidably present in the show's text that cites the God concept in an interesting, problematic, or revealing way.[11]

INTRODUCTION

When religious stuff appears on stage or religious symbols operate in the script, then the interpreter can start to reflect and expand on the theologies these citations carry. Religious imagery points both to God and religiously affiliated audiences for ticket sales. Pressed just a bit further, fruitfully narrow the scope of "God on Broadway" to those moments when God is a character—on stage or off—and to the scripts that take up biblical source materials or moments from religious history. Henry Bial's study of Broadway shows inspired by the Bible offers a rich testament to the importance of scriptural and religious themes on the commercial stage.[12] Such approaches put the emphasis on the ways Broadway *presents* God. Shows like *Jesus Christ Superstar* and *JB* and *The Last Days of Judas Iscariot* and *The Book of Mormon* and *Galileo* present ideas about God explicitly. Shows like *Disgraced* and *Angels in America* and *Gem of the Ocean* and *Hedwig and the Angry Inch* and *Guys and Dolls* and *The Sound of Music* present ideas about God more implicitly amid a sea of religious references.[13]

INSPIRATIONS: THEATRICAL THEOLOGY AND *THEO-DRAMA*

A popular strategy in recent Christian thought has been to think about God in theodramatic terms and attempt a theatrical theology. In other words, dramatic literatures, from the Greeks to Shakespeare to contemporary playwrights, and the practices of theatrical performance like acting and directing provide structures with which to think about God. The most well-known and influential example remains the Swiss Catholic polymath Hans Urs von Balthasar and his five-volume theology called *Theo-Drama*. A theodramatic sensibility considers the "whole theater complex" as offering "dramatic resources" for interpreting God's self-revelation.[14] For von Balthasar, drama presents a mirror of existence that reveals something fundamental about being human *and* the charged love story that is salvation history.[15] Any act of understanding and interpreting God takes place *in the midst* of an ongoing drama where God also plays a role. Both God and theologians are observers and players too.

Von Balthasar begins by finding "dramatic resources" for systematic theology at play in the art of theatrical drama: "No theological textbook has found it worthwhile to refer to the names of Shakespeare and Calderon."[16]

He dedicates the first volume of *Theo-Drama* to a review of the history of European theatre with references to individual dramatists from the ancient Greeks to Shakespeare, Calderon, Claudel, Kleist, Ibsen, Grillparzer, Shaw, Pirandello, Brecht, and Ionesco as well as great theorists of the European stage. At the same time, the *Prolegomena* to von Balthasar's *Theo-Drama* addresses some of the "elements of the dramatic" that can assist theological reflection: how human social roles relate to the idea of mission; the image of the world as a stage; the relationships between actors, directors, and authors; the cosmic consequences of action; and contests of the good. He treats the everyman theme in medieval drama, the Spanish *autos sacramentales*, and theatrical modernism all in search of the way a theodramatic analogy might provide an interpretive paradigm to understand God's action in human history. This becomes particularly important for grappling with the confrontation between the infinite freedom of God and the finite freedom of God's creatures. *Theo-Drama* argues that the world and its history can be both divinely authored (scripted) and truly free (not determined by fate).

Many theologians have taken up some version of the theodramatic analogy, either explicitly or implicitly, as a tool for interpreting classic doctrinal themes and problems. Theatrical images breathe new life into theological reflection. Kevin Vanhoozer, for example, frames the biblical witness as a kind of "script" waiting to be "played" by the acting company that is the church.[17] Doctrine takes a dramatic shape. Shannon Craigo-Snell locates the theories of stage directors as a way to theologically interpret the liturgical performance of Christian worship.[18] Larry D. Bouchard develops both a tragic theology and a theology and ethics of integrity via and with close readings of plays.[19] For other interpreters of von Balthasar, like Ben Quash, dramatic imagery organizes a theology of history.[20] Despite the limitations of von Balthasar's focus on Europe, Todd Walatka and Roberto S. Goizueta both find ways to frame the preferential option for the poor that undergirds liberation theology according to von Balthasar's theodramatic categories.[21]

In each instance, theological interpretation adopts analogies from theatre to make sense of God. Ecumenical interest in theatrical theology—including the 2012 conference at the University of St. Andrews and the Institute for Theology, Imagination, and the Arts and the subsequent volume, *Theatrical Theology: Explorations in Exploring the Faith*—joins a long legacy for Christian use of theatrical imagery for reflecting on all things divine.[22] As Wesley

Vander Lugt and Trevor Hart argue, "Theology is inherently theatrical, and it is by virtue of its object, mode, and goal."[23] That is, the object of Christian theology—the triune God—reveals Godself by *doing* things on the world stage in a theatrical way; theology operates during the very drama of history it seeks to study. The goal of Christian theology is "faith seeking performative understanding" in such a way that the intellectual content of Christian reflection manifests in Christian life, whether moral action or liturgical celebration.[24] Theatrical theology looks to the theories and methods of the theatre for inspiration and illustration. God's story can make a bit more sense when told theatrically.

The impulse toward theatrical theology is nothing new. Indeed, the image of heaven as a theater for God's glory has long been a theme in Christian thought right alongside the theme of the world as the stage for the drama of salvation. The writings and story of St. Paul offer the first theatrical theology. Consider how Paul talks about the spectacular character of Christian discipleship and martyrdom in his first letter to the Corinthians: "For I think that God hath set forth us the apostles last, as it were appointed to death: for we are made a spectacle unto the world, and to angels, and to men" (1 Cor 4:9, KJV). The poetry of the King James Version highlights how Christian discipleship becomes a performance for angelic *and* human audiences.

But the word translated as *spectacle*, here, is *theatron* (θέατρον), a word that appears in the New Testament only three times. *Theatron* occurs once in Paul's Letters to the church community in Corinth. The crucial phrase from 1 Corinthians 4:9 is often rendered in English as the "theatre of the world before angels and humanity." *Theatron* appears twice more in Acts 19, where it describes the literal theater space in Ephesus where Paul preaches to a crowd of gentiles. That evidence gives confidence to believe that the *theatron*-spectacle of 1 Corinthians 4:9—the spectacle of the apostles' lives—works like the entertaining or educational spectacles one might find in a *theatron*-theater.

Spectacles are not only flashy shows but also public demonstrations. Spectacles show something true, even if they might appear foolish at first. Indeed, Paul knows this. The very next verse invites Christians to appear like fools to the world for the sake of Christ. Performance language continues later in the letter. In 1 Corinthians 4:16, Paul will argue that the Corinthians should learn to imitate him. A theodramatic approach can make sense of Paul's charge in 1 Corinthians 9:22 "to become all things to all people" as a way to preach and share the gospel. There seems little anxiety in scripture about theatrical acting as a kind of deception or variations in role as a betrayal of Christian authenticity.[25] Paul directly seems to encourage Christians to become better actors, to render their living into a convincing spectacle of discipleship.

Disciples can perform God's love in the world in a way that can be seen. This theatrical theological praising for spectacle and performance can begin to make sense of famous Christian truisms. Francis of Assisi, for instance, often gets credit for the maxim "Preach the gospel always; when necessary use words," the idea being that a Christian *life* testifies more powerfully to God's love than Hamlet's "words, words, words." But poetry can also open and lift hearts toward a vision of heaven. A theatrical analogy becomes fitting for the interactions between heaven and earth, as a stage for angels and humans alike. Consider the final image of Dante's *Divine Comedy*. The last line of *Paradiso* imagines the saints arranged like a great stadium gazing at the Holy Trinity eternally circulating, "the Love that moves the Sun and all the Other Stars." The movement of love in the world by creaturely actors imitates the poet's beatific bright-blurry vision of the Trinity as an eternally dynamic act.

Theatrics are not limited to Catholic thought. The reformer John Calvin continuously returns to the theme of the created world as a "theater of God's glory" in the *Institutes of Christian Religion* and his sermons. Calvin's preaching on the doctrine of creation includes a consistent reminder of the importance of creaturely praise to sustain the good order of the world.[26] The audience participates with prayers and perhaps even applause for the Creator's glory radiant throughout God's handiwork. The alternative is for human actors to ruin the divine show. God, in God's sovereignty, has created a world saturated with God's beauty, but such beauty has become illegible and ruined by sin. As one commentator puts it, "Earthly beauty participates in that higher, absolute beauty which rests in God alone. It is God's perfect beauty which sends its rays into our hearts through nature and art."[27] Calvin borrows language of the stage to articulate the world's aesthetic participation in praise and thanksgiving to God.

For all these theatrical theologians, however, drama and the structures of theatre-making operate as an illustrative analogy for doing theology.

INTRODUCTION

The first volume of von Balthasar's *Theo-Drama* opens with the proclamation that his theodramatics will take interest in "the whole theatre complex [*der ganze Theater Komplex*]: that there is something that is structured as a process (as a performance) and finally: what is being played" so everything (*Das Ganze*) about drama can be made transparent and useful for theology.[28] Theatrical theology always runs the risk of instrumentalizing theatre for the sake of a theological point. As a result, theatrical theology—especially when it embraces shows as theological partners—grinds against the norms of the very conversations it aims to further.

Like von Balthasar's *Prolegomena*, my project assumes that I will frustrate readers looking for neat and tidy disciplinary procedures or lockstep agreement with his theological conclusions.[29] This book offers a self-conscious development of the approach found in the first volume of von Balthasar's *Theo-Drama*. In the 1973 *Prolegomena*, von Balthasar surveys the European theatrical canon, mostly its play texts but also its theatrical styles, as inspiration for theological work. Von Balthasar's looks to the classics: the Greeks, Shakespeare, the *autos sacramentales* and Spanish Baroque, the German *Trauerspiel*, nineteenth-century naturalism, and the rise of the modern avant-garde. Where von Balthasar prioritizes theatre as one of the high arts primarily in Europe, this book takes the subway to Broadway.

God on Broadway takes theological dramatic theory into areas of theatremaking that elude Hans Urs von Balthasar's tastes, interests, and life. Almost all the plays and musicals treated at length in this book premiered after the publication of the first volume of *Theodramatik* in 1973. Though von Balthasar might theoretically have encountered *Godspell* or *Jesus Christ Superstar* (*Jesus Christ Superstar* appeared on Broadway in 1971 at the very same time that *Godspell* premiered off Broadway), no reference to either musical appears in *Theo-Drama*. Appeals to the mass-market entertainments of the twentieth century are few and far between in von Balthasar's highly cultured prose. I aim to further the theological literary and dramatic attention to theatre achieved in the understudied first volume of *Theo-Drama*, the *Prolegomena*. Theology can work with plays and musicals in ways that are both chronologically and logically prior to doing theology with dramatic resources "after they have been thoroughly modified."[30] What von Balthasar's project lacks—all the more evident from my perspective in the United States—are some of the dramatic resources for theology made available by commercial and popular theatre in addition to the philosophical, literary, and naturalistic European drama he studies so closely.[31] Luckily, von Balthasar and I share the tendency to go on and on.

ON *AND* AND *ON*

God on Broadway proposes a method to interpret a theology on Broadway or a Broadway spirituality that informs theological interpretation. Do Broadway's acts of theatrical faith seek understanding? The work of this book will be to frame theatrical theology and readings of shows in such a way that also provides a working vocabulary to distinguish words that necessarily interchange: *God, Broadway, performance, religion, theatre, theology, drama*. That work will emerge across the chapters still to come. But let's not get ahead of ourselves. For now, it's important to tackle the rhetorical possibilities between *and* and *on*.

There are several ways to render the relationship between God and Broadway. Von Balthasar took the Germanic privilege to coin a neologism that simply spliced two Greek words for God and theatre: *Theodramatik*. (English speakers know it as the hyphenated *Theo-Drama*.) Many others place these two ideas into combination with the word *and*. Rebecca Schneider's short book *Theatre and History* raises some delightful meditations on the *and* of its title: "In a copulative conjunction, one of the words is an add-on, or surplus in some way, and as in all copulation, things get sticky, complicated, and lead to all sorts of family disputes."[32] It would make a lot of sense, following the example of theologians like von Balthasar, to construe the relationship between ritual and performance, religion and theatre, theology and drama. But many such approaches imply false or misleading binaries.[33] As Schneider wittily avers, combining ideas can lead to genealogical debates and "family disputes." The struggle to make sense of the Holy Trinity—the one God who is God the Father *and* God the Son *and* God the Spirit—shows how *and* may accidentally invite questions of logical and chronological priority. What comes first in order of articulation, God or Broadway? Does one side of the *and* govern understanding of the other? Does *and* make enough room for analogy to keep theology honest?

In hopes to circumvent problems raised by disciplinary location or grammar, my title puts God "on Broadway." *On* is a preposition that indicates both a particular location and a relationship with that place. Something "on" can be seen and encountered. A plate of food "on the table" is ready to eat; an idea "on the table" is open for discussion. To look for God *on* Broadway invites us to see God against a backdrop. In New York's American dialect, *on* is also a strange preposition insofar as queuing before the show starts requires one to stand "on line." But *on* also describes lights, anticipating the way any discussion of art and the divine will look to a theology of radiance and splendor that illuminates. And we cannot forget how *on* also means a time of performance and its evaluation as in when I must be "on" at work or "go on" to play my part in the play. To talk about God "on Broadway" means to interpret Broadway as a site for revelation. Broadway provides a space where God is "on" in a special way.

To look "on Broadway" invites pilgrimage, portability, and movement. God's appearance "on Broadway" creates an important theological opportunity.[34] There are consequential differences between the ways God can be seen "on Broadway" from the ways God can be seen "in church." That is, Broadway moves recognizable religious symbols from an ecclesial context to the context of the entertainment industry. From the Broadway producer's perspective, these symbols *must* be recognizable to cite a religious worldview for the audience. A Broadway show may or may not be interested in a transcendental meaning to the word *God* or the reality of God's love for the world, but the religious symbols used in a Broadway show need to be recognizable in order to work theatrically. In *Performing Religion on the Secular Stage*, theatre scholar Sharon Aronson-Lehavi explains "The reasons that theater artists engage with religious representations on the modern and secular stage are complex and at times paradoxical."[35] From this Christian theologian's perspective, those symbols do theological work precisely *because* they can be recognized.[36] The presence of God may well be recognized in Broadway's symbols (in some cases, precisely in the symbolic presence of God's absence). This book interprets that function "on Broadway": a place where the symbol of God appears in the middle of popular culture and entertaining spectacle.

But Broadway itself is also a contested term. As theatre scholar Stacy Wolf argues in *Beyond Broadway: The Pleasure and Promise of Musical Theatre Across America*, "When most people think about musicals, they imagine Broadway, New York City—bright lights and big city. But in fact that lifeblood of the musical is local, in productions at high schools and community theatres, afterschool programs and summer camps and dinner theatres."[37]

Wolf rightly connects the global brand of the "Broadway show" to its perpetuation through local performances and the handed-down traditions of the Broadway canon.

Broadway is to live theatre what Hollywood is to cinematic art: a synecdoche for the heart of the commercial endeavor. While Wolf narrows Broadway to musical theatre, I will also consider some "straight plays" and a few theatrical experiments. The word *Broadway* remains synonymous with theatrical spectacle: big-budget mega-musicals; well-known classics of the 1940s, 1950s, and 1960s; blockbuster shows whose soundtracks capture the national imagination for a while and seem to found and fund all manner of subcultures. Most American theatre audiences and amateur actors will not see a Broadway show, but the *standards and practices* of professional theatre nonetheless make their way into regional, school, church, and amateur productions. This means that symbol of God plays in all manner of houses, riding waves of Broadway popularity to become a fixture of American culture. So, too, then, will Broadway's theologies.

By the end, *God on Broadway* will also reveal itself to be a paradigm to notice God's performances on the world stage beyond the auditorium in the *theatron*-theater of the world. "God on Broadway" means the theophanic conversations that spill over after the show onto the street and the revelations of God that occur on the many Broadways far beyond New York City.

BROADWAY SEASONS OF GOD'S LOVE: 2015–2016

It is not enough simply to report how God happens to be "on" Broadway as if live theatre were the same sort of "on" as other references to the divine through, with, and in the arts. In fact, "God through Broadway" or "God with Broadway" or "God in Broadway" could all indicate a different sort of project. All of these prepositions, like *and*, imply a way that God may be contained or expressed or manifest by Broadway shows. I see Broadway shows as a scene partner for interpreting revelation, but it needs to be made clear that my project is not one that seeks to diagnose the theological preferences of theatre people. Instead, it selects a series of plays and musicals much with the same sort of artfulness as a comparative theologian or religious studies scholar brings different religious phenomena into conversation: "The choice of tradition and topic for comparative theological engagement is often based on chance encounters with particular teachers or programs, and on one's personal religious background, taste, and affinities."[38] So, too, the choice of plays and musicals that appear in this book emerges from my own lived experiences, chance encounters, background, tastes, and affinities. I contend that is one of the benefits of doing theology while "sitting in the house" alongside friends and strangers watching and living the same event of the show. Theologizing God on Broadway reminds all theology to become more aware of the material and human conditions and the context under and within which it is produced.

The downside to being honest about sitting in the house, however, is its necessary finitude and arbitrariness: "Out of the limitless literature of the stage I have selected only meager fragments [... and the] choice of a particular play depends on its theological fruitfulness—an admittedly one-sided approach."[39] No engagement with a particular play will be as satisfying as a full-length critical investigation; no theological move will be rigorously justified across the entirety of the tradition. Theatre, though, recalls that all theological work is already what Willie James Jennings calls *fragment-work*.[40] These are simply some of the fragments I know and teach and love. Risking Broadway's sentimentality, the goal is to help think about God and Broadway anew via the route that fragments open to the whole according to von Balthasar's dictum, *der Ganze im fragment*—the whole in the part.

But while I will permit myself to talk about Broadway's commercial theology, the method at play here is theological. Its subject matter is Broadway in the light of revelation and not the symbol of God as filtered through and presented by Broadway. Historicizing to a particular period would ameliorate some of the concerns about my idiosyncratic selections. One way to approach God on Broadway—and an early spark of inspiration for this project!—would have been to interpret commercial theologies as they operate in any given Broadway season. I was particularly struck by the interest in the symbol of God evident in the plays and musicals of 2016, many of which I treat in this book. Consider just a few of the titles from that season that either opened or played on Broadway in alphabetical order: *An Act of God, Dear Evan Hansen, Fiddler on the Roof, Hamilton, Hand to God, Les Misérables, Spring Awakening, The Book of Mormon, The Color Purple, The Crucible*, and *The Humans*. Many of the runs of these shows overlapped with a musical based on the hymn *Amazing Grace* that ran for 116 performances in 2015. Despite a dominant presumption that popular culture evacuates religiosity, spiritual questions are not strange on Broadway. These shows centered questions of transcendence enough to put religious language in their titles—*An Act of God, Hand to God, The Book of Mormon*—or embrace storied reputations about their religiously inflected content—*Fiddler on the Roof, Les Misérables, The Color Purple*. Limited only to considerations of God's presence on Broadway, the 2016 season made it clear that theology remained both commercially viable and theatrically interesting well into the twenty-first century.

The difficulty with a strictly historical approach is twofold. The first is the temptation to limit the operation of the symbol of God to its citation. These shows "count" in terms of looking for God on Broadway because they feature overt references to the divine or take extensive interest in religiosity. They play with spirituality to interrogate political, social, emotional, and existential ideas. Ivo van Hove's 2016 revival of Arthur Miller's *The Crucible*, for example, (re-)introduced elements of the supernatural into Miller's political allegory. Did van Hove's decision to take witchcraft more "seriously" or "spectacularly" (rather than symbolically as a point-for-point critique of McCarthyism) display a concern for unseen spiritual possibilities? If the magic feared by Puritanical colonists is real, then are their interpretations of God accurate? Any questions about the play's theological details take a rightful back seat to the devils in the storytelling and to current events. Theology loses a contest for attention against far more pressing material and political meanings. While something about God may very well be disclosed by the production, historicizing the spiritual citations in van Hove's choices will not have enough evidence to sustain theological engagement. Analysis of citations quickly slides toward speculation about artistic intent and what the artists were going for.

The second difficulty with a strictly historical approach derives from struggles with methodology and genre. Would a review of a Broadway season's commercial theology be a contribution to theology or a contribution closer to theatre studies? Plenty of theatre scholars do a wonderful job interpreting the way religious symbols, ideas, and structures make their way onto the Broadway stage. For the most part, "God" appears via the use of the Bible as source material (see Bial's *Playing God* or my own engagement with *Godspell* in chapter 3) or the staging of "real" religious phenomena as an element of the world of the play (I treat the latter throughout this book but at length in chapter 6). The second run of David Javerbaum's *An Act of God* in 2016 (featuring Sean Hayes in the role of God) surely fits the bill of an instance of "God on Broadway." That show's interest in biblical interpretation covers territories better mapped by Bial's methods than my own.

INTRODUCTION

But what tools and attitudes would interpret God on Broadway rather than analyze the use of "God" by Broadway? Theatre history of the theology of a Broadway season shifts the object of concern from interpreting theatrical phenomena in the light of revelation to analyzing the symbol of God in terms of preexisting theological options and resources. In his review of *An Act of God*, Zachary Stewart observes, "It's no surprise that this God is a fan of both musical theater and the gays."[41] *An Act of God*'s theology—put most simply as its organizing words (*logoi*) understanding God (*theos*)—reflects the presumed and unsurprising theology of most of the people who would make up a New York theatre audience in search of a comic evening on Broadway. This makes both good theoretical and theatrical sense because theatre reflects the life of the world. God surely delights in the panoply of musicals and sexualities evident throughout creation! The temptation becomes limiting the operation of the symbol of God so to be a fan according to some preexisting *category*: Broadway's commercial theology matches—aligns, reflects, contradicts, undermines, misunderstands, derives, or any other analytical verb—theologies that take their inspiration from elsewhere.

Finding God on Broadway via citation or via categorization are both worthwhile tools for interpreting the symbol of God on stage in the light of revelation and tools that I will use throughout this project. Historicizing the theological concepts of a certain Broadway season (or in various eras of Broadway's history) would make a major contribution to theatre studies, American studies, and religious studies. But subject matter and method differentiate the approach at play in this book. That is, my goal will be consistently to bring *attention* back to an interpretation of God on Broadway that asks theological questions informed by religious studies and theatre and performance studies. This is what makes this book as much a development of a (confessional) theological dramatic method as it is a theological treatment of plays, musicals, and popular culture.

God on Broadway both furthers theological speculation and provides a model for engaging spectacle theologically. The book asks not only how God appears outside the ecclesial interpreting community ("on Broadway" in the sense of the location and a genre of popular culture) but also how God and God's possibility illuminate Broadway shows (in the sense that theology sheds new light "on Broadway"). Enough preshow announcements. Let's go on with the show!

CHAPTER ONE

Broadway's Commercial Theology

Broadway songs have become secular hymns because show tunes are woven into the sonic fabric of life in the United States.[1] The rousing anthem "Oklahoma!" from Rodgers and Hammerstein's musical became that state's official song in 1953.[2] High school graduations and reunion concerts inevitably seem to feature *Rent*'s "Seasons of Love" or *Wicked*'s "For Good" somewhere on the program. Depending on how beloved a leader has been, retirement announcements may be unironically accompanied by spontaneous choruses of "Ding Dong! The Witch Is Dead" from *The Wizard of Oz* or *Evita*'s "Don't Cry for Me Argentina." Fans of American Public Media's syndicated business show *Marketplace* will recognize "We're in the Money" from *42nd Street* as part of the soundtrack to any day when stocks rally and soar.

Ordinary life extracts these songs from the context of plot and characterization to comment on the experience of living on the world stage. Though not a show tune, Shakespeare's version is perhaps the best-known *theatrum mundi* image in English: "All the world's a stage and men and women merely players."[3] But one of the best-known Broadway anthems for show business works, within the plot of its show, to *sell* the idea of work in and as spectacle. How do you convince a poor sharpshooter to leave the town she knows and join a traveling circus? Sing her a song about the joys of a life in show business!

The song in question is, of course, Irving Berlin's "There's No Business Like Show Business" from *Annie Get Your Gun*. Berlin's infectious tune highlights the wondrous near impossibilities of the entertainment industry. Show business means far more than just the performers who take the stage. Show business *includes* the scenography and props as well as uplifting audiences.

The song highlights an intangible and addictive "happy feeling" uniquely grounded in applause and stealing bows. (An early version of the song distinguishes show people from those in other professions that lack the immediate gratification and gift of applause.) Show business promises recognition like a star on a dressing room door.

But the song also presents the ironic truths of show *business*. The lyrics are a bit tongue-in-cheek: Is *everything* about show business appealing? Well, sometimes there are aching bodies and shows that flop. Show business leads to frustrations, lost romance, physical pain, and the ever-present threat of failure. Consider the no-good, very bad day described in a verse: Not only have your parents announced a divorce, but also your favorite uncle just died *that morning*. You learn these personal facts mere moments before the show begins. There's a depth to this dilemma that we might notice if we sit with the truth that a brokenhearted performer must go on with the show. The needs of the show and the company outweigh the passions of the actor. It's not personal; it's business. Show business must attract customers. Show business *includes* closing down a show when there are no more paying customers. And that's the trick of show people. It's not only that show business represents some fundamentally unique industry, but it also attracts a particular and unique set of people that smile even when things go poorly. The whole entertainment industry persists with an ability to see the good, to continue when all else seems lost, to seek after such a pearl of great price that one would not trade the chance to perform a "turkey" (a disaster of a play that everyone knows will go under) for bags of gold.

Perhaps show business's product—theatre—is best defined as an art for *seeing and being seen*. Perhaps that is what it means to make theatre, even Broadway theatre. Such a definition derives from the Greek origins of the word *theatre*: *theatron*, the place for seeing. This word, which moves wholesale into Latin as *theatrum*, refers to both the *place of seeing* (like a movie theater or an operating theater or a theatre of war) and an event that can be witnessed: *a spectacle*. Theatre is not simply about sight, however, because we know that all the other senses are involved: The sound of the music, the feeling of being in a crowded room in uncomfortable proximity to strangers and the warmth of the lights, the taste of a preshow meal or intermission cocktails all contribute to the theatrical experience. An old adage describes the experience of being an actor through "the smell of the grease paint, the roar of the crowd." The event of theatre describes a multisensory experience. And we know that across philosophical traditions, seeing functions as a metaphor for knowledge. Even today, one might talk about the experience of "being seen for who we are." "Being seen" means being recognized or understood, not merely being watched or surveilled or observed. Being seen describes being *known*, perhaps even being loved. Such forms of seeing transcend ocular vision. Indeed, a major theme across the Greek tragedies points out how those who are blind can see far better than those with ordinary sight.[4]

To go and "see a show," especially a show on Broadway, signals far more than merely what visual phenomena hit eyes as sensory data. "Seeing a show" describes an experience that includes bodies, physical presence, travel to a special place of seeing, internal reflection, and dialogue with others. Theatre names a spectacular encounter, a chance to be part of the show's event. Berlin's category of "show people" might be expanded to include the audience, too, because there are consequential differences between experiencing something *live*—to clap or to boo or to laugh or to cry in the same room as the performers—and experiencing something by oneself through a screen or on a page or in the privacy of the mind. Not everyone is going to feel that way; show people remain a particular subset of the human family. But Berlin's tune reminds listeners *not* to imagine the audience as a passive recipient of the show but as its coconspirator. The audience is *part* of the show; they *participate* in the role of audience member. Indeed, audiences *act*, even if the role calls for sitting, clapping, paying for tickets, and paying attention. The Brazilian experimental theatre-maker Augusto Boal coined the term *spect-actor* to describe those in the audience.[5] Theatre is a place of seeing, where the audience gets drawn into the spectacle by playing a role too.

It is crucial to notice the *negations* in Berlin's lyrics. If the song has a theory of theatre, it is articulated according to analogies along the *via negativa*. There's *no* business akin to show business. Indeed, show business lies beyond what can be conceived. There can be no cataphatic analogy to approximate the apophatic totality of the show business experience. But we can press this a step further because the word *business* has two connotations for actors. The first is the obvious way in which theatre and performance remain inextricably caught up in the entertainment *industry* and its need to make money. Buffalo Bill and his partners try to recruit Annie Oakley *because* his Wild West show is a business that needs to attract customers, sell tickets, and make a profit. But the word *business* also refers to anything an actor *does* during a scene. *Business* is the *term d'art* for the ways in which an actor's physical gestures and movements are part of the storytelling. Stage business is what lets an actor add layers upon layers of meaning to a scene or add some schtick to the show. Cleaning up clutter in a living room while having a conversation about marriage? The cleaning bit would count as "stage business." This pun on business—one that certainly takes on more life for me as an *interpreter* of the Berlin ballad than it might for its performer—is what makes this number work so well. The business (economics) of show business requires *showing* business (action). Show business must be *shown* to the audience to make sense or to make money, even if that business is naturalistically depicted human living. Show business presents something of the unnamable and untamable *more* that "gives life" and wonder to our experience. Sometimes show business presents that *more* of life with an appropriate flourish, a little razzle dazzle.

The spectacle of the stage presents the human experience anew. In theory, one could watch Annie Oakley's shooting without the framing of the Wild West show, but situating her action within the context of a spectacle turns the performance into a business opportunity. Audiences pay to witness ordinary human life shown in extraordinary ways. On greater reflection, it makes more sense to applaud the actress feigning Annie's trick shots than to applaud the plumbing of a working water feature on stage. The actress has convinced us of something *different* from ordinary life; the pipes and water merely follow the rules of fluid dynamics. But the spectacle of water as a part of the scenic design begets applause because it delights in similar ways to the spectacle of the actress embodying Annie and pretending to shoot a gun so well.

Water flows in time, and show business depends on the structure of an *event*. Theatrical showing occurs during and within history. Shows happen in time, through time. Shows are performances, after all.[6] A performance can be defined as that which exists only so long as it is done. Like all performances, shows *happen*. A show cannot be a show unless it goes on: The show, to be a show, must be shown. Perhaps that's why "There's No Business Like Show Business" ends with its own liturgical sending, show business's own great commission to Annie Oakley and to the audience to go on with the show.

Like the liturgy, a show does not really begin or end with the event of the show itself. The meaning of the event cannot be isolated to those discrete moments of performance. Seeing a show is an event that brings together the disparate narratives and lives of the show people who have prepared the spectacle and the audience members who make *this* evening with it. The social stakes are high: It is a lot of work to make a show, and it is a lot of work to attend a show. I think that's why Ethel Merman, who originated the role of Annie Oakley, could so thoroughly make this song her own throughout her career. To be a show person *means* one has the capacity to smile when low, to follow through on the commandment that the show must go on, to find life confirmed in the mutual gift of shared show-making.

BROADWAY AND COMMERCIAL THEOLOGY

Show business seems a useful analogy for thinking about God's revealing. While there are keen similarities between theology and drama, there have long been concerns about a separation between church and stage. Broadway serves both God *and* Mammon. Even the word *Broadway* signals commercial theatre as an industry based in New York City. Broadway theatre is commercial. Broadway shows operate under a categorical imperative to make money by maximizing profit. This economic fact, what Keith Hamilton Cobb has called the "American Theatre-Industrial Complex," structures everything about a Broadway performance: from high ticket prices to spectacular sets and costumes to an emphasis on speed and repeatability. As commercial enterprises, Broadway shows aim to be quickly replicable for long runs and tours. A longer run leads to bigger profits. A Broadway show avoids too much deviation from its original staging and interpretation. Why would an audience pay money to see a different version from the one advertised? But, as a result, the same Broadway show can be staged in multiple cities at once, and celebrities can be seamlessly integrated into the company. Successful design choices become part of the show's brand. Broadway shows are a *product* of the entertainment industry, and the Broadway experience offers a commodity to be consumed.

Broadway's schmaltz, glitz, and glamour have been decried as antithetical to artistic and aesthetic achievement. Broadway shows need "to give the people what they want" to be commercially viable. A moment from "Opening Doors" in Stephen Sondheim's *Merrily We Roll Along* meditates on the truth that Broadway producers want a melody the audience can hum on their way home. In some ways, critiques of Broadway's popular sentiments make good sense. Complex plots, subtle symbolism, sophisticated harmonics, and literary achievement rarely lead to a smash hit. But the history of Broadway's relationship to US literature and culture tells a different story. August Wilson,

Tennessee Williams, Eugene O'Neill, Arthur Miller, Thornton Wilder, Edward Albee, Lorraine Hansberry: These *Broadway* playwrights constitute a syllabus of major figures in the American literary canon. The book musical that finds its roots in Rodgers and Hammerstein's (and, for argument's sake, de Mille's) *Oklahoma!* marks a distinctly US contribution to the history of theatre.[7] Like the patronage system that funded the explosion of visual art and music in Renaissance Italy or the prizes associated with the best tragedies in ancient Greece, commercial intent should not in and of itself disqualify Broadway shows from worthiness for scholarly engagement and reflection.

But what about *theological* engagement and reflection? Broadway's theology cannot be considered immune from distortion due to business interests. Commercial purposes sit directly at odds with the plain-sense reading of Matthew 6:24: "You cannot serve God and wealth." Perhaps I would be better suited to look for mammon on Broadway rather than God. Plenty of shows take greater interest in demons or lampooning religion than asking evocative theological questions. At all times, a theological interpretation of commercial theatre will be backed against the wall of scriptural wisdom. Any "god" revealed by Broadway shows can be quickly confirmed to be an idol. Often, the symbols of God that populate the Broadway stage trade are presumed to be easy caricatures or merely confirm the theological preferences of popular culture. Broadway's theology might be wrongly called low-brow, pedestrian, and ultimately uninteresting *because* of its fundamental business interest.

Broadway provides one of the most obvious ritual sites to reinforce Eugene McCarraher's claims about capitalist enchantment in the United States, where the quest for profit and success in business markets adopts the place once held by religion.[8] As a result, Broadway's commercial theology displays many of classic Christian objections to theatre. Broadway privileges sensory delights over spiritual depth. One need look no further than the Rockettes and their Christmas *spectacular* to identify where Broadway-style shows diverge from long-standing Christian worries about "spectacle." By custom, Broadway audiences will clap for a kick line; rarely does a scene of interpersonal charity and social love prompt spontaneous applause. At the same time, Broadway's versions of sacred stories conjure a rush of "religious" emotions that mix nostalgia with felt presence, whether of God or an openness to transcendent Love.

Later chapters of this book will investigate some theological contributions of the revelations, memories, traditions, blasphemies, histories, and sacramental spectacles on Broadway stages. But it will first consider whether show business can, in fact, tell us something about how God shows up. Doing so requires reinvestigating some concerns about spectacle that dominate and dictate engagement with theatre in the Christian theological tradition.

PLATONIC HANGOVERS AND PATRISTIC PERFORMANCE ANXIETIES

Some scholars cite a version of the "anti-theatrical bias" to make sense of the problems posed by Broadway's commercial theology.[9] Shows cannot be trusted because they re-present reality rather than allow reality to reveal itself. Actors, sets, props, and costumes depend on fakery to make Broadway magic. Even the phrase *Broadway magic* threatens to put audiences under a spell. Theatre *always* raises a credibility problem because, by definition, *theatre puts on a show*. That is, theatre tricks the senses into believing the truth of a story "put on" by the performance. An actor represents a character, not themselves; an actor goes on to perform despite their broken heart. Scenery looks like a lush garden, but those plastic flowers and greasepaint will smell wrong. All those '50s "Telephone Hour" phones ringing that Hugo really pinned Kim might work if they were connected to a network. Dancing sailors or singing nuns never *really* earned their uniforms, but they simply put them on display to entertain. Such playful disregard for the meaning communicated by appearance trains audiences to distrust any self-disclosing power of the world. The ability to mimic, to recreate, to "put on a show" risks undoing a social sense of reason or reality. In the wake of Broadway's performativity, what counts as real?

Concerns about deception are as ancient as they are influential. One can trace an origin for the anti-theatrical bias in the European intellectual tradition to Plato, who theorized problems with imitation. Any depiction of something, however beautiful or accurate the image may be, remains a step or two away from the real thing. Plato's right, of course: One cannot eat the image of an apple on the back of a laptop or sit in the painting of a chair. *Mimesis*, the Greek word at the root of both *imitate* and *mime*, refers to this process of representation. Representations will always be fundamentally different from the reality they depict. Indeed, for Plato, our experience of the whole world consists in encounters with shadowy representations of what is ultimately true. Herein lies Plato's famous theory of forms: Every apple we see in the world reflects, in some way, the perfect "form of the apple" that exists in a divine realm.

Humans know that a chair is a chair because of the way each individual chair imperfectly mimics the ultimate truth of chairness: the perfect "form of the chair." There are many dimensions to Plato's theory—including his ingenious mythology in the *Phaedrus* that humans "remember" the forms because our souls once fell through their realm on their way to being trapped in bodies—that lead him to banish poets from his vision for a perfectly just city.[10] Inherited poetic storytelling, even if it sings beauty and goodness and virtue, can only undermine a philosopher-king's confidence in the real. Poetry, if it is to be permitted at all, should be a training in truth from the start. Plato argues that "what poets and prose-writers tell us about the most important matters concerning human beings is bad. They say that many unjust people are happy and many just ones wretched, that injustice is profitable if it escapes detection, and that justice is another's good but one's own loss. I think we'll prohibit these stories and order the poets to compose the opposite kind of poetry and tell the opposite kind of tales."[11] Of course, Plato will make space for the occasional "noble myth" to justify the organization of his imagined city's castes. But, in the training of the guardians and the structure of civic education, it is better to commit to truth and seek after the world as it really is (or should be) beyond any allure of illusion or distraction.

Even beyond the ethical and political problem of poetic representation, Plato issues a fundamental challenge to the artistic choice to represent a different world and the desire to watch those choices be performed. Representations move a step away from the real, so, in order to represent a person other than themselves, actors *voluntarily* subject their psyche to the trauma of a split personality. The imitator will "hardly be able to pursue any worthwhile way of life while at the same time imitating many things and being an imitator. Even in the case of two kinds of imitation that are thought to be closely akin, tragedy and comedy, the same people aren't able to do both of them well."[12] Even those watching shows are not let off the hook. Theatregoers crave a trip back into Plato's cave of illusions. At a basic level, the prisoners in Plato's allegory play a theatrical game. The shapes on the wall are nothing other than shadow puppets![13]

To walk into a theater, then, means abandoning hope that outward appearance necessarily radiates a *singular* inner truth. It means signing up to be distracted and confused by people, objects, movements, sounds, and stories playing at realities different from the everyday. It means paying to look at all the false shadows on the wall. Broadway's spectacles signal the great triumph of ideology: caves of intellectual imprisonment that masquerade as an escape from the mundane through the liberation of entertainment. In the words of one Broadway-cave Emcee from the musical *Cabaret*, "There are no troubles here." (And we are drawn to be distracted from political turmoil and watch the show. As Susan Sontag rightly notes, the aesthetics of fascism are fascinating.[14]) Plato's theory prefigures how spectacle can quickly become a tool to indoctrinate and normalize the logics of oppression. Shows make it easy (perhaps enticing) to ignore who does not get to sing that "Tomorrow Belongs to Me."[15]

Broadway's spectacles, perhaps, should simply be avoided. Such a view tracks with the early Christian critiques of theatre in general insofar as Christians have always gathered to perform ritual actions that recall and re-present the drama of salvation. The mimetic actions of worship must be a constitutively different phenomenon from the mimetic actions of a theatrical performance. Writing in the second century, Tertullian drew a sharp distinction between the holy spectacle of the liturgy and the dissembling spectacles of the arena. The God of truth wants nothing to do with the falsity of professional liars. Worship is serious business, and Christians spoil the celebration of God's glory by shouting hosannas in the same manner at a liturgy as they might cheer on a charioteer. Tertullian may be the founder of a Christian "performance anxiety." In a tract literally titled "On the Spectacles," *de Spectaculis*, Tertullian makes three big objections to Roman shows that are echoed and nuanced across the tradition:

1. Tertullian argues that spectacles create a problem because they rouse the passions and turn our eyes away from God. Roman shows are all the worse because they derive from worship of pagan gods or the glorification of violence. His primary objection is that shows are fundamentally idolatrous: "Every show is an assembly of the wicked."[16]
2. Christians who attend the circus or the theatre tacitly endorse their content as appropriate by their presence. Tertullian argues that cheering for the glory of a gladiator undermines liturgical songs of glory to God. Our applause and praise should be reserved for God alone.[17]

3. Tertullian supercharges Plato's problems with imitation into a claim that all forms of mimicry sin against God. Wearing masks or "putting on of voice, or sex, or age" offends God. As Tertullian writes, "The Author of truth hates all the false; He regards as adultery all that is unreal."[18]

Therefore, any form of theatrical mimesis—including playing with the performance of age or gender—rejects fidelity to God's truth through hypocrisy.[19] Creatures must show themselves in terms of the reality of their createdness. Tertullian assumes that play at being otherwise betrays a loving commitment to God. Tertullian's worries are not as antiquated as they may seem. Some contemporary audiences worry about the ways shows can be blasphemous or mock religious belief. Consider the decidedly mixed reaction to the hit musical *The Book of Mormon* or the clowning Jesus of *Godspell*. These objections mirror Tertullian's concerns about spectacle offending God. Tertullian's objections ultimately trade in the same currency as Plato's: Imitation deviates from reality; show business distorts and derides.

Theatrical spectacles inevitably seem to invite vice and distraction. Anxiety about Broadway's commercial intent merely confirms ancient wisdom about the dangers of shows. The magic of theatre poses a problem because it can convince humans to believe that anything is possible. Theatre might cause us to call into question spectacles of power or long-standing traditions or deeply held values. Theatrical play may even invite us to reconsider our own performances of identity and self. Am I anything more than the characters I play in everyday life? Does the play of the world have any deeper meaning, any truth that lasts? Can I trust the performances I witness? Can I separate a fake spectacle from a real one? What's the difference between an actor from London playing at being the prince of Denmark and an itinerant rabbi from Nazareth *playing* at being the Son of God? Plato's worry about the *political problem* of theatricality quickly found allies in the early Christian church.

The earliest Christians debated core doctrinal questions in the cultural context of the late Roman Empire, East and West. Beauty, rhetoric, images, and *spectacle* mattered in classical Rome.[20] Society remained focused on entertainment, and this posed a concern for Christian worship. According to Blake Leyerle, the early church father John Chrysostom, whose name (*golden-mouthed*) reflects his renown as a preacher and an orator, worried, "What the congregations witness in church is 'not a dramatic spectacle';

nor, he adds, do they 'sit looking at tragic actors' with an obligation only to applaud. Instead of a theater, the church is properly a 'spiritual school,' even as the work of preaching is furthered not by pandering to a taste for entertainment but by fulfilling the need for instruction."[21] But entertainment was not only distraction. One need only think about the importance of mosaic, statuary, and architecture to the Roman project. Rome established its authority with *shows* of imperial power, but these theatrics also entertained. We can imagine the bloody executions of dissidents and prisoners in the gladiatorial arenas, or we can even call to mind the horror of crucifixion as a *display* of the empire's triumph over those who might resist Roman rule. The games and the cross were popular enough to gather a crowd that would watch. Spectacles of violence grab human attention, but the spectacles that abound in Roman culture were not simply blood and gore. Major cities were filled with street performers playing bawdy comedies, lewd romances, and tragic love stories. Sex workers employed performance to grab attention and attract customers. The worship of Roman deities and civic figures (like the requirement to offer sacrifices to images of the emperor) took a decidedly *theatrical* shape.

It can be tempting to read some of these early objections as the retort of non-show people. Theatre presents a problem for philosophical or Christian life because showiness, particularly in the ancient context of sex and gore, is unbecoming of the God who is the way, truth, and life or unbecoming to the life of the cultured and philosophical human in command of their passions. But perhaps it is a biased distaste for shows and the distractions of entertainment rather than unadulterated rational or theological argument that funds their objections. It might be fairer, then, to round things out via the concerns of a platonic theatre lover: Saint Augustine.

CONFESSIONS OF A THEATRE KID

In his major work of political theology, *City of God*, Augustine of Hippo will explicitly connect licentious pagan street performances to demonic possessions as if doubling down on the threat of the diabolical in Tertullian's treatise against spectacles. But just as Roman civil society held deep concerns about the status of actors in public life, so, too, did the early church worry about actors who wanted to be Christians.

Shows belong to the Prince of Lies. *City of God* cautions against theatre's quite literal collusion with the demonic. Those depicted on Roman stages "are not gods, but malignant fiends."[22] Augustine claims unsuspecting pagans get tricked by demons into believing unworthy gods. No real deity would wish to be so disgraced by public spectacles! The stage teaches its own civil understanding of the gods. Spectacles have a theology. In Book VII, Augustine makes the point directly: "Hence it is clear, without any ambiguity, that this 'civil' theology has invited wicked demons and unclean spirits to take up residence in those senseless images and by this means to gain possession of the hearts of the stupid."[23] For Augustine, watching Roman performances— his favorite kinds are the romantic and the violent—can invite evil spirits to colonize the heart.

Augustine, of course, speaks from experience, and there is another side to his writing about spectacle. By the third book of the *Confessions*, Augustine makes clear that his misguided love for stage romances ultimately blocked his desire for God. The Doctor of Grace *adored* theatre. He was, in many senses, one of those show people, what we might even call a "theatre kid." Augustine's theological autobiography, *Confessions*, includes multiple recollections about his desire to watch stories about love and to enjoy a good cry. In fact, theatre served as one of the chief ways that Augustine tried to satisfy his restless heart's longing for God. As a college student in Carthage, Augustine would devour tragic stories about love. Augustine knows that the spectacle on stage produces quite real emotions in its audience. Fake theatre's power to make real feeling is the problem Augustine diagnoses. Love for a fictional character dulls our love for a suffering neighbor. He recycles the platonic worry about *mimesis* into an objection to theatre's pedagogy. Shows train us to love the wrong way. We develop affection for lies over truth, for appearances over depth.

For Augustine, tragedy provokes an empty catharsis for the sake of its own pleasure. Such pleasure *teaches* something about the nature of suffering in the world. Augustine weeps for the actress's lie but ignores those heartbroken by the everyday world.[24] Theatre trains audiences to *enjoy* the appearance of suffering rather than to help alleviate it. This leads to his witty takedown of theatre: the better an actress deceives, the more applause she receives. The theatregoer cries at the feigned death of a character but shrugs off real-world encounters with street performances of tragedy. Augustine identifies how the Roman bread-and-circus policy makes us forget to weep for the too-common sufferings of cruelty, starvation, slave labor, and war.

Augustine's concerns about actors' passions can be rightly extended to their audience. Spectating always already anticipates and includes participation. The mimesis of spectacle invites a similar response through, with, and in its onlookers. The performance demands an immediate response despite the audience's initial desire; such conversions happen in *real time*. Literary critic Erich Auerbach sees in Augustine's mixed prose style a peculiarly Christian turning inward to conjure and consider a richly textured inner life. Auerbach calls Augustine's writing and content—a style both biblical and Ciceronian in rhetorical resonance—"avowedly Christian."[25] The reason, Auerbach contends, is dramatic. Augustine's sophisticated Latin shimmers with parataxis, juxtaposed clauses hurtling at breakneck pace without pause or conjunction. Even in literary form, Augustine's narrative moves; words pounce. Augustine's memorable turns of phrase become turns inward to reflections on memory and, in the *Confessions*'s rhetorical "un-turning" of self-obsession, shifts focus outward toward God.

When Augustine turns to describe the performance of gladiatorial games in the sixth book of *Confessions*, "the tone has something urgently impulsive, something human and dramatic, and the form exhibits a predominance of parataxis."[26] Nowhere is this more evident than the Alypius passage in *Confessions* VI. By now, Augustine has not yet fully converted to God and still struggles with worldly temptation. He pauses his own self-narrating to tell the story of his friend Alypius's struggle with an addiction to Roman gladiatorial games. Augustine's rhetorical strategy performs how the Boalian spect-actor's experience of spectacle overwhelms, educates, and ultimately converts desires. Auerbach calls Augustine's rhetoric a drama. To provide a sense of Augustine's rhetorical effect, I quote the story in full:

> [Alypius] held such spectacles in aversion and detestation; but some of his friends . . . happened to meet him in the street and . . . used friendly violence to take him into the amphitheater during the days of the cruel and murderous games. When they arrived and had found seats where they could, the entire place seethed with the most monstrous delight in the cruelty. He kept his eyes shut and forbade his mind to think about such fearful evils. Would that he had blocked his ears as well! A man fell in combat. A great roar from the entire crowd struck him with such vehemence that he was overcome by curiosity. Supposing himself strong enough to despise whatever he saw and to conquer it, he opened his eyes. He was struck in the soul by a wound graver than the gladiator in his body, whose fall had caused the roar. The shouting entered by his ears and forced open his eyes. [. . .] As soon as he saw the blood, he at once drank in savagery and did not turn away. His eyes were riveted. He imbibed madness. [. . .] He was not now the person who had come in, but just one of the crowd which he

had joined, and a true member of the group which had brought him. [. . .] He looked, he yelled, he was on fire, he took the madness home with him so that it urged him to return not only with those by whom he had originally been drawn there, but even more than them, taking others with him.[27]

Auerbach draws attention to the verbs in this passage. The passive Alypius—an observer—gets transfigured into one of those show people: "What he has despised, he now loves."[28] Auerbach finds the sudden collisions of verbs to be a mode of speech that makes the drama of interiority visible in the *present* tense.[29] Augustine's description of embodied experience re-creates the arena's conflicts of desires and passions. Just as parataxis collapses the grammatical distance between verbs, Augustine's prose identifies Alypius's wounds with that of the warrior and the intoxication of guzzling the spectacle. Alypius, rather than the gladiator, plays the role of a fighter engaged in mortal combat. Try as he might to refuse to watch, Alypius cannot resist the *sound* of the crowd's roar. One imagines he might be drawn in by the smells of sweaty patrons and bloody combatants. When the gladiator falls, so, too, does Alypius's resistance: "The shouting entered by his ears and forced open his eyes." The crowd's roar takes control, but it is Augustine whose prose enacts that same transition from verbal sound into mental sight. Augustine crafts such a vivid description and rhetorically performs the show's power to colonize Alypius's and our minds.

Once looking, Alypius cannot resist the spectacle. His eyes become fixed (*fixit*, riveted), but what begins as an unwelcome assault slides to an inebriating glut of violent aesthetic pleasure. Auerbach identifies the "extremely dramatic" verbs with which the passage concludes: *look, yell, burn,* and *take madness home*.[30] Here, performance externalizes the internal drama of conversion in both form and content. But other sounds and performances can convert toward the good. Later, the apex of Augustine's own conversion will be famously triggered by the *sound* of "chanting" *tolle lege*, "pick up and read."[31] The passage Augustine picks up and reads from Paul's Letter to the Romans instructs him to make something of a costume change, to "put on the Lord Jesus Christ."[32] Conversion means changing *how* Augustine plays his role. Indeed, themes of interior desires made visible in dramatic action and the linkage between spectator and performer are the foundation for Augustine's performance theory.

Augustine remains one of those show people even after his conversion puts aside the temptations of Roman spectacle. The critique of Roman shows in *City of God* and the rhetorical demonstrations of theatrical and gladiatorial spectacle in *Confessions* both rely on a bedrock presumption that performance can educate desire and focus attention. He never abandons this confidence in the power of performance. Though theatre remains dangerous, Augustine locates a proper teleology for performance while preaching on the sacrament of the Eucharist. In Sermon 272, Augustine admonishes the faithful to grasp the deeper meaning of the bread and wine that are ritually transformed into the body and blood of Christ. In another flourish of language "at once dramatic and paratactic," Augustine links seeing and receiving the Eucharist to performing the church's identity as the body of Christ: *Estote quod videtis, et accipite quod estis*; "Be what you see; receive what you are." The words for *to be* that Augustine uses (*estote* and *estis* from *sum, esse*) also hold loose etymological relations with the verb to eat (*edo, edere,* or *esse*). Augustine's theology of the Eucharist intertwines seeing, being, and consuming. With the same rhetorical tactics Augustine used to narrate the sight of blood in the arena that led Alypius to imbibe madness, so, too, does Augustine theorize the vision of Christ's body and blood on a sacrificial altar and the reception of a sacrament of peace and unity. The performance that makes the Eucharist visible also invites transformation into the One whom one is called to be and, ultimately, already is.

LET'S GO ON WITH THE SHOW

The critique of spectacle sourced in Plato, Tertullian, Augustine, and others has prescient things to say about the reign and rise of social media and posting filtered photographs, the power of entertainers to persuade us to believe certain stories, and even the demonic potential to be caught up into cults of spectacular personality. Distractions from God's plan for creation connect theatre and performance rather directly to Satan, the Prince of Lies. This traditional understanding of the Devil as a performance artist persists into the present. Around Easter time, Latin Rite Catholics will renew their baptismal promises. A recent and still used version of this renewal begins with a dialogical rejection of Satan: "Do you renounce Satan? (I do.) And all his works? (I do.) And all his empty show? (I do.)"

But contemporary Christians can, however, work through the performance anxiety inherited from these early critiques of the stage and its power to distort, distract, and defile. Platonic resonances in these objections view Christian life as a zero-sum game, one where spectacle can *only* infiltrate and ruin the ways creation testifies to God's truth. But storytelling and play and creativity are also a part of God's show business. In fact, theatre may sometimes hold up a mirror that shows not only a reflection of nature as it is but can also start to show the promise of the world as it could sometimes be. Theatre's work is never done: The show must go on.

Show business seems also to promise a way to think about the ongoing showing of the world, both in the sense of the world's appearing (as described by analytic tools like phenomenology) and in the sense of the events that occur throughout the world's history. Actions *show* who we are. Paradigmatic for theology, of course, will be the showing of God's self-revelation to the world in the incarnate life of Jesus the Christ. But even before closely considering Broadway revelations, ideas from the Berlin ballad can help us stumble into a theologically rich idea: God's show *goes on*. Indeed, despite the aching bodies and hearts that result from the flops and falls of sin, God goes on showing God's love for the world.

A sense of God's show business recalls the theology of *creatio continua* (continuous creation). The world stage continues to be a place to perform only because God continues to love it into being. Creaturely existence across all of time remains dynamic and contingent to God. All the drama of human history, let alone the history of the cosmos, dwells within the play of God's own life. Consider Julian of Norwich's hazelnut "shewing" where God shows the whole of creation as if a tiny, beloved hazelnut held in the palm of her hand.[33] All of creation's busyness happens within the context of God's business of going on with the show of the world. Show-making calls the audience to participate. So, too, for creation to recognize the truth of God's love for the world. As von Balthasar explains, "The *good* which God does to us can only be experienced as the *truth* if we share in *performing* it. [. . .] This is possible because it is already a reality for God and through God, because he has already taken the drama of existence which plays on the world stage and inserted it into his quite different [*ganz-anderes*] 'play' which, nonetheless, he wishes to play on our stage. It is a case of the play within the play: our play 'plays' in his play."[34] The God who reveals Godself is intimately involved in a kind of divine show business in which creatures are invited to play a part.

The dramatic structure of God's relating to creatures most clearly manifests in ritual actions like the liturgy. Interpreting God on Broadway, however, will consistently face the problem of the root distinction between performance contexts. A liturgical spectacle differs from theatrical spectacle. As seen in Augustine, the problem is not performance itself but the sorts of desires performances educate and the realities theatre mimetically re-creates for all to see and, perhaps, become. But these dramatic concerns did not stop theatre from serving theological ends, even for these critics. The very theologians worried about spectacle also borrowed theatrical terms for debates about the mystery of the Holy Trinity. Theatre-loving Augustine's treatise *On the Trinity* (*De Trinitate*) set the agenda for centuries of trinitarian theological speculation. Tertullian offers us the earliest use of the Latin term *trinitas* to describe the relations between who we tend to talk about as the "three persons in one God": God the Father, God the Son, and God the Holy Spirit. The words *persona* in Latin and *prosopon* in Greek refer to the theatrical masks worn by actors.[35] Later theologians like von Balthasar have used theatrical analogies to explore how God relates in Godself. Perhaps God the Father is analogous to the unseen author of the script performed on the world stage by the visible Son totally aligned with the will of the Father under the inspired direction of the Holy Spirit?

History reports that many Christians anchored these concerns about spectacle in the theatre, but it would be a mistake to mobilize these critiques against Broadway alone. Indeed, Broadway spectacles merely concentrate the culture of spectacle in which we live into one industry and genre.[36] One cannot subject Broadway's commercial intent to theological scrutiny without simultaneously investigating and critiquing the commercialization of all aspects of human life conditioned by capitalist cultures, mediatization, and mass surveillance.[37] The antitheatrical bias continues to bear disproportionate weight. If Broadway cannot be a resource for theology simply because its intent is commercial spectacle, then neither should novels nor poetry edited by the publishing industry, academic research in theology emerging from tuition-driven universities in the higher education industry, or the material cultures of popular religiosity on sale in greeting card bookshops and florists. The problems of consumerism run deep for any theology.[38]

Competing commercial interests infiltrate and infect all sorts of deeply meaningful aspects to Christian life. Indeed, the dominant logic of average Sunday attendance and philanthropic goals operant at most churches seems no different from the commercial "butts in seats" approach of Broadway producers! My goal here is not to intervene about the ethics of the commercialization or aestheticization of religious life. Instead, thinking theologically about God on Broadway in particular (and theology in dialogue with theatre more generally) can provide critical tools to make better sense of Christian life in a world increasingly characterized by constant and self-conscious show business.

Ordinary, mass-produced, and commercial phenomena can *also* prompt reflection about God. They are worthy and worthwhile sites for theological interpretation not least because they so thoroughly saturate the lives, paradigms, and cultural starting points of believers, nonbelievers, and the curious. So, too, God may disclose Godself through a Broadway show even while the producers, writers, designers, and actors intend to make money as an element of show business. Broadway provides an inspiration for thinking deeply about and within the commercialized context of contemporary Christian life. Looking for God on Broadway helps theology become more conscious of the way commercial intent and its ideological distortions influence theological conclusions. In other words, that new understandings about God might be interpreted from Broadway theatre demonstrates that the symbol of God functions theologically *despite and through* commercial endeavors.

What theological insights can derive from commercial theatre? Broadway shows need to be popular, and part of that popularity regards accessibility to a mass market. When God or religious themes appear in a Broadway show, one notices the commercial viability of a story about God. Faith, like sex, sells. But, also like sex, faith sells when it presents a fantasy of perfection and access. Broadway distills and represents theories of God that are accessible to believers and nonbelievers alike. A religious story like *Jesus Christ Superstar* or *Sister Act* or *Amazing Grace* will have an easy marketing opportunity through bulk sales to church groups, but these shows must also appeal to tourists and Broadway fans of all religious and areligious persuasions. So, too, shows that use religion for laughs must walk a fine line between blasphemous offensiveness and sharable humor. Broadway has the capacity to make manifest a popular understanding of God. No business does "manifestation" quite like show business.

This popular understanding of God permits Broadway to ask vital theological questions about life today without the specialist's need to anchor those questions in a history of doctrinal development. Broadway's show business happens outside an ecclesial or academic context. That is, questions about God on Broadway are *live questions* for insiders and outsiders, participants and observers, fans and skeptics. Broadway's theology is, properly speaking, public and dramatic. Rather than find extra-ecclesial appeal as a liability, theologians should interpret commercial spectacles of the symbol of God in the light of revelation. These objections do not stop God's show from going on, and there is much to say theologically about the symbol of God by entering dialogue with its performance on Broadway. But, to do so, we need to first get clear on how a spectacle on a stage can be made ready for theological interpretation.

CHAPTER TWO

Paying Attention to Spectacle and Revelation

Theatre grabs attention. Few Broadway staples argue for this truth more directly than Stephen Sondheim's *Sweeney Todd*. The first line, reprised over and over as a leitmotif throughout the show, commands the audience to attend Sweeney's tale. The instructions are rather ironic for those who have already entered the theater and found their seats to see the production. But the idea of *attending* to the tale elevates the titillation of Sondheim's penny dreadful thriller. A creepy organ prelude sets the mood for attendance as the tale transfigures into a ritualistic summoning of the demonic barber and his anti-theology of service to a malevolent deity.[1]

Actors will "attend" to telling the story, but audience attending also means more than passive presence. Attend, here, means paying attention to the *story* of Sweeney Todd, to learn how, alongside Sweeney, to hear melodies no one else hears. Attention notices allegorical nuance and theatrical conventions, dark thrills and feats of mechanical and performance prowess that make the spectacle. This opening sequence, "The Ballad of Sweeney Todd," prepares audiences with just enough necessary backstory for understanding what will eventually happen to those who sit in the chair of the titular demon barber of Fleet Street. As in any religious drama, the basic outline of the plot will be shared from the start between performers and audience. There will be no surprise that Sweeney becomes an agent of murderous atonement. Benjamin Barker *becomes* Sweeney Todd, as does the actor who inhabits this role. And it is the actor playing (perhaps himself possessed by or being played by) Sweeney Todd who breaks the fourth wall and explains how the company should not reveal too much of the play's plot at its start. The turn to the third person—the actor playing Sweeney *referring* to Sweeney's wishes—is telling. Attending Sweeney's tale is the same as attending the play in its playing. Attention to the play is different from rehearsing a mythological summary offered by the company. Attending distinguishes itself from hearing, knowing, watching. Time spent in the theater will be spent attending Sweeney's story as performed, an act of service and participation. The tale gives itself to be attended by the playing of the play.

As seen in the last chapter, walking a route to revelation via spectacle is somewhat strange for a Christian theology and surely contested. Spectacles are more often vehicles of deception, distraction, and defilement. Anticipating some classic objections, Sweeney and company conveniently identify the demon on Fleet Street. *Sweeney Todd* presents itself for the patristic rejection of theatricality due to the dangers of demonic possession. But might it be possible to attend to spectacles of dramatic revelation that disclose symbols of God? Those symbols could help the attentive to interpret the God revealed by Jesus the Christ to be infinite, self-giving love rather than Sweeney's fictional wicked god of revenge or the demons of antiquity. Aware of the dangers, this chapter pays attention to spectacles of the symbol of God on Broadway.

INTERPRETING THEOLOGY, SPECTACLE, AND REVELATION

Spectacle can be a source of revelation. At least, that is the foundational claim that underwrites theological reflection about God on Broadway. To make meaning about God on Broadway requires a theology of Broadway spectacle. But why take the time to formulate this claim as a possibility ("can be" and "source") rather than a description ("is" or "reveals")? Revelation, in most branches of the Christian tradition, names God's self-disclosure to the world. Revelation describes when and how God communicates something about Godself. And while many different religious traditions speak about gods making themselves known to humanity, Christians understand the fullness of revelation to be found in the person of the Christ. Because the Christ is God in human flesh—God incarnate—the Christ reveals God most fully to humanity. In theatrical terms, the Christ is how God plays on the world-stage and displays and effects God's action in human history.

Consider the concretion of this claim in the language of the Second Vatican Council's dogmatic constitution on divine revelation, *Dei Verbum*: "This plan of revelation is realized by deeds and words having an inner unity: the deeds wrought by God in the history of salvation manifest and confirm the teaching and realities signified by the words, while the words proclaim the deeds and clarify the mystery contained in them. By this revelation then, the deepest truth about God and the salvation of man shines out for our sake in Christ, who is both the mediator and the fullness of all revelation."[2] Humans experience God's self-revelation in the interdependence of deeds and words: God's *action* that intervenes in history and *testimony* about that action's meaning and value. Want to make sense of how God's deeds and words fit together? Look to how God's love for the world gets expressed in the deeds and words of the Christ who shares a human heart.[3] Indeed, it is the Christ—the visible image of the invisible God—that makes God's self-revelation intelligible to God's creatures. In the Christ, God acts and speaks to humanity in a human way.[4]

The trick, of course, is that Christians have long understood the possibility of an encounter with the Christ that exceeds the physical and temporal boundaries of the historical Jesus of Nazareth. Holy scripture contains a record of God's self-revelation handed down across generations to be newly encountered today. The Protestant theologian Karl Barth identifies the "strange new world" opened by God's word.[5] That is, scripture is not simply a dead record of God's prior revealing that can be manipulated and used but offers the possibility of a dynamic participation in God's self-revealing Word in God's own radical freedom. In addition to the Bible, Christians have long highlighted the specific revelatory potential of sacraments as visible signs of invisible realities that communicate God's grace. So, too, Christians in multiple ecclesial expressions have traditions that venerate the images of holy men and women, elaborate ritual practices, and depths of beauty expressed in sacred music, art, and architecture. In a Catholic register, "Sacred Tradition and Sacred Scripture form one sacred deposit of the word of God."[6] *Dei Verbum* nearly invokes the Shakespearean image of the stage as a "mirror held up to nature" but instead reflecting the divine: "This sacred tradition, therefore, and Sacred Scripture of both the Old and New Testaments are like a mirror in which the pilgrim Church on earth looks at God."[7] It would be wrong to say that Christians understand the triune God to be shy about revealing Godself.

There is also a practical and social dimension to revelation: "Christians do not possess, not even by understanding it, the truth that God communicates to them until they succeed in transforming it into a humanizing difference within history."[8] Christians have long connected care for others to the words of Matthew 25. By *doing* works of mercy—feeding those who are hungry, offering drink to those who are thirsty, inviting those who are strangers, clothing those who are naked, visiting those who are sick and imprisoned— one engages others *as* Christ.[9] God reveals Godself in acts of care for those who suffer. This theme reverberates in Christian thought: Dorothy Day's writings on treating poor people as *alter Christus* or liberation theologian Ignacio Ellacuría's idea of those who are oppressed as the crucified people of God.[10] It would be patently wrong to limit God's self-revelation to a point of fact for an isolated theological thought experiment.

My goal is not to offer a literary review of the theological consensus on the interpretation of revelation or revelation's place within the human social situation. Instead, I want to point out the wide varieties of subject matters that constitute information about God's self-disclosure. In short, *any opportunity to know and love God can be interpreted as a human response to God's self-revelation*. If it is right to see evidence of the divine in the care shown to suffering neighbors, ordinary miracles like forgiveness between partners in a sacramental form of life, meaningful liturgical celebration, cherished family moments, beloved stories, and familiar paintings, then it might also be possible to attend to God's self-disclosure in flashy shows. The secular and commercial theatre can be interpreted as a site that "reveals" the divine.

The scare quotes are there for a reason. Suggesting that Broadway reveals God in a straightforward way is a scary thought. There are good reasons to be skeptical about accessing God's self-revelation through spectacle. And I should be honest about the theological sleight of hand in the wordplay. The theory of revelation that informs my argument assumes two things at once and asserts their compatibility: (1) Revelation is God's self-revelation, and (2) the theology that interprets revelation is a human endeavor. The first assumption is that any instance of divine revelation is always and already God's self-revelation. God is not another thing in the world or the finished product at the end of a complicated theological recipe. There are no methods or procedures to *make* revelations happen. If so, God would be subject to creaturely decisions; revelation could be summoned and manipulated like magic. God's freedom to be God, even in the midst of theological speculations and interpretations, means that any discussion of revelation depends on God's willingness to reveal Godself.[11] Luckily, Christians also believe that God's decision to disclose Godself to the world is an act of love. God chose to be known and knowable to God's beloved creatures fundamentally and fully in the incarnate person, life, work, and passionate mission of Jesus the Christ.

The second assumption adds that theological interpretations of God's self-revelation are fundamentally human activities. Meaning made from revelation must be truly *human* meaning. It makes little sense for human creatures to speak about God in the language of angels or mushrooms. If Tony Kushner's angelology is to be believed, humans probably cannot converse in angelic tongues, and there has yet to be a dictionary published by any sentient fungus among us. All theological meaning-making will therefore be *analogous* meaning-making.[12] But analogy will be the case for any and all speech about mystery. Take love, for example. The depth of the meaning of love cannot be exhaustively contained by words of description or even a long series of concrete examples. The manifold and different expressions of love throughout the world and its history crack open ordinary language with calls for poetry. How much more, then, would language stumble when trying to describe the God who is *infinite* love? Words must be finite to communicate as words; infinitely elongated speech becomes sound and mantra. Ultimately, only God—the eternal, infinite, and absolute—could eternally utter God's Word of love and still retain its sense as an act of loving communication. Humans require symbols and poetry to make mystery intelligible, tangible, and meaningful.

But another register of "human meaning" has overtones of hermeneutics, of interpretation theory. How might something new and outside of my own experience become meaningful to me? Interpretation seeks understanding when it generates meaning by working on and with some phenomenon distinct from myself. Interpretation "plays" with a text or with sensory data and so creates new meanings from experience. The play of interpretation brings meaningless material realities to life as meaningful. In theatre, interpretation most directly happens when the company embodies the script in performance. New and differing meanings can come into conversation and so open even more new possibilities for understanding. Interpretation helps make an experience of the world communicable. Humans understand when the previously unintelligible phenomenon becomes not only readable (like a text) but when its meaning can be applied to human living.[13] In the words of the philosopher Paul Ricoeur, interpretation operates when that which is foreign becomes familiar.[14] I interpret some text or object or sound or experience so it becomes meaningful to me. The act of interpretation also lets me share that meaning with others.

The structure of hermeneutics provides the ground to understand *theology as an interpretation of God's self-revelation*. Hans Urs von Balthasar makes the point most plainly in the second volume of *Theo-Drama*. He writes, "All theology is an interpretation of divine revelation. Thus, in its totality, it can only be hermeneutics. But, in revealing himself in Jesus Christ, God interprets himself—and this must involve his giving an interpretation, in broad outline and in detail, of his plan for the world—and this too is hermeneutics."[15] Theology looks to God's self-disclosure and interprets human meanings from it. Theology continues God's work of self-interpretation by learning from the model God provides in the Christ's interpretation of God, a human interpretation offering human meaning.

By calling all theology an act of interpretation, von Balthasar emphasizes contingency, revision, and what I call *interestedness*. First and foremost, theology depends on God's initiative. As an act of interpretation, theology responds to God and remains contingent to God's self-determination. By framing theology as hermeneutics, von Balthasar shows this fundamental dependency on God to set the terms for theological meaning. Interpretations that stray from their subject matter shift from hermeneutics to speculative or constructive theorizing. Philosophers in the nineteenth and twentieth centuries spilled much ink grappling with the problem of a universal method for interpretation theory that might be as true for the study of scripture as it would be for reading a brand-new novel or responding to a work of visual art. It seems that understanding, as a human endeavor, always runs the risk of misunderstanding meaning. Has truth been hidden behind or inside a text? Or is truth a category always in some way relative to power and social construction? Why should interpreters go looking for truth anyway?

Some theories, inaugurated by Friedrich Schleiermacher but echoed in debates in the United States about how to read the US Constitution, aim to anchor the understanding of truth in a text or work of art to the author's intention within that work's original context, language, and situation in the world. Other theories seek understanding as it emerges from the complex interplay of inherited traditions of meaning, personal insights, and social locations. Still others worry about the distortions of interpretation that colonize the complexity and richness of events, lives, and art works by rendering them texts to be extracted, categorized, and repackaged as "readings." These debates continue, but theatre provides an analogy for the way all interpretations remain contingent (even prior to theology's *de facto* responsiveness to God's primary act).

Theatre displays the responsive structure of interpretation. Theatre responds to life, and audiences respond to the performance as played. That is, interpretation always and already logically follows some primary act. Locating the moment of response distinguishes an interpretation—meaning-making in response to some mysterious phenomenon beyond itself—from an "original" creation despite how all creativity, in some way or another, offers interpretations of preexisting matter. Interpretations have power to shape perception, certainly, but interpretation must always remain in service of that which is interpreted. In other words, interpretations shift into "new" creations when the interpreter overpowers the distance and autonomy of the subject matter and sets new terms for the meaning of the one being interpreted.[16]

Further, theology, as an act of interpretation, will be revisable. Human meanings change over time because human cultures develop and language shifts. Indeed, by highlighting theology as hermeneutics, von Balthasar makes room for all the many ways that humans get theology wrong. Interpretation happens in the midst of history and time, so even the church's understanding of divine revelation (its doctrine) develops across the life of the world. The plausibility and efficacy of theological insights will wax and wane with history, but any revisions to understanding happen at the level of human knowledge and not God's self-disclosure. In other words, human theological interpretations can come to new and deeper understanding (or recognize mistakes and errors) without requiring that God develop into someone new or change God's mind. Creatures evolve; God remains constant.[17] Revelation unfolds across history as humans continue to learn more about God, but this does not mean that God has some unrealized potential or needs to grow like humans do.

A fullness of revelation happens in Jesus the Christ (who does, in fact, grow up as a human being), but there may be aspects of God's self-revelation that theologians have not yet cultivated the eyes to see or may have missed due to their own ideologies or even sin. Fullness does not imply totality or exhaustion; otherwise, one might presume God's self-revelation is restricted to a particular version of the Bible or limited to a historical moment in time. Rather than limit God's willingness to reveal Godself, von Balthasar shows how the Christ becomes the norm to interpret all of God's self-revelation. God has not hidden aspects of God's identity from the world, but humans will need more time to understand and interpret the full meaning of the Christ for salvation history.

Finally, and perhaps most importantly for von Balthasar, is that theological interpretation must remain interested in human experience. This is not to say that theology should twist its understanding of God to suit personal desires or social norms; recall that theology, as interpretation, is contingent on God's initiative. Rather, the interestedness of theological reflection responds to the fact that knowing God is always already a form of love for God. Anne Carpenter explains it this way: "Von Balthasar wants to see all knowing as an act of love, not as a 'full, free, and spiritual love,' but as an act akin to love. [. . .] It is not, then, facticity itself or alone that occurs in the knowing of a true thing; it is the loving acknowledgement of what is and what is meant to be."[18] Knowledge of the God who is love (1 John 4:7–12) requires not only that theological interpretations must care for the truth of interpretive statements but also that interpretations do good and express God's glory beautifully. All theology is hermeneutics precisely because theology aims to render God's self-revelation personally meaningful in the present as an act of love. In this way, theology cannot remain aloof from human experience or disinterested in the particularities of the creatures God loves. A human theological understanding does not in and of itself save—only God does that—but theological interpretation might be able to make the mystery of salvation that much more appealing, sensical, and communicable to others.

Where does this leave Broadway? With the understanding that spectacles of the symbol of God are already interpretations of God and give themselves for further theological discovery. God on Broadway is an interpretation calling for further interpretation.

DRAMATIC REVELATIONS

But can spectacle operate as a site for revelation? Would not the symbols of God in a Broadway show be like Sweeney, an idol or a demon? To look at how Broadway shows might "do" theology requires first addressing the central problem of spectacles that do invite a kind of real "religious experience" in response to fantasy. As Jean-Luc Marion identifies, "Revelation, if it can ever be conceived, arises from the question of phenomenality much more than from the question of beings and their being (existence), and certainly infinitely more than from the question of knowledge of objects (demonstration). What do we see, what can one ever see, of the invisible?"[19] My aim is not to assert that revelation always or exclusively phenomenalizes itself as spectacle but to think through how attention to theatrical phenomena might *disclose* rather than *delude*. I want to take seriously the possibility for God to make Godself known through spectacles, everywhere from the sacred biblical theophanies on Mounts Horeb and Sinai to the glamour of Broadway shows. Phenomenological attention to theatrical phenomena may also help clarify how to attend to revelation in, through, and as spectacle without mistaking the entertainment of demons or charlatans for experiences of the living God.

In a general sense, religious experiences might be plausibly considered an encounter with revelation, at least insofar as choosing to name something a "religious experience" describes an event disclosive of the absolute or transcendent or numinous. Experience takes the label "religious" when something conceived to be divine or spiritual or ineffable appears to consciousness. The phrase describes sensorial heights—"the concert was a religious experience"—as readily as it denotes more expected encounters with the sacred that point toward transcendence: rituals, spectral manifestations, sublime contacts with beauty, experiences that reflect the life of a religious community. Religious experiences are experiences, but they exceed the boundaries of the ordinary by way of the ordinary. Applying the adjective *religious* to *experience*, however, signals a depth dimension.[20] *Religious* uplifts the paradoxical capacity for this experience to manifest the invisible (to others or as such). Once further identified as a religious experience of revelation, the experience makes a claim about how one lives. A paradigmatic religious experience, then, would be theophany: a direct manifestation of some god that irrupts into the world and is perceivable in the same manner as other phenomena. But the paradigmatic case of theophany cannot be the sum of religious experiences; otherwise, it would be hard to distinguish between angelic visitation and alien abduction. But one kind of religious experience seems clearly legible: the interpretation of phenomena as revelatory and so disclosive of God.

In the Catholic-Christian paradigm from which I encounter the world, a term for such a phenomenal encounter with God is *sacrament*. A sacrament has long been defined, following Augustine, as a visible sign of an invisible reality that gives grace.[21] Sacraments reveal divine action in a phenomenal way: One can *see* that which mediates unseeable grace. In every case, sacraments manifest the presence of God by means and mediation of created things. The platonic worries about mimesis addressed in the previous chapter produced a real need to keep spectacles far away from sacraments precisely because they can be phenomenologically confused. The Eucharist *appears* to be ordinary bread; a confession *appears* to be an ordinary, if charged and hushed, conversation; a baptism *appears* to make a wet baby, and so on. Sacraments are a strong locus for thinking about revelation because the material (visible) components of a sacrament can be recognized by nonbelievers in other realms of human life or cited in other ritual actions. One does not require the eyes of faith to recognize the phenomenality of a sacrament.

Indeed, unlike the biblical theophanies or a Marian apparition or a mystical ecstasy, sacraments depend on their mundane commonality to communicate grace. *A sacrament without phenomenality is no longer a sacrament.* The logic of sacramentality posits that a disclosure of the divine in the form of a communication of grace can occur simultaneously with the ordinary givenness of phenomena while nonetheless superseding, without eradicating, ordinary meaning. In this way, sacraments reveal the ultimate end of all things in God. For the Christian, every loaf of bread and every cup of wine anticipates some possibility to become more than itself as a communication of grace. Indeed, the bread that performs Eucharist perhaps achieves a more flourishing breadly-ness than the bread that becomes a sandwich. But even a sandwich can be considered a religious experience without any knowledge or participation in the sacramentality of the created world. So what happens when revelatory "phenomena" appear outside the confines of a sacred context or religious intent? Do outward signs still mean inner graces when glimpsed not on the altar or font but on the stage? Play suspends ordinary meanings but puts the same bodies in action. Theatrical play—like all forms of play—allows the event of play to transform into a structure that displays meaning in excess of itself.[22] The reality of a play is not recognized through an examination of the biology of the players or the sociology of the theatre industry or an amalgam of Durkheim's "collective effervescence" with action and poetics and narrative.[23] Rather, in Hamlet's phrase, "the play's the thing." Risking a tautology, it is the *event* of playing that manifests the performative phenomena we call "a play." Like music, a piece of theatre—a play—exists most fully in its being performed. The theatrical phenomenon is, first and foremost, an event that gives itself to be witnessed.

The theatrical phenomenon might be better dubbed a *spectacle*. Spectacle (and its adjectival cousin, *spectacular*) suggests events of entertaining display that can be witnessed: a rock concert, a presidential inauguration, a lightning storm, a parade or protest march, a rocket launch, a lover's quarrel in a public place, fireworks, a liturgy. Any event gives itself as spectacle once framed as an event to be witnessed. There is a sort of theatrical reduction that begins to consider a performance (perfectly ordinary and mundane) as a spectacle to behold, a theatrical phenomenon. Contemporary culture offers a physical, if certainly not phenomenological, form of this reduction all the time. Events are rendered into spectacle by means of the crowds that produce their smart phones and cameras to record pictures and video. By terming the theatrical phenomenon a *spectacle*, it opens up the category of spectacle beyond the genre conventions of drama, theatre, opera, ritual, and performance art. Theatrical language and theory can then be used to clarify spectacles in various contexts beyond the art of theatre-making.

At the same time, *spectacle* nicely distinguishes those performances received as performances to be watched from those performances that are everyday performative phenomena. A performance becomes a spectacle when one stops to watch the show.[24] Some days I am captivated by the ways my coffee maker performs a spectacle of bubbles and drips and olfactory delights; other days I am captive only to my desire for the result and quality of its performance in the event of coffee making. A theatrical phenomenon needs to meet the first criteria, the spectacle. It does not really matter if the coffee maker on the stage in a play brews spectacular coffee, but, as theatrical phenomenon, it always performs its coffee making in a spectacular way.

Consider a different set of examples closer to the theme of revelation. Fire quickly becomes a spectacle when watched—pyrotechnics make for the best bits of magic in *Harry Potter and the Cursed Child*—but a fire can also give itself in ways that fade into the background. Fire might be foreground or background depending on phenomenological focus: as an element of a room's coziness, as a means for cooking, as the source of light from a candle, as a backdrop to a newsreel on climate disaster. In every case, some aspect of a fire may call for enough attention to become the focal point of consciousness and therefore a theatrical phenomenon.

The spectacle of a fire that burns without consuming a bush in Exodus 3:2, at the very same time, seems to have the capacity to reveal God. I am less concerned with the order of manifestational operations: It is clear from the text that burning bush spectacle is angelic in origin—"There the angel of the Lord appeared to him as fire flaming out of a bush" (Ex 3:2). Nonetheless, "God called out to [Moses] from the bush" (Ex 3:4), and the scriptural text attributes the speech directly to God (cf. Ex 3:5–10; 12; 14–22). God seems quite comfortable communicating alongside and through phenomena that give themselves in order to grab attention. Miracles often do. Hence, God's promise to assist Moses with "wondrous deeds I will do in [the king of Egypt's] midst" (Ex 3:20). Yet the same book of Exodus further indicates that God might communicate something of Godself via natural phenomena. The story of the great theophany includes the phrase "Moses was speaking and God was answering him with thunder" (Ex 19:19). God's self-revelation has not been compromised because God mediates God's "voice" via spectacles that, at least on the part of the biblical record in Exodus, do not require supernatural gifts to be phenomenally perceived. Fire and thunder reveal *as spectacles* of fire and thunder.

ATTENDING AND ATTENTION THAT MUST BE PAID

So what would it mean to attend a tale as theatrical revelation? To attend to something or someone means to place them as the focal point of consciousness. In phenomenological terms, attention organizes intentionality and awareness; attention characterizes intentionality toward that which gives itself by considering it apart from what operates as background. Apropos of theatre, this notion of attention sometimes gets styled as spotlighting. The light draws attention to a particular part of the *mise-en-scène*, but a spotlight does not diminish the contribution of the background. Rather, a spotlight places a particular part of the scene into focus. Literalizing the spotlighting metaphor on stage helps clarify something about attention. Sometimes the light of the spotlight is that which is attended to rather than the objects on stage the spotlight touches and illuminates. A spotlight can play a character, like when Tinkerbell flits around the stage in the first scene of *Peter Pan*. The audience's attention recognizes the light as a character by focusing attention on the movement of the light rather than the beds, walls, tables, windows, toys, and lamps that make up the set pieces of the Darling nursery.

Attention is therefore creative in some sense (and some phenomenologists would agree that analysis and description of intentionality do generate something in experience that is the object of phenomenological study rather than phenomena themselves). Attention studies further distinguish between the kind of attention that requires work (such as that which I am devoting to composing this sentence that needs to be grounded in an accurate scholarly reference) and the sort of enjoyable, effortless attention that describes what it means to be caught up in a state of flow (such as when I become so engrossed rereading a scene from a play that I lose track of time and continue reading).[25] Theatre manifests a core yearning of the human condition, one echoed in the child's or lover's cry "pay attention to me!" Theatrical space organizes attention; stages, wherever they appear, align collective attentions onto the single event.[26]

Attention is also a route to prayer. Simone Weil understands "attention, taken to its highest degree, is the same thing as prayer. [. . .] Absolutely unmixed attention is prayer."[27] Attention shifts the consciousness of the attendant to become responsive to the object of attention by placing it as focus. It is attention that focuses and so brings phenomena into the foreground. Through attention, an object becomes present to consciousness and so can give of itself in new and surprising ways. We make discoveries by paying attention. So, too, in prayer. An expansive account of prayer describes humans releasing themselves from ordinary self-possessiveness to become responsive to a divine prompt. Prayer becomes attention to experiences of God that, in the natural attitude, recede into the background.[28] Prayer, in this most capacious sense, attends to God's presence (even in apparent absence). Prayer readies consciousness to notice the phenomenality of the divine within the created world: a readiness to attend to the world as created, as the shared stage for divine action.[29]

A wide swath of religious literature contends all doing can be done as prayer. Practices such as mindfulness, meditation, and contemplation all derive from a fundamental precondition in cultivated attention *away* from the distraction of the world. Paradoxically, spectacles train attending. By orienting attention, theatre thus teaches a mode of potential prayer akin to how Weil suggests school studies "are extremely effective in increasing the power of attention that will be available at the time of prayer."[30] Put another way, theatre's organization of attention trains a responsiveness to phenomena that is ready to become prayerful. Such training derives from the way in which the stage leads objects to "double" themselves.[31] This is Antonin Artaud's idea that theatre presents itself *and* that which it makes present. The theatre becomes the space for the immediacy of *"matter as revelation."*[32] So the actor dancing the part of the Javanese god presents both dancing flesh *and* the god. Doubling applies to all elements on stage. The actor both is and is not the character, at least we hope so in the case of a homicidal barber or a suicidal salesman. The stage makes being ambiguous because stage phenomena never exit their ordinary ways of being. Theatrical objects always give themselves in multiple ways; in the phenomenological language of the theatre theorist Bert O. States, a chair on stage is a chair pretending to be another chair:[33] "What the chair made possible, in a word, was conversation: casual or exploratory talk leading to tension and crisis."[34] But a chair can also play the role of a throne or be made into the driver's seat of a pretend car. As theatrical phenomenon, the chair's ordinary way of appearing falls away without fully disappearing or disintegrating. Instead, the chair becomes transparent to its role as a chair within the world of the play and the world of the stage. The chair never ceases really being and giving itself as a chair even while it plays its role. Theatrical objects (including actors!) thus give themselves in a twofold way—as themselves and as a role in the production. The chair could be conscripted to play many other sorts of roles, but the audience sees the chair as itself and as part of the scene. A more uncanny experience goes to the presence of a real dog, a ticking clock, or running water on stage because they maintain a level of freedom that risks dispelling the illusion of the stage world.[35] Their ordinary phenomenality persists more strongly.

The same might be true about any spectacle of the human condition. Linda Lowman, wife of the titular salesman Willy Lowman in Arthur Miller's *Death of a Salesman*, reminds theatergoers that framing attention as prayer comes at a cost: "So attention must be paid."[36] Her memorable aphorism occurs in the context of theatre's capacity to illuminate human dignity. Attention must be paid to Willy because "he's a human being." The object of Linda's line can mean multiple ways: It can indicate the human actor playing Willy or a reference to a fictional character within the imagined world of Miller's play or some ambiguous combination of the two that reflects the shared human experience on stage. Linda theorizes how theatre's mirroring of human life also issues a demand. Awareness of human performances requires that we pay attention to them. All the more so for performances of suffering. The scene reveals Linda's suspicion that Willy is suicidal thanks to a sales career that fizzles and fades. The whole of Miller's celebrated *Death of a Salesman* explores how such a "terrible thing is happening to him." And, as in ancient tragedy, the audience knows more than the characters.

Linda's prayer to her children that they pay attention to their suffering father inverts the performance anxiety about suffering on stage as somehow blocking empathy for suffering in the world. Linda Lowman might be a better theatrical and phenomenological theologian. For Linda, attention to a human being's suffering—even if that suffering is *performed* as part of a theatrical illusion—uplifts the call of all suffering. Her words have the potential to invite what Nichole M. Flores calls an "aesthetics of solidarity."[37] Miller's play might become formation toward the sorts of attentions worth cultivating after the curtain has fallen. Fiction reveals the value of human dignity displayed simply in being human. If we can learn to pay attention to Willy, we can learn to pay attention to all the miseries that go unnoticed. Attention must be paid.

Such a reading of Linda's aphorism emerges from Miller's poetics and yet turns backward onto the material bodies at play. This reading proposes that the ambiguous doubling of the stage might be productive. The fictional world crafted by Miller's text comments on ordinary human life. My point, then, is not about the attention that must be paid within the "world of the play" to Willy Lowman but rather that Linda's speech materially addresses an audience attending the play in the same way "The Ballad of Sweeney Todd" invites attending his tale. Linda's point becomes about the audience's attention to a human being, not Biff's or Happy's attention (or lack thereof) to their father. Willy is, of course, played by a human actor. So are Linda, Biff, and Happy. The human being who presents Willy's humanity also presents humanity as such. Human dignity gets doubled. Linda's comment to her children expands to be a comment to the audience about attention itself, at least for those paying attention.

The cost of attention arrives in time and talent as well as treasure. Attention functions as a precursor and training for prayer precisely because it devotes the energy of personality toward the object of attention. Attention borrows time from other activities. The ritual structures of theatrical performance make the temporal cost of attention glaringly obvious: The show has a runtime during which the audience attends. A trip to Broadway costs more than the dollar amount printed on the ticket. The same can be said of the players and producers who make the show happen during that same runtime. When attention commands both time and talent, it becomes active even if the heightened experience of attention for a theatregoer or theatre-maker appears in a mode of grammatical passivity to the object of attention.

Attention does not slip into any sense of pure passivity, as if the object of attention acted on the attendant as object. Theatre makes this point quite plain. When we hear the person next to us begin to snore, we know that they have slipped into the passive attention of sleep. It would be wrong to say that the somnolent no longer receives any of the givenness of the show as phenomenon. One remains oblivious to, perhaps even lulled by, the sounds on stage and the darkness of an auditorium. Instead, a sleeping audience lacks the necessary conscious attention to actively receive the show. Those asleep receive all the same visual and aural and sensory data but in nonconscious passivity. The image of a sleeping audience can be stretched to those distracted or preoccupied with a cell phone or a side conversation. Distractions block the awakening to that which is happening right before one's very eyes. Metaphorical waking up means paying attention to what is actually happening all around. Coming to awareness does not change the facticity of the event. The show goes on even for those who sleep through it.

Instead, attention means directed action toward the reception of that which is given to me. That is, attention refers to active reception, perhaps even "full and active participation" in the mode of reception. The oblique reference to the language of the Second Vatican Council's *Sacrosanctum Concilium* 14—most memorably its English construction as "fully conscious and active participation"—underscores that such a view of attention need not mean performing roles identical to the actors in order for an audience to *act*. A phenomenology of the theatrical experience clarifies that even the audience has been doubled. Our attention to the event of the play deepens in the communal experience of attention as in the "collective effervescence" that makes laughing at a joke on stage distinct as an experience from laughing at the same joke while reading a printed version of the script.

This goes further than the literal additive of stage business, sight gags, or the amusement at how many ways an actor can interpret and deliver a line. Laughing as a group occurs differently than laughing alone. A group laughs with and for each other as often as an expression of individual amusement. Our attention to the event of the play and our theatrical experience diminish when other members of the audience divert their attention, whether slipping into the passive annoyance of a snore or the active rudeness of a glowing text message violating the LuPone paradigm. What allows attention to concretize in a fused orientation to the stage is collective attention. Otherwise, the doubling of the audience in view between my seat and the stage that forms some of the "background" to the play shifts to the foreground of my consciousness. Other people sitting in the house become an obstacle, rather than an augmentation, to attending to the event of the play as site of revelation. Critically, this collective attention does not pretend that awareness of the audience or theater space fades away. Attention must be paid to the stage, but this attention binds with the attentions of other people in the audience. One never pays attention alone. Spectacle thus becomes or carries revelation in a communal religious experience of attention.

GOD'S SHOW BUSINESS

Now that I have established some foundations for interpreting theatrical revelations theologically, the chapters that follow will consider some of the ways that Broadway spectacle can become a site for such public revelation. As I suggested in chapter 1, popular plays and musicals cannot be rejected simply due to their commercial intent or due to a simplistic performance anxiety about spectacles. Instead, theologians need to understand that a God who wills to reveal Godself and act on the world stage is a God deeply invested in show business.

Attention to spectacle opens toward prayer, and it is only prayerful discernment that will distinguish between attending to Sweeney's tale and worshipping an antichrist. Consistently, attention needs to return to God as the agent of the transaction, like the early moment from *Les Misérables* with the Bishop's advice about how his precious gift of silver has been paid to buy Valjean newfound time for a life that attends to God.[38] Spectacle can direct attention to God's revelation. If so, Anselm's definition for God in his ontological argument can be modulated into the key of Benj Pasek and Justin Paul's opening number from the 2017 film *The Greatest Showman*. God's self-revelation must be "The Greatest Show," a show greater than which none can be conceived. Ultimately, divine revelation is God's show business and the whole of creation an ongoing stage for its performance. Broadway shows, then, do not sit apart from the rest of the world that God creates, redeems, and sustains. Rather, the symbols of God that appear—whether intentionally or not—in a Broadway show will nonetheless function to prompt attention, reflection, insight, and maybe even prayer.

CHAPTER THREE

Playing with Dangerous Memories

Broadway remembers God. But what or who does Broadway remember when it remembers God?

This chapter goes in search of a more dangerous memory of God on Broadway within all of Broadway's kitsch, mass culture clichés, and even easy good feelings. Like fleeting memories of a night at the theatre, this chapter continues in a series of impressions. As a work of theology, the selection of shows and moments to treat is necessarily arbitrary; the same can be said about the arbitrary citation to a small selection of theological texts and theoretical ideas. But another aspect of that arbitrariness is that Broadway limits scholarly work to the tastes of the mass market in addition to the tastes of the theologian.

Theology conscious of its human origin tastes a bit like memoir, and a theology about mass culture risks replicating worldly assumptions rather than questioning the status quo. But the necessary arbitrariness in selection and personal memorializing can also be, in other senses, a strength of this theological method. Broadway-style shows offer a specific vantage point from which to think about God: Sitting in the house always occurs at a moment in history, and that fleeting moment must be remembered and revived later. More than other dominant cultural modes of production outside religious institutions, Broadway remembers a potency for the symbol of God. Broadway remains a place where the gods are alive.

MEMORIES OF HAPPINESS AND LIGHT

Could a chapter on Broadway and memory begin with anyone other than Grizabella the Glamour Cat?[1] Spandex and whiskers did not stop the Andrew

Lloyd Webber anthem "Memory" from escaping the confines of Broadway. Just before her selection to be the cat that will travel up, up, up to that unseen place of transformation and rebirth—the Heaviside Layer—Grizabella sings her famous ballad. The tune is well-known and the lyrics clearly inspired by one of T. S. Eliot's poems. No longer the beautiful pet she once was, Grizabella feels discarded, left alone with memories of sunnier days. In memory, Grizabella can recall when she had knowledge of happiness. She sings with hope that such a beatific memory might even live again. On stage and in her song, memory poignantly connects touch and life.

Memories of *Cats* also seem to include Christianity. The ballad about memory leads directly to the show's final tableaux: Old Deuteronomy, the mystical leader of the feline tribe, leads Grizabella to a floating spare tire and a staircase that descends from the heavens, a pathway toward new birth. In the original staging, Old Deuteronomy (played by Ken Page) reaches for the hand of Grizabella (played by Betty Buckley) in a conscious citation to Michelangelo's image of the creation of Adam.[2] The other cats sing out in quasi-liturgical mystical exaltation to the eternal life of the feline divine. These hymns to memory and life, to happiness and shouts of "vivat," feature explicit aural and lyrical reference to Christian ritual practice and places. *Cats*, in all its delightful absurdity, concludes with profoundly heightened emotion, a saturation of religious symbols, and an invocation of an afterlife where memory and beatitude will be comingled and healed. The sentimentality borders, for some audiences, on the worst caricatures of Schleiermacherian "religious feeling." Might all lost cats pass away to the Heaviside Layer like Grizabella![3]

The finale of *Cats*, like so many other Broadway spectacles, remembers and exploits religious imagery for emotional impact. (The reverse might be said for contemporary liturgical styles in Christian worship that exploit chord progressions and staging techniques for emotional impact.) Like so many beloved or despised Broadway shows, *Cats* trusts that its audience will remember religious questions and find, in the spectacle, something of an emotional answer. The pattern recalls von Balthasar's warnings about aesthetic theology. Aesthetic theology collects the conclusions of philosophical aesthetics into a theory of Beauty and subsequently applies this theory of Beauty to God as its route for theological understanding. In aesthetic theology, the Bible becomes most accessible under the rubric of art.[4] For aesthetic theology, the world's Beauty becomes the exclusive vehicle of revelation: God and Beauty are experienced as the same phenomenon.[5] Any experience of the beautiful is always and already an experience of divinity. The problem is acute for von Balthasar, who notices that, in aesthetic theologies, God only seems to reveal Godself according to already determined aesthetic categories and artifacts. Aesthetic theology creates a closed system that God can no longer subvert, subsume, or even surprise. Better, for von Balthasar, to craft a theological aesthetics: "By this we mean a theology which does not primarily work with the extra-theological categories of a worldly philosophical aesthetics (above all poetry), but which develops its theory of beauty from the data of revelation itself with genuinely theological methods."[6] Theological aesthetics asks questions about Beauty that start with what God reveals about Godself in order to delight and better understand God.

Memories of God comingle with memories of beauty, but theological aesthetics requires more thorough investigations. Left unquestioned, Grizabella's memory might limit revelations of God to a private emotional experience seeking consolation and renewed happiness. Without discernment about the differences between memories of beauty and memories of God, *Cats* would be a liturgy for monotheistic therapeutic deism.[7] We never get to see Grizabella's experience of the Heaviside Layer or witness feline resurrection in her promised rebirth to new Jellicle life.[8] Perhaps we do not need to see the outcome of the play's theological gestures at all. It is enough simply to remember the possibility of something more than the world as a marvelous junkyard ball.

Doing theology with *Cats* is a (purposefully silly and playful) stretch. But Broadway also remembers God in more direct citations, not the least of which being the seeming omnipresence of dancing and singing nuns. Spectacles of theatrical religiosity include these nuns' references to God in an old-school language that often accompanies their old-school habits. One can find Latin words of praise and thanksgiving from Richard Rodger's and Oscar Hammerstein II's *Sound of Music* to Alan Menken's and Glenn Slater's *Sister Act*. These shows present religiously garbed characters singing tunes that communicate what can be received as overtly theological ideas. While "Climb Ev'ry Mountain" might not contain many lyrics Christian or theological, the Mother Abbess sings this number in the same costume habit she wears to intone the "Preludium" and its full inclusion of the *Gloria Patri* at the show's opening and the wedding scene's *Gaudeamus Domino* and *Confitemini Domino*. But her lines in the script that precede the song make the number's theological context palpable: "What you must find out is—how does God want you to spend your love?"⁹ These nuns sing Latin prayers, and it does not take a profound leap of interpretive imagination to imbue the lyrics of "Climb Ev'ry Mountain" with an Augustinian sense of Christian hope in God's love that does not compete with love in the world. The Mother Abbess lends support for Maria's restless heart on a lifelong pilgrimage to follow rainbows and find dreams.¹⁰ In context, "Climb Ev'ry Mountain" provides the spiritual direction inviting Maria's further discernment of God's will for her life as well as her understanding of God.

Along the same lines, the conceit of a dying Philadelphia parish saved by a lounge singer in the witness protection program—who dons a black habit to masquerade as one of the Holy Order of the Little Sisters of Our Mother of Perpetual Faith—seems even more far afield from remembering the living God. Part of the plot celebrates how nuns who sing popular music can make a church popular again (and, crucially, secure bigger donations). *Sister Act* collapses the distance between the commercialism of the performance of religiosity on Broadway and the real need for religious services to be entertaining to draw a crowd willing to provide financial support. The number "Raise Your Voice," however, integrates Latin text from the liturgy. After a round of hallelujahs, Deloris calls for a Gloria. The elderly Sister Mary Lazarus ups the tempo for *Laudamus Te! Benedicimus Te! Adoramus Te! Glorificamus Te!* The shy Sister Mary Robert finds her voice to belt out the name of the Lord: *Iesu Christe in Gloria Dei Patris*! The staging offers a romantic fantasy for how a predominantly white Catholic community might encounter, recognize, and praise God's glory in the style of a Black Catholic liturgical tradition.¹¹ Far from imperial imposition, the language of the Gloria in Latin crosses cultural boundaries; the show chose this number to be featured in a performance at the Tony Awards. Within the world of *Sister Act*, Sister Mary Clarence's inculturation even receives a confirmatory visit from the pope! In its context of performance, could this joyful noise invite the audience to a moment of prayerful praising, blessing, adoring, and glorifying Jesus Christ in the glory of God the Father? "Raise Your Voice" imagines the glory of the Lord liberated to resound in the midst of the contemporary world's troubles. Members of a marginalized community—be they religious sisters, poor women of color, those oppressed by gun violence—finding and raising their voices is God's glory.

The frequency of Catholic sisters on Broadway concretizes a point: Broadway often trusts that its audience will remember God, or, at the very least, the public performances of communities of faith. Theologically, these passing spectacles of religious imagery seem to remember a God with divine perfections like Rodgers and Hammerstein's "happiness and light." Indeed, the God remembered by *Cats*, *The Sound of Music*, and *Sister Act* might be most readily presented as a God of sentimentality and bourgeois comfort rather than the God revealed by and through Jesus the Christ. On Broadway, it can be hard to distinguish religious feelings from aesthetic delights. We find God on Broadway when the show confirms who and what we want God to be. Such an aesthetic theology, to borrow von Balthasar's category, does not get God totally wrong. God does grace God's people in palpable and affective ways. But religious sentimentality is not and should not be the whole theological story because it cannot be communicated or shared with a public. That is, these citations of God only work theologically as an interpretation of revelation via some sort of confirmation bias on the part of their audiences. Any depth in the religious symbol remains opaque for those who lack eyes of faith.[12] Religious aesthetics—in this case, Christian aesthetics—can be fruitfully employed as ornamentation and setting.[13] But the citational memory of God in these sorts of shows does theological work only when further funded by the theologies of its audiences outside the world of the play. These shows offer little to critique or nuance the reign of religious aesthetic emotivism. There is nothing categorically wrong or evil or silly or absurd about a theology informed by the pleasure of a beloved Broadway show or the memory of a show tune that sometimes transfigures into prayer.[14] All sorts of Broadway shows remember God, but sometimes those memories are, simply put, safe.

DANGEROUS MEMORY PLAY: LIVE!

An alternative to a "safe" memory of God might be a version of what Johann Baptist Metz calls "the dangerous memory of Jesus Christ." There is the chance to notice that dangerous memory hidden even in *Cats*, *The Sound of Music*, and *Sister Act*: Each show might be contorted into the story of God's unconditional love extended to those oppressed and forgotten. But the entertainment industry does not hold any inherent responsibility to carry dangerous memory. Instead, this is the "ancient unchanging task of Christian theology: to speak about the God of Jesus by trying to make the connection between the Christian message and the contemporary world visible, and trying to articulate its tradition as an unrequited and dangerous memory in this world."¹⁵ Metz contends that Christian faith expresses itself fundamentally in and as memory of God's liberatory actions and promise. The church bears a memory of Jesus that "is no bourgeois counterfigure to hope. On the contrary, it holds a particular anticipation of the future as a future for the hopeless, the shattered and oppressed. In this way it is *a dangerous and liberating memory*, which badgers the present and calls it into question, since it does not remember just any open future, but precisely this future, and because it compels believers to be in a continual state of transformation in order to take this future into account."¹⁶ Metz provides a clear way to distinguish between sentimental memories of God that provide happiness and light only inwardly to the individual and dangerous memories of God that provoke social responsibility to act. Danger persists in both the willingness to bring human memory close to God and the risks presented to the status quo. Sentimental memories try to replicate the past in the present moment; dangerous memories promise a new future to those who are suffering.

There is an obvious historical connection that accounts for some of the ways Broadway remembers God. Danger refers to proximity. Broadway can play along with a genealogy for Western theatre-making that keeps ritual, religion, myth, and entertainment in close company. Theatre brings divine mystery into the midst of human experience. According to von Balthasar, "The cultic origin of our theatre is beyond doubt; the *risky* undertaking of a synthesis between the way man sees himself and his encounter with the divine myth as it manifests itself to him . . . takes place at the *dangerous* borderline where magic and revelation cannot be told apart."¹⁷ This version of the story gathers the tragedies of ancient Greece, the pageantry of imperial Rome, the mystery plays of medieval Christendom and finds the great theatrical synthesis for English speakers in Shakespeare's Wooden O. Broadway inherits the long-standing connections and anxieties among players and prayers, gods as characters, and entertainment within an act of worship. Like all genealogies, this history of theatre layers a convenient narrative on top of family resemblances. One can draw a deceptively straight line of transtemporal westward migration from Aeschylus's Athens to Hildegard's Rhineland to Marlow's London to O'Neill's New York. Such simplistic origin stories ignore the spirits that walk about in Noh drama or performances that manifest local deities in India, but it makes for a compelling narrative of fictive kinship.

Rather than rehash that European theatrical genealogy, it makes more sense to be informed by work in theatre and performance studies on the rich ways that religion and theatre intertwine with cross-cultural complexity. Antonin Artaud found inspiration for his "theatre of cruelty" in Javanese dance.[18] Richard Schechner grew performance studies out of seedlings from anthropology.[19] Indeed, David V. Mason argues for a "performative ground" for both religion and theatre as human practices of making—*poesis*. The divinities encountered in theatrical performances are decidedly "not fake."[20]

Religion and theatre scholarship housed in the fields of theatre or performance studies typically focuses on the material conditions of theatre-making. That is, theatrical drama's central convention is that it happens in the present and the presence of an audience that could, at any moment, become a part of the event. But this fact does not elude even a theologian like von Balthasar: "There is a certain hubris involved in showing the point of encounter between the human question and the divine answer in an event performed by human beings. This hubris will always be there in the background in all theatrical performance, awakening in the spectator a tense expectation that he will learn something revealing about the mystery of life."[21]

The material condition of theatre-making in "tense expectation" also holds true for drama as a literary genre; dramatic texts, including philosophical or theological dialogues, are scripts that invite readers to perform. Drama includes and leads to productive tensions and sharp changes. And it is performance theory that reminds us how the capacity to join in a play at any moment is material. Only good social and cultural formation stops the audience from rushing on stage to stop the tragedy of Othello, or Hamlet, or Jesus, or Antigone, or Orpheus. The great Brazilian theatre-maker and theorist Augusto Boal calls everyone who attends any performance a spect-actor, always already ready to join the drama.[22] Only the conventions of the LuPone paradigm stop Broadway audiences from intervening in the action on stage. Drama, at perhaps its most basic level, demands being swept up into the moment *now*.

Drama symbolizes a human event that brings memory into presence. Memory also works as a kind of making present. At first blush, memory brings an image of separation. Memory recalls the past that is no longer living present by re-presenting it, making it live. Broadway remembers how God used to be relevant to extra-ecclesial life or uplifts nostalgia for a bygone childhood. It would be easy to see how religious citations, then, invite audiences to reflect on religious ideas as part of the spectacle but to keep theological realities at arm's length. Memory accesses something located apart in time and space. That which is remembered is past, perhaps dead, and brought back to life through human doing.[23]

Theatre brings memory to life, perhaps even literally as theatre's memories are presented before and with a living audience. Theatre not only reflects the life of human existence but also demands human liveness as its artistic medium. Broadway memories live in the liveness of performance. Peggy Phelan describes performance's fundamental connection to liveness: "Only life is in the present. Performance cannot be saved, recorded, documented, or otherwise participate in the circulation of representations of representations."[24] Performances disappear. When one encounters a recording of a performance, one mediates performing via a different artistic genre and material condition. Broadway has always held a close connection to mass media, especially television.[25] Watching a Broadway show at home on screen—even if it is a filmed version of the original cast, as in the streaming version of *Hamilton* I will discuss in a later chapter—enables theatrical remembering differently from an experience of the performance live.

Broadway, as treated in this book, demonstrates how theatrical memories of God can start to shed what José Esteban Muñoz calls the "burden of liveness" by means of Broadway's close connection to mass media.[26] I have taken Muñoz's term slightly away from its context. He describes the burden of liveness as a disproportionate expectation placed on performers of color to create entertainment by means of their bodies, but liveness as "burden" extends to analyses of Broadway. The cost to attend a Broadway show in its ritual context places a disproportionate burden on making sense of God on Broadway. Liveness contributes much to the meaning-making of a Broadway show but significantly decreases its accessibility. Theological work with Broadway in all its various forms and legacies needs to remain aware of liveness as a burden rather than an ontological premise. But even a recording of a Broadway show remembers its liveness, the fact that it was done in a place and time in mutual copresence.

Remembering a show, then, projects a kind of participation within its event continued, even now, in the present of my experience of it. As performance theory explains, theatrical performance eludes freezing. The point is not at all alien to von Balthasar's theological dramatic theory: "The central issue in theo-drama is that God has made his own the tragic situation of human existence, right down to its ultimate abysses; thus, without drawing its teeth or imposing an extrinsic solution on it, he overcomes it. [. . .] The whole question is this: Is there some standpoint from which we can observe and report on this dramatic sequence of events?"[27] There is no external standpoint for reading the drama of the stage or the drama of salvation history. No theologian—not even von Balthasar—can really step outside the theater of the world's space-time in order to comment as if from eternity. Those comments would still spring from a particular historical person (hence von Balthasar's need to develop his category of *supertime* to describe God's eternal action of loving). This includes no external standpoint from the materiality of the body that remembers. Theology done while sitting in the house might be "external" to the world of the play on stage, but theology's position can never become external from the shared event of the play.[28]

STAGING A THEOLOGICAL MEMORY PLAY

Broadway knows how to stage memories. Tennessee Williams's *The Glass Menagerie* makes visible the struggle to make sense of the body's place between memories of the past and desires for the future. The play opens with its narrator, Tom Wingfield, explaining his role as stage storyteller and master of this play's memorial magic. He admits, "I am the opposite of a stage magician. He gives you illusion that has the appearance of truth. I give you truth in the pleasant disguise of illusion."[29] Tom draws a sharp distinction between performances that entertain, where the basic reality is a trick aimed toward fleeting delight, and the sorts of truths that can only be made visible in spectacle. For Tom, perhaps channeling Aristotle, poetry and stage magic illuminate rather than undermine the content of memory. Tom designates the play "a memory play."[30] Tom's brand of theatrical memory relates directly to liturgical *anamnesis*: The performance of this narrative makes present again a retelling of Tom's past.[31] We learn that Tom is a poet who yearns for distant shores; other workers at his warehouse call him Shakespeare. This memory play, then, becomes Tom's poetic history of the Wingfields.[32] Tom cannot write his identity *ex nihilo*, but he constructs a future on the foundation of memory. He must mythologize (make public) his private dream to flourish.[33]

Memories of the play need to be mythologized, too, because Williams purposefully troubles easy correlations between the printed version of his play and its performances. A theatrical convention of quasi-Brechtian projections—title cards and images for "memories"—was cut from the original 1945 production, and the 2013 revival I saw on Broadway similarly disregarded Williams's suggestion. Yet the playwright includes stage directions for the projections in the printed text as if rubrics for a liturgy of the future. An introductory comment on "The Screen Device" reads, "An imaginative producer or director may invent other uses for this device than those indicated in the present script. In fact the possibilities of the device seem much larger to me than the instance of this play can possibly achieve."[34] The play anticipates multiple stagings and interpretations and revivals, but Williams's first Broadway success contains within itself the hope for renewed afterlives.

Hope in the world of the play comes from Tom's mother Amanda's memories of gentleman callers. On the one hand, the gentleman caller is dubbed "the most realistic character in the play, being an emissary from a world of reality that we were somehow set apart from."[35] Jim O'Connor cracks the insular concerns of Tom's memory-dreaming; he warns Tom, "You're going to be out of a job if you don't wake up."[36] The "reality" of the gentleman caller does not grow from the misty uncertainty of Tom's memory; rather, Jim becomes a harsh catalyst of destruction and irrevocable change. Jim's presence is a crisis of reality in a world of illusion. But, on the other hand, Tom notes the gentleman caller's symbolism as "the long delayed but always expected something that we live for."[37] Later in the play, Tom extols, "Like some archetype of the universal unconscious, the image of the gentleman caller haunted our small apartment. An evening at home rarely passed without some allusion to this image, this spectre, this hope."[38] Amanda's memories of gentleman callers ground a family eschatology realized in messianic expectations of fairy-tale consolation, a return and restart to the idyllic perfection "remembered" in a nonexistent past. Her attempt to resuscitate that past describes dead memories that lack liberating-transformative danger; they recapitulate the idolatrous and empty desires of "systems of the present." Metz writes, "Outside the realm of human freedom and its conflicts, all power for fulfillment, for reconciliation, and for peace is reserved by this memory to God."[39] But Amanda locates salvation in marriage for her daughter Laura. Communal responsibility might be cleansed by shifting care to another. Jim's inability to serve as messiah gets confirmed at the end. He is already engaged to marry Betsy; hope has been misplaced.

Williams loads the play with even more Christian references. Tom's opening story about Malvolio the stage magician includes overtones of Jesus's miracle of turning water "into wine and then it turned to beer and then it turned to whiskey" as well as his escape from the sealed tomb of a nailed coffin: "But who in hell ever got himself out of one without removing one nail?"[40] Amanda's salvific gentleman callers always came on Sundays, and she wears a cotillion dress she "resurrected" from an old trunk.[41] The gentleman caller scene, though, deploys what I read as a warning about an inversion of Metz's dangerous memory of freedom. Williams's "Screen Device" makes the Christ-figure connection obvious. The title card for the gentleman caller's arrival reads "Annunciation."[42] The messianic Jim delivers his gospel of self-superiority.

The scene leads to Laura showing her collection of figurines, the titular glass menagerie, to Jim. She was especially proud of her favorite, a tiny glass unicorn. Despite her "inferiority stuff," Jim convinces Laura that she should get up and dance. The Broadway revival in 2013 allowed this moment to swell into a larger-than-life spin around the living room; Laura and Jim swirled with abandon until the tragic accident. They slam into the table, knocking the glass unicorn to the ground. It breaks; the horn has fallen off. Laura brushes any sadness aside. Glass breaks. She can tell a story to make it better: "I'll just imagine he had an operation. The horn was removed to make him feel less—freakish!"[43] Tragedy comes in the way sharing the menagerie leads to the loss of magic, a return to the mundane. The gentleman caller who sweeps in with an air of reality only shatters fragile happiness. The unicorn—a medieval image of Christ—gets sacrificed into an ordinary horse, but nostalgia for a lost past cannot bring about liberation or resurrection.

Why does Tom tell this story to an audience? Various productions can achieve different answers, but the set of the 2013 revival helped to underscore the play's role as Tom's confession. At the end of the plot, Tom abandons Laura and his mother to join the Union of Merchant Seamen.[44] But he offers an epilogue. Even away from the apartment, Tom must grapple with memories he cannot jettison: "Oh Laura, Laura, I tried to leave you behind me, but I am more faithful than I intend to be."[45] Zachary Quinto delivered these lines dressed in the costume of a sailor, looking out over a pool of water that, for most of the show, seemed a bit of overdone stage spectacle. This moment now recast the entire *mise-en-scène* as a vision of the hull of a ship. Throughout the play, characters would seem to fly across the room as if shifted by the weight of memory. In the end, we see this story told from a man sailing across the open sea toward greater devastation.

Throughout the script, Tom makes frequent reference to the destruction of the Spanish Civil War and anticipates the coming violence of World War II: "In Spain there was Guernica! / But here there was only hot swing music and liquor, dance halls, bars, and movies, and sex that hung in the gloom like a chandelier and flooded the world with brief, deceptive rainbows. . . . / All the world was waiting for bombardments!"[46] The modular woodwork over reflective waters suggested a ship in the middle of a starry ocean. In the end, Tom's memory play becomes an attempt to manifest his guilt to be resolved in communal cathartic confession.

But this kind of memory play does not achieve the liberation Metz contends must be dangerously remembered about God's action. Like Williams, Metz notices the potential to imagine memory as a kind of screen with stage magic, but such a play would not be the dangerous memory that liberates: "A specific memory of this kind breaks through the magic spell cast by the ruling consciousness. It lays claim to history as more than a screen against which we project our present interests."[47] Perhaps that is why memories of the tragedy of a broken toy sting more powerfully than symbolic readings that project onto Laura's plight the loss of innocence, stolen purity, or disenchantment. Gentleman callers are not saviors. Metz would underscore that the sorts of emancipations Tom, Amanda, or Laura envision are simply movements from one place within an oppressing situation to another. Tom flees but cannot free his memory. This memory play limits possibilities of freedom to those constructed within the confines of this-worldly logics: "Its eschaton is boredom[,] its mythos a faith in planning."[48]

But Williams's play does something live that is perhaps different from its *memoria*. The show points toward the possibilities of dangerous-liberating storytelling: "Proclamation and pastoral action do not really seem to be in crisis because there is too much storytelling, but rather because it is hardly possible anymore to tell any stories correctly, with a practical-critical effect, with a dangerous-liberating intent."[49] Williams supplies Broadway with personal mythologies weighted under the pressures of the present and hopes for the future. Tom's autobiographical poetry of memory reveals fragile identities broken as easily as glass animals. The play becomes one of reflection and confession when its narrator-character refuses to occupy some standpoint external to the actions of history. Tom can thus ask audiences to gaze alongside him into looking glass pools and wonder, if they took up the challenge to tell their own memorial narratives, who they would see and into whom they might become. Remembering our stories becomes dangerous-liberating because it calls into question the futures our choices remember or fail to remember. All the more so during times when we remember the danger brought by gathering bodies to tell stories. The remaining sections of this chapter will look to how Broadway shows remember God dangerously.

WE'VE GOT GODS IN THE HOUSE TONIGHT

Adding some gods more explicitly to the mix makes theatrical memory even more dangerous. Theatrical remembering challenges necrotic theologies. That is, liveness describes the material conditions of a Broadway show. Liveness, then, becomes an analogy for what it means for the dangerous memory of God to live on stage. Broadway remembers the gods *live* and, in that live remembering, can incorporate the dangerous memory of Jesus Christ. The structure of embodied performing together in this set-apart place of seeing—that is, theatre—makes Broadway's revelations the symbol of the living God.

Anaïs Mitchell's concept album turned Broadway smash, *Hadestown*, retells the myth of Orpheus and Eurydice to the sound of a swinging New Orleans jazz band. The very top of the show is remarkable for its revival of the Greek sensibility. "On the Road to Hell" sets the hard times tone with both text and trombone. Hermes introduces each of the show's characters, gods and men, including the hard-working chorus and band. The telling of the story is theatrical-liturgical *work*. Lest we forget, Hermes invites the audience to tip, both money and hats in recognition. The opening number presents theatrical contradictions. Claims of the sadness of the tragedy clash with claps and hollers. Telling the story, even in its tragedy, is a kind of dangerous-liberating memory—dangerous because the story will most likely turn out poorly, liberating because maybe this time it will turn out well. But these gods are live and in the house alongside us. The show places no aesthetic distance between the deity and performer; Hades, Hermes, Persephone, and the Fates are present, live, tonight alongside those mortal men and women like Orpheus, Eurydice, the chorus, the band, and the audience.[50]

So that audiences cannot miss the point about performance storytelling's potential to remember theatrical intermingling divinities and humanities,

Persephone opens the second act by really naming the band in the style of a jazz bandleader.[51] She is, after all, "Our Lady of the Underground." The second act becomes a critical hinge between styles of narration. Hermes and Hades set the tone, but it is Persephone and Eurydice, so often rendered silent as objects of a masculine lover's gaze, who offer the play's final toast to the audience.

Like the Orpheus and Eurydice myth, the show is as much about the stakes of creativity as it is a quest to hell to harrow the dead. Orpheus's descent into hell to save his beloved by means of his love carries an obvious family resemblance to the Christian story. The myth is a favorite of poets and philosophers, especially in the twentieth century. Maurice Blanchot, to choose only one example, explicitly situates Orpheus as the center of *L'Space Literaire*.[52] Indeed, the story of Orpheus and Eurydice is the only myth to be told in two different versions in Mary Zimmerman's playful version of Ovid's *Metamorphoses*.[53] Mitchell joins many others in finding this tale of forgetting, love, descent, and looking backward as an archetypal myth for the postindustrial and technologized modern world.

Hadestown might be a parable about climate change or the factory commercialization of art or the power of music to force us to recognize what is really important or the plight of love in a capitalist culture that commodifies even relationship. Mitchell's version presents an Orpheus whose gifts as a Muse's son are not limited necessarily to artistic genius or perseverance. He is a poet who remembers the future dangerously. The words of Orpheus's toast articulate a kind of utopian realism—the dangerous memory of hope—that exceeds even his actions in the play. He raises his cup "to the world we dream about! And the one we live in now."[54]

Hadestown sings a memory of the world alive. The dialectic between underworld and surface shows aliveness as freedom in the concrete. Voluntary slavery to build the wall of Hadestown—alternatively symbolizing various disordered addictions to consumption, materialism, industrialized energy, alcohol, work, security, hierarchy—offers a full belly and warmth alongside the heads down work chant and forget your name. Crucially, the play does not judge Eurydice for her decision to take a place on the factory floor. The Fates directly address the audience, asking whether they would have acted in the same way if in Eurydice's shoes.[55] But the storytelling brings with it a dangerous-liberating memory because its plot does not work out the way we want it to. In fact, the myth remains dangerously free to be itself. Its narrator-character, Hermes, who becomes the solemn judge of the Orpheus test, makes the stakes and outcome of its ritual performance obvious from the outset. The musical does not promise happy endings if the future will be a continuation of the world as it is now.

The story of Orpheus and Eurydice is a tragedy. It is sad to sing, yet it is a song worth singing again. *Hadestown* invites audiences to remember a different kind of bright burning and unquenchable hope that radiates from Christian tradition. Like when churches celebrate the dangerous memory of the crucified Christ, the show displays the fact that such a story could be told again and again and again with such energy, joy, and life. But the festival celebration of the story does not in any way negate its sadness. The tragedy is the impossibility of a different ending; here, then, is a script that remains honest to the Fates. But the play's hope breaks in from *outside* the boundaries of the Orpheus and Eurydice myth. It shines through the wall's cracks. It resonates in the sound of a band introduced by name at the top of the second act and the voices of silenced women that retell the conclusion. Hope resides not in the comfortable feeling of a pleasant ending but in the communal will to have knowledge of the ending and nonetheless start telling the story once more with theatrical hope for a different conclusion.[56] Such a collaborative work to sing the tragedy over and over and over again precisely offers a model for the kind of hope that can remember a possible future for the world despite its current ways of being.

If it's right to read *Hadestown* as a parable of ecological havoc, then the structure of the show enacts something like the arc of Gerard Manley Hopkins's "God's Grandeur" and its curling confidence that nature never fully spends itself away no matter how humans smear it with waste and toil. So, too, the renewable energy of human love enflamed by the divine glory that charges all that is. In Christian theological terms, the Christ is Orpheus's song that will put the world back into tune. The song achieves an expression of love that reestablishes a community of creation among humans, gods, birds, waves, trees, tables, cellos, drinks, Broadway seats. The uncertain community of cooperative creativity promises a deliverance from Hades's society of endless production and certainty secured only by the threat of its loss: That's "Why We Build the Wall."[57]

In Christian terms, Orpheus bears the dangerous memory of the possibility of social and material harmony through a fragmented melody he can never quite complete and a story never quite finished. The end begins again, just as spring comes. Only the Christ fully descends into the hells of our creaturely making to lead us home to love without also looking back. The Christ harrows hell in a way Orpheus cannot. But Orpheus might teach us to view Jesus's harrowing as a singing creation into tune rather than a conquering and repression of the hells within ourselves. The Irish ecological mystic John Moriarty would call this integrated vision of the cosmos on the other side of descent with Christ a "commonage consciousness." As Moriarty writes in *Turtle Was Gone a Long Time*, "So let us imagine it: sitting there like Orpheus, lyre in hand, Jesus sings in our underworld and round about him, placated and peaceful, all the malevolent-potent powers of all past ages, kainozoic, Mesozoic and palaeozoic."[58] Mitchell's Orpheus describes such a world as the radically realized eschatological banquet of paradise now in the world we have once we sing it back into tune. Rivers provide marriage bands, trees lay out the wedding feast, and birds prepare a nuptial bed.[59] We already have more than enough for a good party.

But *Hadestown* does not present itself in Christian terms or in the language of Irish theopoetic ecological mysticism. The plot is Greek, the aesthetic and music are Great Depression-era New Orleans-inspired folk, and the theatrical style is Broadway spectacle. The show, rather, commends an interpretation of the world ready for divine intervention. It remembers how the gods still have a place in the house. In the materiality of its performance—that is, the human bodies who do the work of enacting the drama, manipulating the set pieces, dancing the choreography, singing, and playing the music *and* the tangible pieces of scenery, props, instruments, costumes, merchandise, and stage—the storytelling overrides the reign of Fate toward freedom. That is, the script and score dictate a narrative and a sound world, but the *performance* indicates something beyond seen through cracks in its walls. And that crack lets in light from outside. In literal terms, the crack in the wall might let in light from outside the theater (a theme investigated in a later chapter).[60] The nonplace near the road to hell with a railroad station stands in for the globalized industrial arc toward inevitable planetary ruin. The trains are already running us all to Hadestown, but maybe a community can learn to sing tragedy differently this time. Any resurrection must be a surprise.

History certainly lent *Hadestown* an unintended existential weight that could not be predicted. The musical opened just before the outbreak of the COVID-19 pandemic and won its Tony Award for best musical while Broadway remained dark. But, momentarily, the play brought something of the world back to life.[61] That moment of life is a transient point in *Hadestown*'s retelling of the myth—Persephone's presence on the surface preferred to her exile below ground, her meeting Orpheus so she knows who he is for the bargain with her husband later, the promise of spring and summer abundance after and prior to the cyclical threat of winter's winds and scarcity. But this ephemeral moment of life, here in the house together, gets expressed in an event of dancing, movement, trombone solos. The theatre becomes a temple to celebrate dangerous remembering and returning to life made possible by the materiality of performance where gods and mortals dance and players and audiences raise glasses together to Orphic poets and to everyone present.[62]

BACK TO LIFE: THEATRICAL REVIVALS

How does theatre remember?[63] Both Williams's memory play and Mitchell's sad song are retellings that can be retold. The term for a theatrical retelling calls to mind bringing back to life, *revivifying*. A theatrical revival offers a fascinatingly normative distinction between theatre-making and other sorts of human creativity. A revival is neither an adaptation nor a translation. Revivals are reinterpretations within the boundaries of the infinite reservoir of the script's potential. Revivals return to a play's liveness, its freedom to be staged and manifest in innumerable good ways. Revivals can, thus, make changes within the act of interpretation. Revivals might adjust the music and orchestration of a musical, or reset the play in a different time or place, or make minor adjustments and cuts to a script to make it more readily available to a contemporary audience. In each case, the givenness of the play becomes a source of freedom, an opportunity for creative collaboration. A revival is not a recreation of the original staging or a national tour, a movement of one version of an interpretation of the play on the road for more and more new audiences and new venues. A revival is closer to a cover of a song than a remake of a film: It takes and refashions the already given with obvious deference to the source material. A revival stands in absolute continuity with its original as an *expansion*. If that continuity is severed, a revival becomes an adaptation. A revival is another production of the original. By reviving, returning the play to life, the company engages the play with creative freedom.

Revivals create scholarly difficulties for an academic community beguiled by the romantic promise of the "original." Lingering Neoplatonic fantasies of emanation as diminishment and the zero-sum logic of economic scarcity also collude to make scholars skeptical. A revival is not lessened by the fact that it performs theatrical choices differently from the original production, but a revival must be inextricably indebted to the original production. Indeed, any production of a play in the Broadway canon by a regional theatre or a high school is a revival in the technical sense that I mean it.

As a heuristic portable across cultural and professional structures and national styles, a piece of theatre comes into being either by devising or reviving. Both bring theatre to life. Devised theatre names practices where an ensemble creates a show from their own collaborative creative work.[64] Sometimes devising operates according to the image of a playwright as a literary author or musical composer creating in isolation and then handing a text/script/score over to a company to rehearse and perform. On Broadway, the company collaborates with the writers during rehearsals and previews. Scripts and songs might be changed based on an audience response or actors' suggestions until the version is standardized by the opening. Every original play emerges from a devising relationship among directors, actors, designers, producers, and the writer. So even the imagined traditional practice of theatre-making, where an author hands over a script to be brought to life, interpreted, and performed for an audience, is a practice of devising theatre.

More experimental theatre companies do collaborative work with greater intentionality. Many scholars and theatre companies refer to devised theatre as *collaborative creation*. Devised theatre emerged across the twentieth century as a mode of creative practice at great distance from a singular author. Devised theatre companies, themselves, create the text of a playscript based on contributions from the entire ensemble. Devised theatre takes its cue from other modes of creative work like jazz, where improvisation and interaction provide opportunities for discovery. Even if there are more skilled writers among the ensemble, devised theatre may not locate authorship in a particular person whose role is "author." But any reflection on the history of theatrical praxis makes abundantly clear that collective devising best names a transcultural process for performance-making. Everyone involved in crafting the show plays a role in devising it, even if some member of the company—somebody like William Shakespeare—had such significant talent as a writer that a record of the devised piece, a script, bears that writer's name. In any case, the new play has been devised through a collaborative process that receives and responds to the given circumstances of the world in order to tell its story.

Shows that are revived also proceed through a collaborative creative process, but the process begins after the moment the script has been fixed. In other words, revivals inherit the final product of the originally devised show as the given circumstances for their creative work. The boundaries for a revival's creative choices are set by the inherited script. The given circumstances of the play are conditioned by the choice to enter into the performance history of *this* script, *this* play, *these* words.

Like all interpretation, revivals have incredibly wide creative freedom but must remain faithful to the script as given. A company that strays too far from the inherited script shifts from reviving into adapting, the devising of a new show using fragments of the original as inspiration. There are no hard and fast interpretive rules (as Schleiermacher says, hermeneutics is an art) that can universally distinguish a revival from an adaptation.[65] On Broadway, legal protections from the estate of authors usually restrict revivals to artistic choices that work the words of the text. Samuel Beckett's estate, for instance, is especially protective of the authority of the script to shape a revival's choices. Revivals intend for the audience to receive an encounter that intends to do what this show does. In other words, revivals consciously enter into what theologians and philosophers call a tradition. There will be much more to say about theatrical representations of tradition and theological revival (*aggiornamento*) in the next chapter. But, before we close this chapter, I want to linger for a bit with one Broadway-adjacent revival of the dangerous memory of Jesus.

GOD IS LOVE IN A TIME OF COVID-19

Just as *Hadestown* performed a revivification, for a moment there, in the midst of plague, so, too, did the Berkshire Theatre Group in Pittsfield, Massachusetts. The Berkshire Theatre Group represents the kind of regional theatre that revives Broadway shows in new productions. It secured permission to be the first professional musical performance sanctioned by Actors' Equity after Broadway shut down due to the pandemic and staged a revival of a devised musical about Jesus in August 2020.

Godspell adapts the Gospel of Matthew (with cameo appearances from Luke's prodigal son and good Samaritan) into a musical revue that alternates teaching, storytelling, and singing.[66] Jesus and his disciples play-act the parables, sing a mix of reorchestrated hymns and original songs, and enculturate the Gospel to the energy of the 1970s. Almost all the musical numbers are led by a single character with the rest of the cast providing backup. The plot (if there is one to be found) loosely follows the life of Jesus, beginning with a "baptism" sequence to the tune of John the Baptist's "Prepare Ye the Way of the Lord" and concluding with a "crucifixion" and cries of lament for the death of God. The only characters with biblical names are Jesus and John/Judas (shared by the same actor); the remaining characters traditionally go by their given names from everyday life. The show is frequently revived in both religious and secular spaces because its telling of the Gospel story carries as many memories of hippies and low-budget Broadway as it does the Savior of the world. But the play is also incredibly flexible: Its performance script retains much of the sense of a devised theatre piece inspired by the scriptural text and offers the right for an ensemble to adapt the jokes and contemporary references to the present moment. A Broadway revival in 2011 added the sound of beeping cell phones to its opening number and shifted many of the play's pop culture references to the early 2000s.

This flexibility inspired the Berkshire Theatre Group's production. It switched familiar stage pictures of secret handshakes and cuddles to social distance, plexiglass, and masks. I saw the show on August 13, 2020, snagging my ticket before the size of the audience was reduced to make more room for social distancing. The play happened outside in a tent. The simple stage was divided into acting areas six feet apart or dutifully separated by movable clear shields. Each member of the cast had their own zone. The vaudeville-inspired number "All for the Best" used yardsticks instead of canes—six feet!—and had a can of lemon-scented Clorox wipes with a yellow lid appear alongside a phrase about conjuring buckets of gold. *Godspell* met the audience where we were.

This included more than pandemic-era references and personal protective equipment requirements. This production consciously and intentionally cast with wide gender, racial, and sexual diversity—the role of Jesus particularly, played by the Black actor Nicholas Edwards. It placed representatives of the Sanhedrin (in many productions signaled by anti-Semitic stereotypes) and Roman Empire in police hats and aviator sunglasses. The Berkshire Theatre Group changed the opening sequence from a rundown of the history of ideas into true stories from the cast's young actors. Cast members told stories about the fear brought about by the unknown virus, blossoming careers slamming to a halt due to lockdowns, and their reflections on the murder of George Floyd and the realities of racism in the theatre industry. These histories and the show's displays of community without physical connectedness invited the Gospel to speak to the present. It proposed theatre as an antidote to the twin plagues of systemic racism and COVID-19.

Theatre and plague go together well, at least according to the influential and problematic theatre theorist Antonin Artaud. His work, most famous in the collection of essays *The Theater and Its Double*, develops his theory of the "theatre of cruelty." But what is fascinating about Artaud's theatre-making and theatre theorizing is, in the words of his foremost English-language champion, Susan Sontag, "both in his work and in his life, Artaud failed."[67] Rejected by the Surrealists for his love of the bourgeois fanciness of the theatre stage and rejected by theatregoers for his bizarre and confusing stagecraft, Artaud finds himself most influential in the realm of high theory and dramatic criticism. He sought to revitalize the stage: to move away from stodgy play with form into something revelatory, shocking, and new. Artaud wanted theatre to be dangerous.

Artaud offers a surprising juxtaposition between the metaphysical or spiritual experience of theatre and that of plague. Both rip away the sense of normalcy; both challenge our categories. By looking to plague, Artaud reconceptualizes the purpose of theatrical possibility and performance. Plague permits theatre to reclaim its ground as sacred, risky, contagious, and full of life. In short, the context of plague makes even sentimental memories into dangerous ones.

Artaud's spectacularly confusing short essay "The Theater and the Plague" sits next to his more well-known provocative ideas: two manifestos for a theatre of cruelty and his theory of shadows or "doubles" of true life that appear in theatrical performance. The whole book drives toward a central thesis: Theatre is about more than dramatic words. In fact, speech and language can get in the way of theatre's manifestations of the really real. Artaud writes in the preface to *The Theater and Its Double* that true theatre is never repeatable—"The actor does not make the same gestures twice, but he makes gestures, he moves"— because "the theater, which is *no thing*, but makes use of everything—gestures, sounds, words, screams, light, darkness—rediscovers itself at precisely the point where the mind requires a language to express its manifestations."[68] The same sort of irruption of the real into the delirium of the everyday belongs to the city or industry besieged by plague. It has its own *mise-en-scène*, its own design, look, and aesthetic. In other words, plague captures theatre's capacity to cut through the intellectual noise of everyday language and see or feel something real. *Godpsell* brought the plague aesthetic to the musical.

Artaud's essay circles around observations about plague from the ancient and medieval world. But he begins with a mediation on a story that he supposedly finds buried in the archives of a small town in Sardinia. In May 1720, some unimportant regional middle manager dreams about a ship carrying plague on its way to Marseille. Our friend the viceroy knows that this plague ship will need to dock in Sardinia along the way, but his dream influences political action. Like so many cruise ships refused ports of call at the start of the Coronavirus pandemic, the viceroy refuses to allow this ship to come to Sardinia. The dream is a nightmare, one where nearby plague *communicates* even if it does not get close enough to infect.

The mechanics of contagion are unremarkable: A virus moves unpredictably and without clear reason. Physical contact matters but is not the only means of contagion; the mere *threat* of plague undoes social order. Artaud returns to the image of the plague ship as a symbol for the incommensurable and uninterpretable difference between cultures: an ominous vessel that appears godlike in the harbor and sends forth invisible angels of death.

This story about plague's proximity and spiritual communication (the ship comes close enough to cause a dream) invites Artaud to reflect on the purpose of theatre. As in Tom's observation about his memory play in *The Glass Menagerie*, theatre stages a kind of waking dream wherein we come to proximity with a vision. Plague does something to the social order: an unnamable scrambling of priorities, expansions of governmental power, changes to our day-to-day lives, upheavals of culture.

There are three areas of Artaud's theory that are instructive. First, plague exhausts us with images and forces of "physical disorganization." Theatre, however, offers images with a "spiritual force that begins . . . in the senses and does without reality altogether." In other words, Artaud suggests that theatre might conjure the same sort of emotional or spiritual energies in us to uproot preconceptions as the plague. Theatre stages "virtual" violence to disturb the repose of our senses.[69]

Second, Artaud writes that theatre is not like plague because of its contagiousness but because theatre, like plague, becomes a site for revelations of the real: "the bringing forth, the exteriorization of a depth of latent cruelty by means of which all the perverse possibilities of the mind, whether of an individual or a people."⁷⁰ Theatre does not represent or point to something unreal. Theatre *reveals* the reality of cruelty in the world, the possibility for the unimaginable to unfold in a world aflame, a world teetering on the edge of unimaginable loss. This is not a fantasy but the reality of this world with its compromised religious and civic institutions that violate and profane the public trust.

Third, Artaud argues that "the theater, like the plague, is a delirium and is communicative."⁷¹ He invokes the great antitheatrical argument of Augustine: Theatre performs all the good stuff—sex, violence, tragedy—and so trains us in feelings and perversions that corrupt the body politic and threaten the soul. Theatre *fascinates* and leads us to fascinate others. Whether Bacchic rituals that invite parties on the mountainside or secret mysteries that initiate cults of some unknown god, theatre confounds confidence in the real and so readies us to ask better questions.

These observations do not seem to be entirely right about theatre; Artaud appears sadistically bent on forcing his audience to undergo some sort of emotional or traumatic experience (reminiscent, perhaps, of the forcible march from the dark of Plato's cave into the blinding light of the forms). Better, I think, to be taken with Bertolt Brecht's call to rupture our mundane sensibilities with laughter and musical numbers and awareness of the work that goes into making spectacle. But Artaud does teach us to be a little more skeptical about the spiritually antiseptic, about the kinds of plays that scrub away the dangerousness of the divine. Artaud argues that theatre allows audiences to see, in the gathering to watch stories unfold by others, something *inherently risky*. We might become delirious and want to communicate the vision of our ecstasy.

Artaud becomes useful to interpret *Godspell* at the Berkshire Theatre Group because he challenges the temptation to sanitize the dangerous memory of Jesus Christ into only comforting "happiness and light." The performance's adherence to the sacred rites of social distance, masks, quarantine, and testing became part of the theatrical/religious ritual. The teachings of Jesus fell flat in this production, at least for me, because they felt evacuated of their transcendence. Stories about discipleship and the kingdom of heaven felt like a vehicle to talk about the immanent threats of plagues and the sinfulness of white supremacy in police violence. *Godspell* has long faced controversy.⁷² The show presents stories of Jesus more human than divine. Performance editions of the script include an explanatory note on the play's explicit and intended lack of a resurrection scene. Jesus dies, the company sings long live God interlaced with a reprise of "Prepare Ye the Way of the Lord," and the show ends with a newly formed community, both in the company and in the audience.[73]

The production I saw did not alleviate these concerns and may have unwittingly amplified them. The play's religious themes were overshadowed by the idea of musical theatre during pandemic and the resurrection of an artistic practice rather than the body of the Christ. The play's references to Jewish religious authorities in antiquity explicitly linked the Pharisees to contemporary police violence against persons of color. The production seemed to find its room to make the play relevant in those very places where revivals of the show require the most theological and religious sensitivity.

Yet the scenic design placed the whole performance of the COVID-19 era musical in front of a dogmatic theological claim: "God is Love is Love is God." The backdrop made explicit the connection between the Jesus character on stage and the symbol of God. The show's themes of love and the divine were unmistakably important even if the performance did not invest those moments of teaching, verbatim quotations from the Gospel, with the same emotional energy as song lyrics. Scenographic theology is, perhaps, the least interesting way that the symbol of God can take the stage. The words concatenate references: "God is Love" from the First Letter of John (1 John 4:16), the phrase "love is love" that operates as a shorthand for recognizing the love expressed between same-sex persons, the phrase "Love is God" as a claim about the divinity of love, and an *is* in the middle that equates the equations "God is Love" and "Love is God." Scriptural references and theological premises juxtapose with activism and the deployment of "love" as a language for inclusion.

The backdrop phrasing can be critiqued for its theology, particularly as to whether "God is Love" really is the same thing as "Love is God."[74] God's love precedes human acts of loving because God's priority extends even to conceptual formulations about God's very being as an act of love. Claiming "Love is God" performs the same order of operations as von Balthasar's concerns about aesthetic theology. It limits God to the boundaries of a creaturely imagination. All of the world's love reflects God because God is an absolute love greater than anything that which is within the world could ever conceive. The various ways in which the backdrop theology can be read indicate whether Gospel memory the play performs will be sentimental or dangerous-liberating. God becomes background, relativized to a concept like "love," safer and more familiar.

But given the manifold failures of Christian communities to show forth the love of the God who is Love, perhaps "God is Love is Love is God" is an even *more* effective way to call audiences to think differently about God and to exegete the Gospel story according to the "signs of the times."[75] The Berkshire Theatre Group performance was a literal tent revival, after all.

So how might the theatre prepare the way of the Lord with dangerous memory in a time of plague? Perhaps by revealing a truth deeply felt and still sacred: We *can* be together, tell stories, and feel in common with Durkheim's "collective effervescence." Energies swirl together to invest religious artifacts with totemic, even transcendent significance. The most powerful part of this *Godspell*, for me at least, was that chance to feel alongside others in the presence of others. To remember the strange danger of liveness. To hear beloved music sung and sacred stories told under a tent with total strangers I was too hesitant to greet. My sentimental religious experience remained private, both socially and emotionally distant. But the performance of *Godspell* made love and hope feel a bit more contagious than the virus in that moment. Love and hope returned to be transgressive and essential feelings while telling a story that made the memory of Jesus live. Joy bubbled, a little. And it felt risky. Maybe here is Artaud's genius hidden under his maddening fascination with cruelty, his rage at a theatre made boring by convention and normalcy. Theatre reveals to us the world as it truly can be, mask, meter stick, and all. And in that dangerous world, God was no less present and the good news of salvation no less proclaimed.

Godspell concludes by singing about how proclaiming God's life ("long live God") prepares the way of the Lord. The music and lyrics suggest a movement forward, a turn outward from the individual's experience of Jesus toward a community formed by shared struggle and love. It is, perhaps, a similar community to the one on the road to Hadestown that tells a love story over and over again in hope that the future might remember and enact our hopes rather than our current sufferings. It is, perhaps, a community that could teach the very lesson that Tom needs so that his memory play would liberate rather than suffocate. It is, perhaps, the kind of community that holds dangerous memory right alongside Broadway's sentimental safety in its memories of the symbol of God. The kind of community ready for memories of a living God. In the end, Broadway remembers God in ways that theological writing cannot, in the dangerous and risky spaces between bodies telling stories again and again. These are the kind of communities that hand on dangerous memory as a living tradition. These are also the kind of communities that can fail and can calcify both sentimental memories and dangerous memories of God into nostalgia for a bygone culture. The next chapter looks to the way Broadway shows stage, develop, and query tradition and doubt with two large Broadway set pieces that directly raise an important objection about "instrumentalizing" theatre and religion for theological interpretation that needs to be first addressed through a short interlude.

In-One[1]
On Instrumentalizing

If Broadway retains something of a dangerous memory of the living God, as discussed in the previous chapter, surely that memory manifests most abundantly in the explicit staging of religious traditions. We briefly encountered these "safe" memories of religious life in costumes and harmonies of cats and nuns singing Latin prayers. Broadway also remembers the power of divine presence via the ritual actions, beloved songs, famous characters, central stories, and sacred costuming that mark a religious community. Perhaps God shows up on Broadway most abundantly when shows stage religious traditions outside their traditional context. The trappings of religious life make their way outside their natural habitats and migrate to Broadway. As Misty Anderson contends, recognizable religious symbols are portable: They appear just as readily in the front of an audience as they can in front of a congregation.[2]

It is not that hard to dress up an actress like a flying nun or don a prayer shawl with tzitzit. These costumes carry immediate meaning for audiences because they bear the weight of the traditions that they cite. But the context of a Broadway show alleviates actors from needing to keep kosher or profess vows of poverty, chastity, and obedience. Does the actress playing the nun in charge of a Catholic school need to be Catholic herself? Does the actor offering Shabbos in Anatevka need to be Jewish? Is religious identity exhausted by costumes and gestures and songs? Broadway shows seem, on first glance, to dilute the potency of religious symbols by permitting their instrumentalization for the sake of plot and setting rather than as visible signs of a particular way of life in relationship to God. Theatre that stages religious symbols also unmasks the theatricality of religious practices. Broadway's citations of religious tradition can domesticate the dangerous memory of God into playacting the antiquated beliefs of a bygone era. All that remains of dangerous memory is nostalgia for a time and place when this playacting was real.

Staging tradition stops nostalgia from retreating into "safe" memory. I want to draw a distinction here between the notion of a dangerous memory of the living God articulated through Broadway's creative nostalgia and what I called "safe" memories of religion in the previous chapter. Broadway's sentimental approach to religious questions will always try to color nostalgia with warm and fuzzy feeling, but tradition holds nostalgia open to critique in the present. Nostalgia imagines a past that nonetheless grounds the dangerous memory of a different future. Nostalgia can be porous and inclusive. Nostalgia invites a wider audience than "safe" memories of God. "Safe" memories rely on the audience members to supply their own experiences to make theological interpretations to religious symbols. "Safe" memories of God remain personal and privatized.

At first, this distinction between safe citations and dangerous nostalgic traditions seems to make no difference because Broadway's use of props, costumes, language, symbols, or gesture instrumentalizes religious phenomena for a commercial and entertaining end. Plays are not religious rituals, and religious rituals are not theatre. There will be great overlap between these two spheres of human activity, but theatrical traditions do not propose to speak religious truths. Broadway instrumentalizes ritual as a symbolic shortcut. The referent of these rituals cited on stage remains the world of the play and its narrative rather than the world we inhabit and its God.

Looking for God on Broadway necessarily invites a similar critique that I have "instrumentalized" theatre for the sake of my theological point. That is, intellectual work presumes an understanding of the divine derived from academic theological materials, loads that theology into a particular take on the God concept, and then finds instances where that concept of God performs on the commercial stage. The accusation assumes an order of authorial operations: (1) Gather esteemed and trustworthy accounts of God, (2) use those accounts to develop a theory for how God might show up in a play, and (3) apply those insights to concrete examples from Broadway shows. Such a process, in other contexts, might be called eisegetical (reading God *into* Broadway) or ideological (imposing a fantasy paradigm that obscures the reality of the play as an act of hermeneutic violence). This sort of critique can be well-founded. Theologians rarely allow the profanities of popular culture to make theological meaning with the same freedom afforded to sacred texts, histories, peer-reviewed journals, artifacts, and performances. Entertainment distracts from the seriousness of an academic endeavor to interpret revelation. Popular images of God merely simulate the "real thing" discerned by the experts. Filtering theological ideas through Broadway, so the accusation goes, seems only yet another attempt to give 'em the old razzle dazzle by dressing foregone theological conclusions in the sequined costumes of something a bit more engaging.

The instrumentalization objection can be levied from all directions. Instrumentalization is a problem for theatre lovers because it refuses to appreciate a given play on its own terms as a nonreligious work of art. That is, Broadway theatre does not presume religious commitments on the part of its audience or actors: It's a theater and not a chapel! Pressed further, scholars of theatre and performance can point to the material realities of Broadway shows that become public school plays across the United States. Such performances could only be legal (in light of the non-establishment clause of the First Amendment to the US Constitution) if the religious references or themes in a show function artistically rather than religiously.[3] By instrumentalizing those artistic choices into resources for theology, I choose fundamentally to alter the genre of a Broadway show. A show makes all sort of unintended meanings, but any religious meanings are only religiously meaningful to *me* as interpreter. I am, of course, free to draw theological meanings from these plays, but I do so as a private reader and thinker. My work functions with far different intent and theological foundations than the 2022 illicit Christianization of *Hamilton* by the nondenominational community The Door McAllen in Texas. The megachurch adjusted lyrics and added an anti-LGBTQ sermon to the Broadway show (but has since apologized and paid damages). Their interpretation, however, saw *Hamilton* as a vehicle to communicate their private theology. But Broadway shows do not intend to be moments of revelation. Indeed, Broadway's broad and public appeal explicitly resists transfiguration into something religiously revelatory. So goes the objection.

Instrumentalization also creates a problem for religionists. If Broadway functions as a site for revelation, and I consider that revelation according to its Christian character, I have thereby instrumentalized an open set of resources for a presumptively closed religious theory. Why not also consider God on Broadway from Jewish, Islamic, Hindu, or neo-pagan theological perspectives? Further, why not keep revelation at a general, theoretical, or philosophical level? Indeed, as many religious studies scholars and many theatre and performance scholars argue, Broadway plays make more sense interpreted within a nonsectarian and pluralistic frame of reference. Better to focus on material and empirical data like audience demographics, ethnographies of actors' experience, economic analyses, and literary treatments of scripts according to their religious source materials. In some respects, the next chapter will undoubtedly instrumentalize the Yiddish production of *Fiddler on the Roof* when I argue for its contribution to a Catholic-Christian theology. Such interreligious instrumentalization is not ethically neutral. I have instrumentalized profane entertainment into a quasi-sacred resource and exoticized the religiosity of Jewish culture in the US, Eastern European, and diaspora contexts. There are also concerns about Christianizing non-Christian materials through an act of intellectual colonization. I have instrumentalized one religious set of identities for the sake of making meaning for another. Instrumentalization risks an implication that a non-Christian identity remains "incomplete" until fulfilled by Christianity. These problems will continue to amplify in future chapters with more explicit attention to the bodies performing on stage and in the house. A second objection.

To view Broadway as a site for interpretations in light of revelation requires considering these plays against their theological rather than theatrical horizon. The method requires more than simply exposing the theological import of religious themes, symbols, and citations from within the boundaries of the materialistic theatrical horizon or interpreting spirit according to what Donalee Dox identifies as the "paradigm of performance."[4] Rather, a play prompts theological construction and reflection. The move includes a shift of horizon that becomes particularly noticeable when treating only moments of a play—or the form of a play—as a key into the whole and composite experience.[5] As I explained in the introduction, *God on Broadway* explicitly aims to continue the work of von Balthasar's *Prolegomena* to *Theo-Drama*. Like von Balthasar, "out of the limitless literature of the stage I have selected only meager fragments: moreover, I have not treated them from a literary point of view but have been obligated to select and present them for my theological purposes."[6] I have already confessed my role as the arbiter of selection. These are the plays that I choose to write about—that I want to write about—and so my selections reveal biography and bias as much as they reveal God. Like any actor, I disclose my character via my performance choices.[7]

But my selections are also the assembly of a set of theological resources. My choices, in Anne M. Carpenter's language, perform the theological task of *resourcing*.[8] Critiques of theatrical theologizing deploy the metaphor of instrumentalization to mean the treatment of a play as a tool, like the surgeon's or inquisitor's instruments shown to frighten Galileo in Brecht's theatrical version of the story. Instrumentalization dissects, deconstructs, tortures; the materials instrumentalized are conscripted into forced servitude and complicity. Instrumentalization interprets in such a way that violates a play's integrity as a play on its own terms within its own religious (or irreligious) and cultural contexts. My work to find revelations of God on Broadway cannot avoid shades of this critique of Christian theological interpretation as a mode of hermeneutic violence.[9] So, too, any attempt to read and construct meanings against the grain of implied genre, means of production, cultural context, and professed intentionality.

But instrumentalization may have another connotation. To instrumentalize also means to play with as an instrument of performance: to transform into the structure of a scene partner.[10] We instrumentalize guitars and xylophones and trombones when we play music, but we can also instrumentalize rubber bands, variously filled glassware, and paper towel tubes to make music. Every time I pound on my desk in time with rhythm, I instrumentalize my desk as a drum. This mode of instrumentalization discovers excesses of possibility latent within materiality. Ordinarily, the charge of instrumentalization implies diminishment, contortion, or restriction by limiting the meaning of the object to the intentionality I impose on it as my tool. Ironically, to instrumentalize my desk into a drum expands its potentiality to perform a new role. In theatrical terms, I have turned my desk into a prop by playing it and playing with it. But this expansive, playful meaning nonetheless treats the desk as a tool for my own ends. I have still instrumentalized the desk-as-drum prop, but a playful interpretation interprets the desk against a horizon of unforeseen possibility. How else might I play this instrument? How else might this instrument play me? *Sed contra*.

Some critique of instrumentalization cannot be dodged because my work brings multiple artistic and theoretical genres into conversation, but perhaps the more dastardly modes of instrumentalization can be avoided. Methodologically, it remains important to reinforce that I see Broadway-style shows as opportunities for revelation and therefore invitations to expansive and playful theological interpretation. To treat drama as a theological resource means to instrumentalize theatre as a scene partner for improvising and playing theology anew. My aim is not—nor has it been at any point—to load Broadway theatre with a prepackaged theology, to instrumentalize the plays I chose into illustrations of a theology that might be just as well articulated another way. Broadway has undoubtedly shaped my understanding of God. Broadway distinctively reveals God and contributes its own voice to theology.

I minimize the negative risks of instrumentalization by performing my interpretations playfully, by insisting, over and over, that my choices sit among a larger set of interpretive possibilities. Most centrally, I engage in theodramatic conversation where these shows provide dramatic resources for the work of theology. That means treating these Broadway shows as theological conversation partners that present an interpretation of divine revelation that furthers, complicates, and challenges inherited and calcified understanding and promises new constructive directions.

This excursus to muse on instrumentalization uncovers the spatial fact of interpreting God while sitting in the house rather than in the pews. There are traditions all along Broadway, in its theaters and in its churches, on street corners and on the clothes of passersby. God's play on Broadway will thereby contribute to a tradition's ecclesial and communal discernment, self-recognition, and development. Traditions forge links between memories of God on stage and in the house. Tradition brings the dangerous memory of the living God to life through action. Tradition is done, enacted, performed. *Respondeo.*

CHAPTER FOUR

Tradition and Traditions

Broadway shows happen in the same history as the church. Encountering the symbol of God living—rather than as instrumentalized referent—blurs lines of demarcation between sacred and profane, theology and entertainment. But theology that embraces Broadway as a dramatic resource also blurs lines between communities, between liturgical and theatrical settings. The symbol of God plays on Broadway in many religious registers and for audiences of mixed religious and cultural affiliations. Broadway theaters are filled with pluralistic publics invited into the ongoing movement and contestation of traditions.

This chapter considers two shows about tradition after and during disaster.[1] God on Broadway might keep the symbol of God alive outside an ecclesial context even when religious institutions seem untrustworthy, lost, destroyed, or broken. These shows conduct theological inquiry into the nature of traditions precisely because any given performance is not a religious event or liturgy. Broadway remains, by definition, outside the religious community. Neither show asks to replace rituals, prayers, or communal practices. Broadway's traditions do not supersede religious ones. Yet these shows can operate as theological events, invitations to query God and tradition, to enter constructive dialogue even if the community doubts where it should go next.

A commercial theater needs to be more comfortable with doubt than a church. Broadway has its own extra-ecclesial traditions that interlace with the church's. What might it mean to see the dynamism of tradition on stage as a partner in theological contestation and doctrinal development? This chapter juxtaposes *Fiddler on the Roof* and *Doubt, A Parable* as dramatic resources for theology, scene partners for interpreting the symbol of God while sitting in the house of a Broadway theater.

"HOW DO WE KEEP OUR BALANCE?"

There may be no better testament to Jerry Bock's artistic achievement than the power of the solitary sound of a violin. The Fiddler's tune wriggles home into memory from the very first time one hears it. Those first few haunting notes of the "Tradition" theme recur, again and again, as a leitmotif to signal the fragile continuity of a distinct community and tradition's inevitable and yet surprising transformations over time and life in diaspora. Perhaps this very same tune plays perpetually in shared places: Anatevka and innumerable theaters around the globe. To remember the Fiddler's tune connects us across time, space, context, and distinct traditions. The memory takes residence not only in the mind but also in performed action, a tradition continuously embodied whenever someone gets caught up in humming the tune to themselves: walking out of a middle school theater production, in excitement while making popcorn to enjoy while watching the 1971 movie, or in the parking lot after listening to the musical's soundtrack during an ordinary morning commute.[2]

The music of *Fiddler on the Roof* extends beyond Anatevka. Any performance, on stage or screen, can begin someone's initiation, by Tevye, into the tradition that organizes and structures life in the shtetl. But we know this tradition to be both religious and entertaining, both of Jewish and of Broadway origin. *Fiddler on the Roof* performs these traditions simultaneously—so, too, the elements of *Fiddler* that cling to the memories of its fans, cast members, and devotees. Could the same be said of Flo Milli's sampling of Zero Mostel's singing "If I Were a Rich Man" in her song "Roaring 20s"? Does it matter for Flo Milli's interpretation if one hears Mostel's nonverbal syllables as liturgical cantillation and recalls "If I Were a Rich Man" as a moment of prayer? Could a Broadway show tune capture a "real" memory of a religious tradition? Who should feel nostalgia and for what?

Yair Lipshitz argues, "*Fiddler* treats religious tradition with loving affection and nostalgia, but it also portrays it as a world clearly left behind."[3] Nostalgia calls to mind and transcends a perceived gap between the present moment and some lost past. The pleasure and pain of nostalgia consist in crossing a distance of memory. The 2016 Broadway revival for *Fiddler on the Roof* complicates what Lipshitz sees as the "secularization narrative" in *Fiddler*'s reception history by framing the performed story as a journey "home" to Anatevka.

Tevye's character begins as the image of an ambiguous but contemporary tourist, researcher, or descendant. Perhaps the play opens with an actor studying for this classic Broadway role through travel. The scenic design presented an Anatevka train station and the actor playing Tevye in a bright, modern raincoat reading from what appeared to be Sholom Aleichem's stories. The implication was clear: Seeing *Fiddler on the Roof* (by extension, anyone playing a performance of *Fiddler*) makes a homecoming. Performance brings Anatevka to life. Indeed, *Fiddler* brings Anatevka and its "Tradition" to its place of performance. The 2016 revival concretizes questions about *Fiddler on the Roof*'s reception history. The Fiddler has arrived in New York, after all, in order to play for the assembled audience. Tradition begins with, and in many ways *is*, the sound of that all-too-familiar tune. Tradition has resonance.

Few critics capture the multimedia influence of *Fiddler on the Roof* with the same care as Henry Bial in *Acting Jewish: Negotiating Identity on the American Stage and Screen*.[4] The book analyzes "acting Jewish [as] a critical formulation of Jewish American identity in the latter half of the twentieth century"[5] through what Bial calls "double coding." Bial writes, "It is necessary to address the way the work speaks to at least two audiences: a Jewish audience and a general or gentile audience. [. . .] Selective attention to these two admittedly idealized and imaginary reading positions [a 'Jewish' reading and a non-Jewish or 'gentile' reading] is itself a strategic choice."[6] The same performance—be it on stage or screen—will lead a mixed audience to construe Jewishness differently based on their subject positions. Indeed, Bial's notion of double coding aims to show how "the Jewish reading of a performance is most commonly *supplemental* to the dominant or gentile reading."[7] A work of popular culture needs to have mass appeal, but Bial argues that this commercial intent (one that necessarily requires buy-in from gentile audiences) need not negate or compete with Bial's so-called Jewish interpretation, understanding, or importance. Bial explicitly takes up *Fiddler on the Roof* (and the interaction between the stage musical and the 1971 film) as an exemplary case.

Bial both summarizes the production history of the musical's premiere on Broadway in 1964 and also engages in a lengthy comparison between Zero Mostel's and Topol's Tevyes. Bial highlights that some "traditions" around Tevye's casting can be traced to Mostel, notably the idea that Tevye should be "played by a heavyset (or heavily padded) actor"[8] or that Tevye will pause to sit in the midst of a scene. Mostel's choices to sit on the wagon for some monologues emerged from his need to rest an injured leg. The body of the actor contributed something to the tradition of this character: Tevye wears the physical toil of life in Anatevka echoed in later interpretations.

For some critics, Topol's performance in the film demonstrates a more youthful energy and masculinity. But Mostel's stage choices, stemming from his body's material need, nonetheless captured something true about Tevye that later actors continue to choose to echo. Marvin Carlson identifies how the stage remains "haunted" by history, both a play's performance history and the wider history of the world.[9] All performances of Tevye will be "haunted" by Mostel and by Topol. Previous iterations of the stage musical and the film all contribute to contemporary interpretations. Nostalgia about *Fiddler* oscillates between stage and screen, and the close connection between the play and the film indicates how porous nostalgic love for *Fiddler on the Roof* can be. Such nostalgia stretches through space and time. It might be extended, even, to the Yiddish-language version directed by Joel Grey and performed off Broadway just before and after the COVID-19 pandemic.

But are there boundaries that separate *Fiddler*'s interpreting communities? A boundary, presumably, across which the meanings of language, theology, tradition, and nostalgia require translation. The Yiddish *Fiddler* was hailed by the *New York Times* critic Jesse Green as offering "a kind of authenticity no other American *Fiddler* ever has."[10] Its language connects the musical to Green's own memories of Yiddish-speaking grandparents and the pain of forced migrations, then and now. The movement from English into Yiddish in New York is an innovation to the show's tradition. But the Yiddish version—even for my own goyish interpretation—captures a sense of spiraling elevation. *Fiddler* may have begun as a citation of the "old country" in the "new world," but *Fiddler* can be an open expression of cultural presence on and adjacent to Broadway. Nostalgia need not follow neat and tidy historical lines. Translation interprets, modifies, and applies. Tradition occurs during time by carrying the past into the present, but this past need not be an "authentic" replication of the play's own performance history to become nostalgic.

Bodies remember, however, and even a Yiddish-speaking Tevye needs to sit down. Clearly, an actor does not need to have an injured leg like Mostel in order to play Tevye well. Actors embody traditions via their performance choices. But does *Fiddler on the Roof* need to perform some tangible connection to Jewishness in order to succeed? Norman Jewison, the director of the 1971 film, was a gentile. But should the actor playing Tevye be Jewish? A test case emerged in the 2004 revival, which cast the gentile Spanish-British actor Alfred Molina as Tevye. Bial writes, "Still, in spite of all the 'goyim on the roof' cracks, the [2004] production has done well critically and commercially. Audiences and critics, Jews and non-Jews, have found much to enjoy in Molina's performance. Does this suggest that audience tastes have changed since 1964? Since 1971? I think not. Rather, I believe this revival, like many revivals of 'classic' shows, serves as a kind of screen on which audiences can project their nostalgic feelings about the original. [. . .] The musical about tradition has itself become one. And you don't have to be Jewish to love it."[11] The translation into Yiddish further serves Bial's point: You don't have to understand Yiddish to love it. Increased specificity clarifies. The scenography placed the story under the letter of the law, literally the Hebrew word *torah*. For moments in the script when Tevye speaks about rather than sings about tradition, the word is, instead, *torah*. Tradition is not merely that which cites the law; it is the law itself. Tradition hands on the law. The Yiddish production subverts the erstwhile Christianizing impulse to view emphases on law as restrictive, stultifying, and oppressive. Torah and tradition give meaning and purpose.

Bial's double coding can become a means to dislodge the presumption that mass appeal (the "gentile reading") operates to secularize the show. *Fiddler* not only cites religious phenomena in its performance of Jewish symbols, but the event of performance also makes religious or spiritual meaning through the show's traditions. This includes the expansion of the show's traditions by the Yiddish-language production to enfold *Fiddler on the Roof*'s ancestral Yiddish vaudeville. The play's traditions bespeak a nostalgia for the shtetl, nostalgia for midcentury Broadway, nostalgia for low-budget camp theatre, nostalgia for childhood singalongs, and nostalgia for a sense of uncomplicated belonging. Rather than suggest that these affects remain separate and index to the disposition and positionality of the interpreter, *Fiddler* crafts a porous nostalgia where the manifold meanings of its traditions are mutually reinforcing. Meanings and memories, including religious meanings, migrate across categories. According to theatre scholar Stacy Wolf, many Jewish summer camps in the 1970s began to use *Fiddler on the Roof*'s number "Sabbath Prayer" for Friday evening services, "marking the strong affiliation among Jewishness, Broadway musicals, and summer camp."[12] Nostalgia for religious and cultural and ethnic histories intermingle with nostalgia for popular entertainment and childhood.

Meaning emerges in the intermingling of performance and performance history, echoing Hans-Georg Gadamer's hermeneutics of tradition. For Gadamer, an apprehension of truth happens through a fusion of horizons between the present experience of a work of art and the history that the work carries. Interpreters discern the "truth" of a work of art through reference to the author's biography, expressed intent, and historical context but also in and through the way that work of art has been received, interpreted, and handed on as part of a tradition.[13] In other words, truth cannot be reducible to the creator's intent. Understanding depends on the encounter between interpreter and work. Traditions of interpretation stick and become a part of that work's meaning. What Gadamer calls a "history of influence" (*Wirkungsgeschichte*) becomes a route toward understanding in the present by enabling an interpretive conversation.[14] Theatre, as an interpretive art, makes an extremely good example for the influence of performance history on a work's meaning, and the haunting presence of Mostel's large body and injured leg in later interpretations of Tevye becomes a case in point. There are some well-known problems with Gadamer's hermeneutics of tradition, especially regarding tradition's apparent lack of a capacity to incorporate critique and its tendency toward deference to authority and authoritarians. Jürgen Habermas, among others, raises the need for critical attention to the ways a traditional understanding may also distort meaning as a mystification of oppressive power.[15] Too strict or unreflective a reliance on inherited understanding can sanction harmful prejudices and replicate oppressive ideologies.

Fiddler on the Roof's plot stages such critical negotiations of tradition within ongoing traditions. The play stages Tevye's struggle to accept and integrate his daughters' choices about marriage that differ from the expectations of tradition: from Tseitel's love match to Motle the poor tailor, to Hodel's to the revolutionary Perchik, and Chavah's betrothal to a gentile Christian. Tevye negotiates each bending of tradition through monologic prayers. At the same time, the musical and its reception raise questions about representation and kitsch. The plot depends on depictions of the ordinary and extraordinary sufferings of Eastern European Jewry.

Porous nostalgia leaves room for a critique of ideological distortion by situating a tradition in a pluralistic context. That is, *Fiddler on the Roof*, by virtue of its double coding, never limits its audience to one dominant religious or theatrical ideology. Indeed, the power of *Fiddler*'s traditions may well derive from the fact that the performance occurs at historical, aesthetic, and physical distance from the historical antisemitism and violence the show depicts. The play's journey to Anatevka happens in a Broadway or local theater: a public space for Jews and gentiles, believers and nonbelievers of all sorts. Porous nostalgia includes the double coding of violence and exclusion. All members of the audience play silent witness to the destruction of the wedding presents, banishment from Anatevka, and the slow walk of exile. Porous nostalgia begets an awareness of both painful loss and complicity.

In fact, the play relies on a dynamic account of tradition as something done in the present. How do we keep our balance? Movement, life, and play. Tevye demonstrates his own amalgam of *Yiddishkeit* stand-up comedy that meets prayerful halakhic reasoning. The balance of tradition requires constant engagement, perhaps including the way that engagement migrates from ordinary life onto a Broadway stage and back again. Consider the play's concluding procession. Emigration to America shows how tradition lives on in the present, how tradition moves from place to place. The character of the Fiddler on the Roof embodies and *plays* the tradition leitmotif—both in the sense of playing the violin to resound the tune and playing a dramatic character loaded with symbolic weight. The final stage direction describes how Tevye turns to invite the Fiddler to follow the family off-stage and bring the fiddle along with him.[16] The location of the shtetl rooftop matters far less than the playing of the theme. What *Fiddler* promises is the possibility of tradition continued (and perhaps modified) in and through the performance of the musical itself.

One could just as easily point to the significance of Jerome Robbins's choreography and the "bottle dance" that functions as a sign of both Jewishness and *Fiddler*ness during the musical Monty Python's *Spamalot*. Or the fact that "Sunrise, Sunset" continues to be sung at real weddings. *Fiddler on the Roof* conjures a porous nostalgia that calls into question the strict separation of spiritual meaning and empty spectacle. Donalee Dox argues that performance can be "a membrane between people's inner lives and the materiality of the social world." Dox writes, "Reimagined as a membrane or helix, performance is not only a site upon which to read the play of social forces and identity formation, but also a means by which people put the ineffability of their spiritual experiences into dynamic play with the materiality of discourses and material culture."[17] *Fiddler* models a version of Dox's membrane in the affective experience of "porous nostalgia." On the one hand, the musical invites a specifically Jewish diasporic community to identify with the old country. Staging Jewish material cultures alongside fictional memories of Anatevka can locate, concretize, and celebrate what has been lost and now found in America.

On the other hand, the musical resists ethnic or religious exclusivism by presenting its collection of cultures and rituals for the sake of entertaining a public audience. Nostalgia must read as sentimental and fun for both those inside and outside the community in order to remain profitable. *Fiddler* has been stridently critiqued for its assimilationist tendencies. Nevertheless, amateur productions of the musical (especially in schools) train non-Jewish communities to develop affection toward its representations of Judaism and Jewish history. On the *other* other hand (*pace* Tevye), the musical generates its own mutually reinforcing feedback loop between Broadway spectacle and lived experience. Varying and complex nostalgic feelings flow out from and through any performance of *Fiddler* much like the catchy melodies of its musical themes.

Fiddler on the Roof crafts porous nostalgia precisely because it continues as a living and transnational tradition in itself. *Fiddler on the Roof* demonstrates how Broadway's performative belonging—a feeling of community constituted by, with, and alongside the musical's performance—drives porous nostalgia. David V. Mason's theory in *The Performative Ground of Religion and Theatre* helpfully distinguishes between a sense of performance as that which masquerades something unreal as real and a sense of performance as that which brings into being.[18] Mason argues that both theatrical and religious creativity spring from the same poetic, rather than mimetic, human impulse.[19] Mason avoids the binary where theatrical signals fakery and religiosity signals authenticity; instead, "*performance* is always explicitly just what it is, because it *does* what it is."[20] What a performance of *Fiddler* does is create a sense of performative belonging. Insofar as an audience gathers to remember Anatevka, this memory and tradition belong to all.

Some critics have taken *Fiddler* to task for implying some necessity in assimilation in this movement from shtetl to stage. That is, what were once "real" and "binding" traditions have been rendered into mere entertainment. The "religious" value of dress, movement, story, even God falls away. But Lipshitz, building on the work of another theorist of tradition, Hizky

Shoham, argues, "On the one level, *Fiddler on the Roof* seems to advocate the secularization thesis, by situating religious tradition in the past. On another level, ironically, it serves as a ritual for a modern secular society, as it repeatedly conjures the very same past it allegedly leaves behind."[21]

I contend that *Fiddler*'s traditions go even further, filling a purportedly "secular" space with a possibility for religious tradition replayed anew. Over time, *Fiddler on the Roof* moves from (1) representing "tradition" as a rarefied object that remains distinct from the artistic event in which it is depicted (Mason's *mimesis*) toward (2) a ritual performance of a "tradition" that includes the audience, dynamically develops over time within history, and interfaces with other cultural phenomena (Mason's *poesis*). To perform *Fiddler on the Roof* is to continue its traditions now, not to present religious simulacra in exilic search of their "real" referent.

Fiddler's audience, therefore, keeps balance along with Anatevka's citizens, mixed and performative communities of Jews and non-Jews, Chavas and Fyedkas, mutually cheering dances "To Life" and shedding tears in witness to communal loss. It would be wrong to suggest that an experience of porous nostalgia at a performance of *Fiddler* renders a gentile into someone who can lay claim to this distinct religious and cultural "history" as my own. It would be equally wrong to say that *Fiddler* remembers any religiosity other than that of the world of its own play. Like any nostalgia, porous nostalgia is always and already constructed. Belonging to Anatevka and its memory subsists in performing, in doing. That is, the sense of belonging to nostalgia depends on inclusion in the tradition of the play itself, a tradition that always performs here and now. It makes great sense, then, that Tevye opens the play by teaching the audience how to keep its balance between entertaining surface and spiritual depth, audience and co-player, individual and community, love and duty, insider and outsider. The method for balance keeping comes down to one word: "tradition."

Pressed a step further, Tevye's public prayers become instructive for theologically interpreting the symbol of God on Broadway. First and foremost, Tevye directly addresses God, but no character or figure incarnates divine life on stage. As spoken prayers, Tevye's monologues are simultaneously public and private. Within the world of the play, these asides could be manifestations of a kind of interior speech. Within the physical conventions of theatre, it is not possible for the audience to overhear Tevye's thoughts unless the actor speaks these words into the world through performance, a sound effect, or some other stage device like a supertitle. Tevye's wrestling with change matches his relationship with God.

Phenomenologically, interior monologue exteriorizes at the material level of performance. A simpler, but perhaps more theologically complex interpretation, presumes that Tevye speaks to God aloud by turning his attention to the balcony. Tevye frequently addresses God directly by commenting on his own suffering, pleading for some consolation, making jokes as if with a good friend. God is an offstage character. The audience witnesses a prayerful closeness characterized by observational humor about the God who observes and knows all. When Tevye prays, however, the actor physically addresses the audience. Tevye frequently breaks the fourth wall for the sake of a joke. Some are less rigidly scripted but nonetheless inevitable. Right before "If I Were a Rich Man," Tevye explains to God that God made more poor people than rich people, including Tevye.[22] From his seated position, the line often soars upward to the rafters of the theater, to the balcony, where it reminds those in the cheap seats of their solidarity as one of those very many, many people that God has made who perhaps could not afford more expensive tickets.[23]

The sound of the tradition leitmotif signals the blurring of lines between the world of Anatevka and the event on a Broadway stage. Tevye's many reprises of "Tradition" are sung as self-referential monologues precisely at those moments when he is asked to permit action beyond the tradition as he inherits it. He interlaces with the tradition as a part of the tradition. Tevye models theological reasoning reminiscent of scripture and rabbinical argumentation rather than a questioning that undermines the validity of God's reality. To reason with God and about God is traditional, especially in those moments when theological reasoning discloses the necessity for those who perform the tradition to develop it over time in order to remain faithful to who God is rather than who one wishes God might have been.

Prayers as addressed to the audience are even more pronounced during Act II.[24] At the top of the act, Tevye's prayer attempts to make sense of the pogrom at the wedding. According to the stage directions, Tevye addresses this prayer to heaven. Tevye speaks directly to the audience asking God about the necessity of violence at the wedding. His question rings with threefold irony. This negative wedding dowry further impoverishes Tzeitel and Motel; the audience watched the destruction of the gifts immediately after a scene of their presentation to the newlyweds. Tevye calls the pogrom a dowry and so interprets persecution as perverse gift, one that perhaps leads to such happiness because destitution has no alternative comparison. Tevye seemingly admits the Job-like difficulty in praising God's gifts in the midst of the world's catastrophes allowed, ultimately, by God. The Act II monologue promises a quotation of the Good Book, but why quote the Torah to God? The question of necessity furthers dramatic irony. The constable "apologizes" for the pogrom while citing his need to follow orders.[25] The violence presents itself as necessary due to institutionalized antisemitism. But, structurally, the pogrom is fated by the script. Performance after performance, God's inverse dowry for Tzeitel and Motel *necessarily* ends the first act. But even within the plot of the play, the pogrom is not strictly necessary to further the plot. Showing the wedding violence serves to foreshadow the forced exile of the play's conclusion, but it offers nothing necessary to further the plot of the story. The wedding violence performs contingent to the whims of the playwright of this particular Good Book—script or scripture.

Evidence for Tevye's self-reasoning monologues as extended prayers appears in the most dramatic decision of the play: Tevye's choice to treat Chava as dead to the family due to her marriage to the Christian Fyedka. When Tevye admits he has no other hand of argument to bend rather than break, the final bit of reasoning has been similarly offered to heaven.[26] The song "Chavaleh" ends with the "Tradition" theme as Tevye draws a transparent curtain between father and daughter. Importantly, this veil is neither necessarily permanent nor impenetrable. In the end, Tevye appears to recognize God's capacity to remain with Chava in spite of or even through her religious intermarriage, communicating his hope and blessing via Tzeitel. Chava and Fyedka report they, too, will leave Anatevka due to widespread silence in the presence of the community's oppression.

What of the audience's silence throughout the play? God appears as and perhaps even in the audience, who has borne witness to Tevye's and Anatevka's prayers, celebrations, and pains. Locating the role of God in *Fiddler*'s audience invites two theological interventions, one open to various theological paradigms and the other more explicitly Christian. The first identifies tradition as the vehicle whereby God's presence becomes both legible and contestable. *Fiddler* displays how tradition carries testimony to relationship with God, but tradition is not coterminous with God in Godself. Tradition relates humans to God in the same way it relates humans to other humans across time and space.

Much to Durkheim's chagrin, the gathered audience does not bring God into being any more than the performance of the "Tradition" theme creates a newly Jewish community. Tevye's prayers are theatrical monologues, but they nonetheless reflect human relationship with God in all of its anguish. Tevye responds to a tragic impossibility in conflicts of parenthood, tradition, and the freedom of children.[27] Faithfulness and peoplehood coinhere for Judaism. If the audience remains aloof from or outside the events on stage, porous nostalgia invites that audience to co-participate in the fusion of religious and ethnic identity, at least for the length of the show.

If the audience plays the role of God, however, *Fiddler* invites a different form of theological solidarity. Silent witness bespeaks a kind of divine permissive will, one that reserves comment on the supposed necessity of suffering or intervention to change the course of events. Instead, Tevye's wish that God be with Chava offers the reply when bending tradition breaks. Might Tzeitel's communication—a handing on of the tradition—extend beyond Chava? Might it be to the whole audience, the very bodies who have, for a time, heard Tevye's prayers? Who, then, will be called on to answer them, if at all?

If the audience members can be interpreted as players in *Fiddler*'s theatrical event, they do so in a strange way. A crowd actively performs God's role passively without explicit intentionality or awareness. Any of the crowd's "choices" lack self-consciousness of the part they play. To see the audience as playing God, in some sense, instrumentalizes the material conditions of the Broadway space for the sake of new meaning about the world of the play. Performance becomes, yet again, like Dox's porous membrane flowing meaning between the narrative content of the play and its material form. Tevye's actor's choices "give" the audience their role much like in an improvisation where one's scene partner suggests characteristics to be played. Very little about the meaning of the plot of *Fiddler on the Roof* shifts if God can be found sitting in the house with the audience.

Yet there are theological suggestions latent in an audience that plays the God to whom Tevye prays. *Fiddler* already argues for the enactment of tradition as a conduit of porous relations. There is porous nostalgia at the level of a performance event and a porous theological possibility at borders between worlds "of the play" and "of performance." The God who the audience plays is a symbol of the God who is nonetheless present in the theater. In language reminiscent of Karl Rahner's phrasing, the symbol of God played by the audience thematizes the unthematic omnipresence of God.[28] Unlike a theological thematization, however, the symbol of God that *Fiddler* makes present through the theatrical traditions performed exceeds the limitations of the narrative, the location, the temporality of the play's showtime. Rather, *Fiddler*'s invocations disclose the dramatic nature of theological reflection on Broadway. God is in the house with us watching the play, just as God is with those going into exile, just as God is with the crucified peoples of the world's history, present, and future. God's reality moves across the porous membranes of performance, as real for these beloved imagined characters as for us.

Fiddler demonstrates how interpretations of the symbol of God cannot happen outside of the history that God has made. Indeed, the portable sound of the tradition motif corrects theological mistakes. Theology sometimes pretends to consider God without simultaneous consideration of the creaturely contexts and historical contingencies within which prayerful theological considerations transpire.[29] One imagines a theology that emerges from the ideal Anatevkas of imagined pasts. As von Balthasar reminds, dramatic theology remains aware that there is "no external standpoint" from which the theologian pronounces. All theology happens during the drama of history, inheriting and handing on tradition in time. *Fiddler* further teaches, however, that questions about the tradition can be asked from beyond the boundaries of the communities and institutions any tradition builds. *Fiddler* shows there is no external standpoint from which to interpret the symbol of God, but there are external standpoints from a religious community from which to query the doubts raised by suffering, by failure, by disaster.

"IT'S A PUBLIC THING"

Sean Patrick Shanley's theatrical response to the crisis of compromised institutions begins with a literal disaster: a sermon illustration about a sailor who loses sight of the stars. After a shipwreck, this lone survivor sets a course based on the night sky, but clouds soon roll in to cover the celestial map. He must sail based on trust in his original perception of the true way. Eventually, this lost sailor will experience a crisis of faith not unlike those in Father Flynn's congregation or the audience gathered to watch Shanley's play. Indeed, Flynn argues that doubt weaves connections as powerful as faith. But the audience of Father Flynn's preaching remains porous.

A priest directly addresses his congregaudience.[30] The sermon opens the play. Before any context of story, Flynn speaks as if in the given circumstances of a Sunday homily. He will preach again—on gossip—and sermonize to the boys' basketball team in the locker room.[31] But this first bit of preaching also interacts with the play's original performance context. Shanley has Father Flynn set the events of *Doubt, A Parable* in the fall of 1964, around the same time that *Fiddler on the Roof* opened on Broadway:[32] after Kennedy's assassination and in the midst of the third plenary session of the Second Vatican Council and its adjustments to the course of the church's history. Flynn is a proponent of the council's spirit of *aggiornamento*; we come to learn that Sister Aloysius is significantly more suspicious.[33] The play makes obvious that the concerns of the modern world reflect both theological issues and racial integration of the community. Donald Muller, the unseen young boy at the center of the play's dramas of potential abuse, is the school's first and only Black student. The stakes of how the school treats Donald could not be higher; as Flynn says, "It's a public thing. A certain ignorant element in the parish will be confirmed in their beliefs."[34] This priest has a particular concern for publicness, that which is outside the walls of the bastion of the church. Flynn also calls the feelings of "profound disorientation" at the assassination of President Kennedy "a public experience, shared by everyone in our society."[35]

The Second Vatican Council opened the windows of the church for fresh air, in Pope St. John XXIII's phrase. This young priest (the *dramatis personae* list Flynn's age as "late thirties") seems ready, like Hans Urs von Balthasar, to join the work of *Razing the Bastions* (first published in 1952) of the church's alienation from culture to aid the "descent of the Church into contact with the world."[36] Father Flynn (or Shanley) may well have prepared for this opening homily by reading some von Balthasar. Flynn addresses themes of God's direction (i.e., the theodramatic transition from role to mission), the drama of emotionally charged religious experience, theology's attention to God's kenotic experience, and understanding of what Flynn calls the "affliction" and "pain" of the "secret of an alienating sorrow."[37] Flynn recapitulates von Balthasar's theology of the cross and Holy Saturday in God's forsaking cry of dereliction in silence. For von Balthasar, the human experience of alienation from God participates in the Son's ultimate experience of abjection and rejection by the Father. God knows, intimately in Godself, the depths of Godforsakenness. Shanley, through the voice of Flynn, addresses divine silence in the experience of Doubt.

The play premiered in 2004, only a few years after the September 11 terrorist attacks and the first reports by the *Boston Globe* of widespread clergy sexual abuse. Shanley sought to dramatize his own theology of Doubt's (always with a capital D) superiority to certainty. He writes in the print version's preface, "Doubt requires more courage than conviction does, and more energy; because conviction is a resting place and doubt is infinite—it is a passionate exercise. You may come out of my play uncertain. You may want to be sure. Look down on that feeling. We've got to learn to live with a full measure of uncertainty. There is no last word. That is the silence under the chatter of our time."[38] To confront the silence of omnipresent Doubt requires becoming present to dramas of change: "It is Doubt (so often experienced initially as weakness) that changes things. [. . .] Doubt is nothing less than an opportunity to reenter the Present."[39] Flynn announces, "Your *bond* with your fellow human beings was your *despair*"[40] to an audience in the Manhattan Theatre Club, a room full of still-rattled Catholics and their neighbors, still-anxious New Yorkers and their neighbors. Doubt, too, can become the site for porous community.

The parable provides access to this Doubt that murmurs below the surface of an age that demands ever-increasing certainty. The political reality of the 2024 election invited Roundabout Theatre Company to do a twenty-year Broadway revival. But *Doubt, A Parable* opens up an essential distinction between the credibility of the church as a theme for theological reflection (what theologians might locate as an ecclesiological and pneumatological question) and the credibility of the church as an institution working in a pluralistic and uncertain world. Shanley's play makes abundantly clear that the credibility of institutions and leaders will be evaluated by both that institution's members (an in-group) and its neighbors (an out-group). Doubt operates in public.

The sermon from the stage pulpit makes a spectacle no less revelatory of Christian life for the non-Christian as the sermon from the church pulpit. The credibility of a religious institution as it performs amid other global and political institutions can be, and indeed has been, compromised across history. Tradition safeguards credibility; so, too, does God's Spirit safeguard credibility.[41] Spirit and institution go together within Christian thought, but there are various and contested questions about how these themes relate, including fundamental concerns for ecumenical theology and issues of religious authority.

The connection between spirit and institution, for von Balthasar, can be explained via his christological trinitarian pattern: The Holy Spirit is the person of the Trinity who illuminates and interprets the self-revelation of the invisible Father in and by the visible Son. As the love exchanged between God the Father and God the Son, God the Holy Spirit incorporates the members of the mystical body of Christ (i.e., the church) into the triune life of God. To enter into the love of God is to be enveloped in this movement of the Holy Spirit. So any attempt to analyze a theology of the church (an ecclesiology) already embarks on the task of a theology of the Holy Spirit (a pneumatology) because it is the Holy Spirit that inspires the church's authority and secures (salvific, transcultural, transhistorical) unity.[42] Discussions about the political reality of the church in the world (that which can be measured by social scientific research, legal argumentation, anthropology, documentary evidence, material culture, and stories of lived experiences) are related to ecclesiology and inform rich ecclesiological discussions but remain distinct from theologies of the church as a mystery.

The mysterious church that is also a public reality can be hard to describe. This play about doubt becomes a parable for the increasingly ubiquitous experience of compromised institutions in the United States using the church as its imagery.[43] These institutions have always compromised those on their margins. Awareness of the complex histories of compromised institutions belongs to modernity's signs of the times. Compromised institutions mar any community's *prima facie* worthiness for belief, trust, celebration. Compromised institutions are those that once held unquestionable power, prestige, and value but now must constantly re-legitimate themselves.

In moments of crisis, the weight of the evidence against the institution compounds with the reality of a damning history that was previously ignored and dismissible. The compromised institution does not signal a total rejection of traditions or social structures but reveals the inalienable complicity of its members who desire continuity with the past and a fidelity with it toward its future. Compromised institutions mean that *every* member now faces public questions. There cannot be any strategy that operates as a call to look away or keep Doubt hidden. My account of the compromised institution applies as readily to Christian churches as it does to any inherited and historical institution (e.g., universities, nation-states, economic systems, methods of research and teaching, political treaties, family systems, normative forms of social life). Shanley's play offers a parable for what it means when solid foundations become shaky.

Shanley's play is not a work of Catholic theology done as an ecclesial exercise within the church, but it *does* Catholic theology. The parable offers a response to the mystery of faith and Doubt that persists despite the compromised institution tasked with transmitting the tradition. But, as von Balthasar wrote prior to the council, "A truth that is merely handed on, without being thought anew from its very foundations, has lost its vital power."[44] *Doubt, A Parable* rethinks the very foundations of where an agent of tradition sits. The play does not try to speak about God outside the world that God has made but does move theological discussion outside the walls of the compromised institutional church. The play diverts the tradition from its mainstream but still puts God on Broadway by staging dramas of tradition.

STAGING THE TRUTH

Parables and theatrical dramas are closely related literary genres. Both can foreground the experience of self-understanding, but I mean two senses of self-interpretation. The first is key to what makes a story fit the characteristics of a parable and a playscript fit the characteristics of theatrical drama: the ontological (or conventional) requirements for interpretive choices. Parables and theatrical drama are self-interpretive insofar as no parable can be told without a wider narrative setting to provide interpretive clues. An act of interpretation precedes the primary act of reception. In the Gospels, parables often respond to questions or as expositions about Jesus's notion of the kingdom of God.[45] While the history of theatre presents more than a few plays that respond to eschatological questions (the medieval mystery *Everyman* trope or the Spanish baroque drama of Calderon de la Barca), all theatrical drama similarly responds to the prompt of inquiry. Stanislavsky called this the "magic if" that inaugurates the actor's work. Performers take hold of the text and its given circumstances and ask, "What if?" and respond with their performance choices.

Parables tell stories drawn from the experience of everyday life to illuminate and disclose inarticulate truths. I call the truth expressed by a parable inarticulate because parabolic storytelling simultaneously operates in symbolic, allegorical, and affective or personal modes. Let's begin with the obvious: Parables tell their stories using a symbolic language. We know this from the basic goal of a parable: to illustrate something, for instance the kingdom of God, through metaphor. Jesus *like* tells us *like* the kingdom is *like* a mustard seed, *like* a camel-threaded gate for the rich, *like* something better expressed through image and story than a discrete data point. Parables confirm that most of what we know that God reveals of Godself will not work identically to knowledge derived from empirical or observed data: Jesus can say, "The kingdom of God is among you" precisely because the kingdom of God is not of this world, not "coming with things that can be observed" (Luke 17:20–23).

Theology needs to tussle with the many different and overlapping meanings that symbols prompt. Parabolic metaphors do suggest some particular symbolic referents to be more important than other interpretive options. Parabolic stories can, of course, be read extratheologically, that is, the parable of the prodigal son is a good story worth interpreting on its literary and ethical merits in addition to any potential symbolic meaning for Christian theological interpretation. The situation of that parable within the framing narrative of Jesus's preaching and the situation of the Gospel within Christian life provide sufficient clues to the parable's theological-symbolic referent to call parables *allegories*. Pressed further, through this clarity of theological-symbolic referent—but inarticulacy of theological-symbolic *meaning*—parables can be understood as allegories meant to provoke action. A genre often compared to fables, parables include criticism of social organization and hierarchy, ethical and religious values, and frameworks for moral decision-making.

Parabolic speech—however surprising, poetic, enjoyable, or confounding it might be—enacts an intervention by pointing beyond itself toward some action or change in the world. The parable remains inarticulate as to the quality of that action. This inarticulacy of quality renders parables portable across existential situations, even amid a common audience. Parables speak differently to different people thanks to the parabolic resistance to disinterestedness: Parables address real existential concerns and real consequences. The parable might be a good story, but what renders a story parabolic is its capacity to grasp attention with affective and personal meaning.

The truth of a parable matters, especially because of the emotions and moral choices the parable discloses. Parables confront those who hear with questions of identity, belonging, relationship, desire, and reality—questions whose affective and social consequences remain contingent to individuals and groups. The parables of Jesus confront rich Christians *differently* from impoverished Christians, *differently* from ways they confront ordained or theologically trained Christians, *differently* from lay or nonprofessional Christians, *differently* from ways they confront nontheistic Buddhists or Orthodox Jews. Parables express inarticulate truth precisely in and through the complexities brought by their human receivers. On stage, parables create the conditions for porous nostalgia open to all the communities addressed in public.

The inability to articulate truth as a premise, however, should not challenge the existence of truth as such. As the premier genre for Christian theological speech, parables safeguard this inarticulacy of truth. History, and plenty of its theologians, demonstrates the problems that arise when the plurality of symbolic meanings in a phrase like "the kingdom of heaven" elides with the pragmatic and finite singularity of worldly dominions. But inarticulacy creates problems of its own. Doubts bubble to the surface when expressions of truth become too fuzzy around their edges. Inarticulate truths can stumble into incomprehensibility, mystification, and ideology. Power speaks more directly than truth, perhaps one reason for the *via dolorosa* from parabolic preaching to the cross. Indeed, the abuses of power can render truth's inarticulacy into silence, the sanction of unspeakable evil, passionate but ineffective platitudes.

Sometimes it takes a parable to speak what cannot be adequately named. Shanley consistently uses the architecture of the play to prepare audiences to understand the play's status as parabolic. Throughout the plot, Flynn's sermonizing employs made-up stories that consciously evoke Jesus's preferred method of teaching. The play begins with a homily. For the Christians in the house, these sermonizing moments feel familiar. But preaching trains the whole audience, Christian or not, how to interpret the entirety of the show.

Doubt, A Parable undoubtedly focuses attention on the clerical sexual abuse crisis in the Roman Catholic Church, even if Shanley, in recent conversations, distances himself as playwright from abuse as his topic of highest interest.[46] What does it mean to doubt a person's motives and actions? Who determines certainty? Can the church hold any religious authority if its leaders protect those who do violence against children instead of protecting the church's most innocent victims? But the play resists any slide into a whodunit even while the script drops crumbs and clues, stages interrogations and confessions, and lingers with gestures and evidence. Audiences (and classrooms) love to debate a central question of Brechtian judgment: Is Father Flynn guilty of the charge that he did something to Donald Muller, always presented through a circumlocution like "taking advantage"? The script leaves everyone, including Sister Aloysius, in doubt. The play offers no neat and tidy resolution; no moment leaves a character unmasked as the ultimate villain.

Parables make revelatory the masks we wear every day. Father Flynn offers the importance of parables that press to say more than the historical record: "What actually happens in life is beyond interpretation. The truth makes for a bad sermon."[47] Parables lack those direct analogs that make allegories easy to diagram. Instead, parables open mysteries for endless overlapping interpretations. Staging the truth—presenting the truth in all its complexity, horror, and grandeur—overwhelms. Flynn articulates that truth might make for a bad sermon, and the occasional bad play, because truth purportedly resists the work of interpretation. Truth-speak promises "seeing is believing," but parables recall the truth of faith beyond sight. The issue is, perhaps, more to do with the fact that the sermon is a monologue. In the memorable phrase of von Balthasar, truth resounds symphonically.[48] Flynn introduces parables to his preaching so to make the moment polyvocal. His two formal homilies are as much the words of Father Flynn as they are the characters of the shipwrecked sailor or nameless gossiping woman or the Irish-brogued confessor Father O'Rourke. Storytelling teaches human complexity more clearly than technical arguments can, and the play continually shows that the spectacle of a Catholic homily can descend from the stage as easily as from a pulpit.

Documentary theatre, like the process used by the Tectonic Theatre Project to create *The Laramie Project*, brings evidence from interviews and research to the stage. One can imagine a devised version of *Doubt* based on interview transcripts, court testimonies, and archival images. Such a play would have imbued Shanley's memories of Catholic schooling with a transparency to the reality of clerical sexual abuse. Shanley wrote *Doubt, A Parable* prior to the explosion of grand jury reports and other governmental investigations in the United States and abroad. Agencies outside the political authority of the church created public access to unequivocal evidence of the epidemic of clerical sexual abuse and its cover-up by the Roman Catholic Church. *Doubt, A Parable* grapples with both the particularities of abuse (whether sexual, spiritual, economic, interpersonal, academic, or corporate) and the power structures of patriarchy, clericalism, and hierarchy that create abuses' conditions and perpetuate them. But the play can be about many things, and it achieves its openness to interpretation as a parable.

The parabolic nature of the stage version also strongly contrasts with the film adaptation that Shanley both wrote and directed. *Doubt, A Parable* features only four actors. None of the schoolchildren is ever seen. The original Manhattan Theatre Club production and the more recent Roundabout revival benefited from the theatricality of absent children's bodies. The theatre of the mind can conjure greater horrors than can be shown on stage. The film, by contrast, lingers on close-ups and makes arguments without words. In the movie, Donald Muller can be seen on the altar behind Flynn during the first homily and is conspicuously absent during the second. Sister Aloysius wanders the aisles of the church scolding distracted little boys and girls during the first homily; the second homily breaks realism and displays the spectacle of feathers fluttering amid Bronx rooftops. Both are striking cinematic moments, but both subvert the transformation of the audience into Flynn's congregation. Given naturalistic choices on Broadway stages, the two sermons *can* perform with phenomenological similarity to a homily at church. A man in religious garments says words, and those sitting in the house hear them from across space-time. The stage version hovers closer to the lived experience of preaching than the film version ever could. The preached parable opens up a Catholic religious world, a New York world, a strange new world of the play.

The play is a parable; it is not history. But what, if anything, might be gleaned from a thought experiment that attempts to corroborate rather than doubt the historicity of the context that surrounds the events of the play? The historical moment of *Doubt, A Parable* matters perhaps as much as its geographical setting in the Bronx in terms of how it contributes to interpretations of the symbol of God. The timing of the events of the play can be non-precisely divined from some evidence in the script and suggested scenography, but I make no claim that Shanley or the designers intended to drop these clues for an overdetermined academic analysis. Instead, I mean only to show that the parable provokes special meaning under the scrutiny of Catholic theological interpretation. I have already discussed how the play opens with Father Flynn reminding the congregaudience about the disorienting feelings caused by the assassination of President Kennedy "last year" on November 22, 1963. It makes sense for the events of the play to happen close to that anniversary. November 22 did fall on a Sunday in 1964, and Flynn's sermon may use the theme of Doubt to anticipate the disorientations of the new vernacular liturgy about to be introduced the following week, on the first Sunday of Advent, November 29.[49]

Let's imagine a version that stays slavishly loyal to the evidence of the printed script's costume choices.[50] At the top of the play, Flynn wears "green and gold vestments."[51] This is the sermon Sister Aloysius and Sister James discuss in the next scene: "This past Sunday. What was he talking about?" "Well, Doubt."[52] We know from subsequent scenes that the play takes place in the early part of the school year, in the fall. Scene 4 begins with Sister Aloysius wrapping rosebushes to *protect* them from the first frost that has, importantly, not yet come.[53] Yet weather records indicate that the first freeze of 1964 occurred on Saturday, November 21, 1964.[54] Adjunct to this bit of meteorological data, Sister Aloysius uses the upcoming Christmas pageant as a pretext to confront Father Flynn in scene 5.[55] The first few scenes make much sense if they were to take place in mid-November 1964.

A wrinkle appears in the temporal fabric of the sixth scene because it features Father Flynn preaching on the theme of gossip—presumably his "intolerance" sermon idea made manifest—while wearing "blue and white vestments."[56] These are the traditional colors of Marian devotion. This may well have been one of the daily mass sermons brought about by a *moto proprio* of Paul Pope VI that introduced preaching to all celebrations of the liturgy beginning in February 1964. If so, these vestments could track with the weather reports and make sense for Saturday, November 21 and the presentation of the Blessed Virgin Mary.[57] Sister James brings up the accusatory nature of the homily, wondering if it might be about "anyone in particular" and by referencing the "big hand pointing a finger" in Flynn's parable illustration.[58] If the sermon appeared at a daily mass attended mostly by the religious community of St. Nicholas School on the weekend, then it makes it much harder to imagine that Flynn meant to indict anyone more than Sister Aloysius. The theme of gossip is also germane to the story of the presentation of the future virgin mother of God and its relationship to the apocryphal protoevangelium of James. Theological and mundane questions about paternity are always a rich source of gossip.

But it makes much more sense for Flynn's gossip sermon to be a homily for the whole community—clergy, religious, and laity—both calling to mind Sister Aloysius's accusations of Father Flynn and, at the same time, serving as his public attempt to quell rumors about why Donald Muller had been removed from the altar boys. The film version and the Roundabout production do not include the white and blue vestments, but the choice to set it on Sunday in the movie makes it clear that even Shanley imagines this moment for the whole of the community. Where would it fit with the white liturgical color? That would require some time to pass and accounts for Flynn's line that "I actually avoided [Donald Muller] the other day when I might've passed him in the hall."[59] A more public occasion would put the gossip homily on a Sunday or some other holy day of obligation.

So there is another route to dating the events of the play. Sunday, November 22 would have been the final Sunday of the liturgical calendar but would still have called for green vestments in 1964.[60] As the exact one year anniversary of the Kennedy assassination, this date, though it confounds the weather records, would be the most natural place for Flynn to talk about feelings in the aftermath of Kennedy's death and preach on Doubt during the conciliar reforms of the liturgy. We know that Flynn follows and supports the work of Vatican II. The young priest explicitly references the "message of the Second Ecumenical Council" in his arguments with Sister Aloysius.[61] (A parable should be forgiven its lack of regard for the real weather report.)[62]

Situating the first Doubt sermon on Sunday, November 22 means that the subsequent Sundays (November 29, 1964, and December 6, 1964) are the first and second Sundays of Advent, respectively. They would feature violet vestments in addition to the new vernacular liturgy. The most proximate day with an obligation for the laity *and* prior to the Christmas pageant *and* that calls for white vestments happens to be a major Marian feast traditionally associated with that blue tinge: the Solemnity of the Immaculate Conception of Mary.[63]

Immaculate Conception, the patronal feast of the United States of America, fell on Tuesday, December 8, 1964. Immaculate Conception also provides ample theological foundations for Flynn to take on the theme of gossip, perhaps even addressing the entire school community in attendance. How do Catholics reckon with rumors about the Blessed Virgin Mary? What happens to Mariology as the church lurches toward the modern world? Those following the events of the council probably knew about the great debates on the status of a Mariological constitution, with the council's Marian teachings ultimately folding into its document on the church, *Lumen Gentium*.[64] Placing the gossip sermon on Immaculate Conception also makes it far less likely that Flynn could be credibly accused of singling out Sister Aloysius.[65] Instead, the pillow parable becomes a vehicle to hold rumors about the change in altar personnel in addition to changes in which direction the priest faces during the consecration. Surely then as now there were rumors that Catholic Mass in the vernacular appeared too Protestant.

A savvy reader might be confused as to why I have spent so many words on historical trivia surrounding Father Flynn's costuming if the play is a parable. Parables *do not* neatly index to their referents as a part of their genre. Few audience members would notice any performance choices informed by this kind of hyper-particular dramaturgy; few theologians and theatre scholars take solace in the small-talk question "How's the weather?" But the ecclesial context matters as much as the political one for a theological reading.

This parable does theology despite the wishes of its producers. At a talkback I attended after a performance of the Broadway revival of *Doubt* on March 2, 2024, Shanley suggested that he did not consider his play to be "about" the revelations of sexual abuse by Roman Catholic clergy. Shanley took more interest in locating the play within the emergence of conspiratorial thinking after the Kennedy assassination and the problems of hierarchical control over what counts as the truth. For Shanley, the play is public, and so, too, are its meanings.

The play's religious dimension becomes a matter of the playwright's memory (he went to a school called St. Anthony staffed by the Sisters of Charity that inspired the play's St. Nicholas School) and an excuse for a richly realized world of religious habits: costumes, prayers, and symbols. It makes for lush visual theatre, especially in the beautifully designed Roundabout revival. But in that production, the Catholic world remained invoked rather than replicated. Aloysius's elegantly decorated office made basic mistakes for a character depicted as a theological conservative in the age of Vatican II: Its cross had no corpus, and the principal's shelf held a picture of Pope St. John XXIII but no image of the reigning Pope St. Paul VI. Few in the house would notice or be thrown by the scenography in the same way the professorial Catholic author of a book titled *God on Broadway* might.

So even in 2024, this parable has its own version of porous nostalgia. Perhaps the Catholic nostalgia appears to be for a time when "the faith, which held us together, went beyond the precincts of religion. It was a shared dream we agreed to call Reality."[66] Yet the traditions depicted on stage are living symbols of a church still negotiating the aftermath of liturgical reforms and revelations of clerical sexual abuse. The tradition promises Reality still, but it is a child's promise. Perhaps the religious themes matter less *because* the church matters less when culture "outgrows" old religiosity.

But faith is not limited to religion. If the political backdrop of the 2004 premiere included unfounded rumors of weapons of mass destruction that sent US troops into Iraq, then the political backdrop of its revival twenty years later must include Doubt prompted by misinformation about vaccines, QAnon, echoes of the January 6 attack on the US Capitol, and elections in an era of deepfakes generated by artificial intelligence. The parable addresses Doubt of all sorts.

Shanley argues in his preface, like so many Enlightened playwrights, "The beginning of change is the moment of Doubt."[67] A very different parable, Octavia E. Butler's speculative fiction novel *Parable of the Sower*, imagines a religion built on the claim "God is Change." No diversion into Earthseed is necessary to highlight that parables radiate their meanings in unexpected directions. Butler's apocalyptic parable reveals the ordinary horrors faced by climate migrants just as readily as Shanley's vision of a church filled with predators. Change and Doubt do not necessarily evacuate the symbol of God from communicating grace. On stage, a man in a chasuble nonetheless makes a sign of the cross and intones, "In the name of the Father, and of the Son, and of the Holy Ghost." On stage, two nuns are dressed in black and white capped with the bonnets of the Sisters of Charity and talk about the obligations of religious life, vows, and service to God. The play's questions about Doubt, sin, trust, vocation, damnation, and relationship reverberate with potential for theological meaning. Further, this play's porosity to the tradition it depicts hands on its reflections back to that tradition. Broadway can ask questions and entertain Doubt that the church should not but must.

BENEDICTIONS

A sort of truism from Rev. Theodore M. Hesburgh, CSC, the former president of the University of Notre Dame, often winds its way into conversation about Catholic schools: "A Catholic university should be a place where the Church can do its thinking."[68] Broadway seems also to be such a place, though plays and musicals think differently from scientists and scholars. I am one such scholar instrumentalizing. Instrumentalization further invites Doubt into regions beyond its own interests to make meaning about the symbols of God the compromised institution hands on via its tradition. As we saw in *Fiddler*, that tradition can move, even onto the Broadway stage. On Broadway, Doubt seeks understanding as readily as faith. Broadway theaters *are not* "communities of Doubt" in the sense of a religious community, a congregation, a church. But they are places where the churchy questions arising from Doubt can be asked and answered, can be ritually enacted and offered, can be prayed and rejected.

Revelations of evil perpetrated in the name of God call institutions who name God into radical question. Over time, that questioning settles in to the order of the day, where the church faces a fundamental burden of proof that confounds the Christian understanding of faith as gift. Questions that undermine the viability of the tradition are fair and long-standing, but the church has few resources from that tradition to answer them. Doubt asks questions from outside "the faith." As a result, revelations of evil perpetuated in the name of God call participation in the church's project to name God as a kind of complicity in the church's evil. Place those revelations in a cultural context where religious affiliation has become a choice among identity choices on the drop-down menu, and theology faces a dilemma it cannot solve other than by dodging the question. In the church, God can be easily distinguished from the sinful actions of free human beings. Grace empowers the good of the institutional church; sinful abuses of freedom lead to the evil done by human beings who also happen to make up the people of God. Christianity and its Edenic fall make sense as a religion of a few bad apples. These answers are ultimately unsatisfactory in public because they are not public answers. They speak from within the tradition and within the church. So what does it mean to invite the church's theology—the interpretation of the symbol of God in the light of God's self-revelation—to take a *literal* step away from the church onto the stage?

Theological dramatic theory, von Balthasar's and others', contends that the stage shows the human experience. Theatrical parables become mirroring, the stage showing the world back to the world. Humanity recognizes itself. As von Balthasar writes, "In the theatre man attempts a kind of transcendence, endeavoring both to observe and to judge his own truth, in virtue of a transformation—through the dialectic of the concealing-revealing mask—by which he tries to gain clarity about himself. Man himself beckons, invites the approach of a revelation about himself. Thus, parabolically, a door can open to the truth of the real revelation."[69]

Von Balthasar identifies the kind of meta-parable that *Doubt* presents. Religious symbols operate parabolically in reference to themselves by using religious symbols at a distance. As Shanley contends, "I've set my story in 1964, when [. . .] the old ways were still dominant in behavior, dress, morality, world view, but what had been organic expression had become a dead mask."[70] The play allows that "dead mask" to convey something vital *because* it steps out from the church and onto the Broadway stage. The nun's habit becomes not Shanley's "dead mask" but von Balthasar's "concealing-revealing mask" both for the actress and for religious life. For Catholics, *Doubt, A Parable* became a site for God's revelation in the midst of revelations of clergy sexual abuse. The danger remains treating revelation instrumentally and so indulging in Pollyannaish equivalences. Revelations of clergy sexual abuse are not revelations of divine origin because evil does not break into the world but emerges from within its order.[71]

But learning about a compromised institution does demand acting differently toward it. Sister Aloysius, the school's headmistress, argues that "innocence can only be wisdom in a world without evil. Situations arise and we are confronted with wrongdoing and the need to act."[72] That action, for Aloysius, undoes the comforts of walking alongside the Lord: "When you take a step to address wrongdoing, you are taking a step away from God, but in His service."[73] Aloysius sees action as mission, a sending *away* from God to do God's work. Her orthodoxy might depend on how the line is played. If you take the step away from God, it is hard to see that choice as anything but Augustine's *incuravtus in se*, the turning into oneself that is sin, justified *ex post facto* as service to the Lord. The parabolic nature of the play keeps the arising situation ambiguous and interesting; we are never confirmed by wrongdoing during the play. If Flynn is innocent, the play confronts the audience with a series of false allegations. The evidence for Sister Aloysius's decision to take action against Father Flynn remains offstage. We never learn, conclusively, whether Father Flynn really "interfered with Donald Muller"; Sister Aloysius has proven it only to herself.[74] We only know that Father Flynn has left St. Nicholas to be appointed by the bishop to be "the pastor of St. Jerome Church and School. It's a promotion."[75] But Sister Aloysius's step-away-from-God line returns, with gusto, as the play's final benediction on the costliness of pursuing a credible attestation of a compromised institution:

> Sister Aloysius: In the pursuit of wrongdoing, one steps away from God. Of course there's a price.
> Sister James: I see. So now he's in another school.
> Sister Aloysius: Yes. Oh, Sister James!
> Sister James: What is it, Sister?

> SISTER ALOYSIUS: I have doubts! I have such doubts!
> (*Sister Aloysius is bent with emotion. Sister James comforts her. Lights fade.*)
> END OF PLAY

To risk a step away from God is to step outward toward the world and its doubts.[76] To act in accord with one's role in mission invites the experience of alienation. The parable that Shanley creates in *Doubt* physicalizes Sister Aloysius's step away from God toward "such doubts." Signs of Catholic religious aesthetics parade on a secular stage; there is no real presence to adore or avant-garde theatrical invitation to pray. Perhaps some Catholics instinctively do the sign of the cross along with Father Flynn at the end of his homilies, but this spectacle is not a liturgy (for spectacles of liturgy, I will look at theatrical sacraments in a future chapter).

The play thus concludes with the same ambiguity about spectacle and liturgy with which it begins. The audience plays congregation to Flynn's preaching and sits in judgment of the righteousness of the actions taken by the play's characters. As in *Fiddler on the Roof*, it seems that the audience unwittingly performs a role of God in a spectacle about a religious community. *Doubt, A Parable* presses this point even a bit further.

Much of the play resonates with overtones of the Second Vatican Council, but it also performs one of Vatican II's most profound ecclesiological interventions, as articulated in *Sacrosanctum Concilium* 7. The Christ is present through the prayer and song of the gathered assembly of the church. That is, the Christ is present in the person of the priest ministering *in persona Christi*, the sacrament of the Eucharist understood to be the real presence of the Christ, and the proclamation of sacred scripture that is "his word, since it is He Himself who speaks when the holy scriptures are read in the Church."[77] But the Christ is also present during the collective gathering. This parable of a play is neither scripture nor liturgy; the actor in the robes is *in persona Flynni*, not *Christi*. But *Doubt*, like any Broadway spectacle, performs in the created world that God has loved into being. Broadway spectacle invites an encounter with the God that undoubtedly must be present outside the church's boundaries, languages, and practices in ways that can only be recognized as the God revealed in the Christ by reference to the church's tradition. The play calls into question religious institutions and ecclesial communities and, in so doing, invites interpretations of God in light of the doubts brought by God's faithful ones.

But the play nonetheless ends with Sister Aloysius's doubtful benediction, her own prayer of confession, her testimony to Doubt's enduring presence. Prayers born out of Doubt are no less prayers. A step away from a closed ecclesial community need not also be the same as a step away from God. Plays like *Doubt, A Parable* may reveal something of God missed by the insularity of church culture. It becomes the best of what Vatican II achieved, the recognition of the church *in* the modern world full of shared doubting, "joys and hopes, griefs and anxieties."[78] Sister Aloysius offers a final sending.

Doubt, A Parable is only one act. An apocryphal story recounts that the ensemble talked in interviews about a post-curtain second act: the conversations between people sharing their impressions and judgments about Father Flynn's guilt or innocence; their own complicated memories of nuns like Sister Aloysius or Sister James; their own confusions or discoveries made while navigating the play's intersectional questions of race, class, sexuality, church reform, violence, patriarchy, and theological credibility. Shanley's parable invites those post-performance conversations in the world to become dramatic acts of theological interpretation. The play ends, and yet, in Hamlet's phrase, "time is out of joint." The next chapter, after another short scene, thinks about how Broadway reveals God's time. When a curtain falls, the show continues. Tunes from *Fiddler* continue to reverberate and resonate. *Doubt* makes the reality unavoidably theological. Audiences keep talking about Father Flynn's guilt or innocence, the credibility of institutions after revelations of abuse and failure, the difficult choices faced by parents and educators, the histories we remember and those we prefer to forget. The play keeps playing even after it ends. Paradoxically, only through conversations had while leaving the theater, after the dramatic revelation of the "facts," can theology start to interpret the doubts staged by Broadway spectacle as a resource for understanding questions anchored by faith.

In-One

On Blasphemy

Where shows like *Fiddler* and *Doubt, A Parable* hold religious imagery in care, other Broadway shows seem only to confirm the earliest Christian objections to theatre as a place for blaspheming the divine. A major recent example of the symbol of God on Broadway belongs to *The Book of Mormon*. And the symbol of God is *powerful*.

Elizabeth Johnson asserts, "The symbol of God functions."[1] Johnson's magnificently productive phrase sums up her point that a community's speech about God influences action, beliefs, and worldviews. Words about the divine are "neither abstract in content nor neutral in its effect, speaking about God sums up, unifies, and expresses a faith community's sense of ultimate mystery, the world view and expectation of order devolving from this, and the concomitant orientation of human life and devotion."[2] For Johnson, such speech emerges from and circulates within the "faith community." The predominance of masculine language for God *functions* within church communities to produce a male image of God. That imagery embeds itself into structures and presumptions. Theological rules might shout that the infinite God transcends creaturely sexual categories, but theological and ecclesial speech nonetheless prefers male pronouns and words as symbols for speaking about God: "The symbol of God functions. Upon examination it becomes clear that this exclusive speech about God serves in manifold ways to support an imaginative and structural world that excludes or subordinates women."[3] Johnson demonstrates how patriarchal ideology occludes and distorts theological reflection. Over time, the ubiquity of certain symbols for God makes it harder and harder to parse differences between God's self-revelation about God's identity and human intellectual comforts and cultural norms. Theologians, Johnson says, must pay close attention to how the symbol of

God functions, how it gives rise to meanings, in order to speak rightly about God. Theologians serve faith communities to provide language and imagery that continue to speak rightly about God in the present. Theology interprets.

The symbol of God also functions on Broadway. There, the symbol of God functions for a wider audience than just one community of faith. The symbol of God functions *without* regard for a "faith community." Like the ceiling of the Sistine Chapel, the symbols of God that appear on stage contribute to a cultural imaginary that influences the imaginary of believers and nonbelievers, Catholics and non-Catholics, show people and those who prefer a quiet night with a book to a night on Broadway. It may be tempting to simply substitute a religious community of faith for a cultural fandom; indeed, amalgamated fandom in the service of positivity and care and emotional acceptance in a utopian future seems to be the theological conclusion to *The Book of Mormon*, with the hope that "Tomorrow Is a Latter Day." Maybe a better religion would come from the well-meaning nerds like Elder Cunningham or the theatre people: those lovers of show tunes and good stories, generally open to and accepting of challenges to cultural norms, fun to have at a party and dangerous for their defensiveness and ability to stir up interpersonal drama.[4] There may be good reasons that many, many civilizations have refused actors the right to vote or participate in government. I want to suggest that Broadway reaches beyond even the analogous "community of faith" that is show people. As a commercial operation, Broadway aims to be accessible to the widest possible audience.

Sister Aloysius steps away from God toward a play quite literally dedicated by its author "to the many orders of Catholic nuns who have devoted their lives to serving others in hospitals, schools and retirement homes."[5] Little of *Doubt, A Parable* rises to the charge of blasphemy despite its use of theological ideas. Importantly, the symbol of God does not require a religious context in order to function. Artists, writers, politicians, parents, courtrooms, game designers, travel companies, and journalists all invoke the power of the symbol of God with frequency. For insurance companies, the symbol of God functions to hold space open to be absolved from covering those unimaginable and inexplicable "acts of God." So what differentiates these invocations of the divine from religious use? A commonsensical answer points to intention or the presence of faith. That is, the symbol of God becomes religious when its users *intend* it to be religious (whatever that slippery word *religious* happens to mean). The sentence "The bread tastes like God made it" has a different meaning for the restaurant critic who intends it as a compliment to a pastry chef than it might for a Christian who intends to describe the gustatory experience of the Eucharist.

An often (but not exclusively) Christian corollary to this argument adds that the symbol of God becomes religious due to the presence of something like faith. The symbol of God only makes a transcendental reference to God through an act of faith. Faith that is a participation in the reality of God secures the meaning of the symbol of God. In that sense, faith is properly a great gift of the Holy Spirit, who sustains the symbol of God's reality. But when deployed without faith, the symbol of God becomes an empty signifier pointing only to a fictional projection of an idea.

The category of blasphemy calls both explanations deeper into question. The nonbeliever blasphemes by intentionally sullying, mocking, defaming, and deriding the symbol of God. But blasphemy suggests that one can intend to use the symbol of God religiously without believing in the truth of its referent. Concern for the nonbeliever's blasphemy implies the existence of faithless religiosity rather than the faithful doubt depicted in both *Fiddler* and *Doubt*. For Christianity, this would look like participation in the symbolic system without the assistance of the Holy Spirit to ensure the symbol system's truth.

Consider some contemporary examples of "invented religions" like Pastafarianism, where practitioners ground belief in demonstrations of empirical data rather than a theological virtue.[6] Here, the symbol of God functions without need of faith as an additive to orient the word rightly to the divine referent. The website for the Church of the Flying Spaghetti Monster plays with Michelangelo's imagery—substituting the deity's noodley appendage for the hand of a white bearded man—aiming to dislodge literalism in the interpretation of the symbol of God.[7] The elaborate costumes and playfulness of the Pastafarians can invite simplistic comparisons to theatricality. Despite their legal right in some states to be photographed for government identification cards wearing the "traditional" Pastafarian headdress (a colander, of course), many reject the public events of the Church of the Flying Spaghetti Monster as nonreligious performance art. Accusations of blasphemous theatricality aim to undo the function of the symbol of God.

In its contemporary expression, many Satanists explicitly reject that the mythological symbols in religions correspond to any ultimate reality. Joseph Laycock argues for the need for subtle understandings able to negotiate between atheists participating in the Satanic Temple and other neo-pagan

Satanists who do hold a transcendental referent for devilish symbols.[8] According to the Satanic Temple, religion's protected status oppresses nonbelievers. The Satanic Temple therefore offers atheists the cultural privilege of a religious community and tradition that can exploit religious freedom laws. Contemporary Satanism proposes a set of counter-symbols to quell the allure of Christianity or other religious beliefs. Satanists, for example, have developed twelve-step sobriety programs that debunk the need for belief in a higher power in order to manage addiction. Indeed, the symbol of Satan functions as a counter-symbol to undo the function of the symbol of (the Christian) God, including practices and rites meant for atheists. The ultimate goal of a statue of Satan at a courthouse might be the removal of all religious symbols, particularly the symbol of God retained in a placard of the Ten Commandments. Like the erection of satanic monuments on public land, even a contemporary celebration of the so-called Black Mass may invert the symbolic order (including its requirement for a validly transubstantiated host) as a provocation to worldly authorities rather than as an act of worship for God's mythological adversary. But certain Satanists' nonreligious performance art nonetheless also operates within the Catholic-Christian symbol system. With neither intent nor belief, the symbol of God functions both within and beyond the faith community.

The symbol of God functions regardless of intent or belief, but I want to leave space open for questions about the theological efficacy of that function. Determining what counts and what does not count as a "religion" remains one of the most vexing questions for religious studies as well as theology (even before it appears in legal or literary theories). This point rings especially true if one holds that the explanatory power of terms becomes diluted when that term might apply to anything and everything: "If everything can be 'religious,' then nothing is 'religious' enough to be worthy of study as such." The same formula attacks performance studies: "If everything can be a 'performance,' then nothing is 'performative' enough to be worthy of study as such." Therefore, I want to sidestep the quagmire of "religion" and "performance" in favor of the significantly more fruitful fields of theology and theatre. This book has looked to how spectacles of the symbol of God function theologically when they appear in Broadway theatre. Terms from religious and performance studies operate to disclose quite particular meanings within the realms of theological and theatrical phenomena. Regardless of the intent or belief of theatrical creators, the symbol of God functions to show something about God.

The problem, of course, is that some of the most interesting, entertaining, and provocative disclosures of God are rather blasphemous. The desire to protect God from blasphemy instills a standard of purity for theology regarding its tone rather than its content. Blasphemy spreads beyond the boundaries of a religious community to impose a standard of reverence on public debate and conversation. Extra-ecclesial theologies need to meet the minimum standard of reverence: One might not pray like the believers, but one must respect the dignity of even the symbol of God. Speech about God, even for the non-pious, must strive to be pure.

Broadway—like all extra-ecclesial popular and vernacular theologies—eschews purity as an a priori goal. Broadway spectacles undo restrictive purity that limits theologies to propriety or convention. That is, standards of social propriety are historically and culturally contingent and mutable. The very same idea that strikes as a blasphemous affront to Christian sensibility in one century signals the in-breaking of renewing grace later; what operates as an unexamined cultural norm for theology in one era appears to be an obvious error in a later time as the church develops its doctrine and understanding. Blasphemy names the indecent until it doesn't.[9]

The next two chapters investigate how Broadway spectacles provide symbolic resources that help theology interpret God in terms of *time* and *stuff*. The spectacular arrival of angels opens theodramatic reflection on apocalyptic temporality, and the spectacular staging of sacraments will call to mind ritualizing bodies. But the use of religious symbols in these shows steps even further away from God than paying prayerful attention to dangerous memories live on stage or the investigations of communities, faith, and tradition in previous chapters. Broadway shows refuse to allow theological interpretations to be sanitary from the contagion of the world and its many differences. Luckily enough for Christian theology, this contagious world is the one that God has made.

To address the charge of blasphemy calls for either its own book or a brief detour, but one show can well set the stage for the spectacles to come *because* of the way it plays with time, stuff, angels, bodies, and blasphemous combinations. *The Book of Mormon* deploys religious ideology for big laughs. The show lampoons what is laughable about religiosity and reframes what it takes to be beautiful about believing. But the exemplar of the show's critique of religion—Mormonism—becomes just as much a critique of Disneyfied Broadway and American culture. Heaven sounds a lot like Orlando, Florida;

creator Robert Lopez and original cast star Josh Gad are themselves part of the creative team behind Disney's *Frozen* franchise.

The Book of Mormon is as much a send-up of the religious text, the book of scripture, as it is the book musical and its structure. Multiple numbers find their inspiration directly in well-loved Broadway moments: "You and Me (but Mostly Me)" evokes *Wicked*'s "The Wizard and I"; "Joseph Smith American Moses" loudly echoes a patter song retelling of a nineteenth-century American story reminiscent of the "Uncle Tom's Cabin" sequence from *The King and I*. But no theme more explicitly or directly calls to mind the nexus of American religion, Disney, and Broadway than the recurring use of *The Lion King* as the show's hermeneutic for Africa. A Rafiki-like character appears intermittently to intone the sound of the savannah through references to the ritualized opening of "The Circle of Life." But the connection to *The Lion King* lands explicitly in one of the show's most memorable numbers and musical leitmotifs.

"Hasa Diga Eebowai" works both independently and within the plot as a conscious send-up of *The Lion King*'s "Hakuna Matata." The Swahili-sounding (but gibberish) catchphrase swirls through catchy layered harmonies. The connections become kind of overt when Elder Cunningham asks if these special words also mean "no worries" in English. This phrase works similarly to Timon and Pumbaa's philosophy of life. "Hasa Diga Eebowai" responds when things go bad, a way to cope with hardship. Of course, a big laugh arrives in the form of what "Hasa Diga Eebowai" does happen to mean as a response to God. I'll hide the translation in a footnote for the sake of propriety and so not to spoil the fun for someone who has never heard the song.[10]

The number intends to be as offensive as possible. Humor derives from its shock value. It juxtaposes the sufferings of crowded and delayed travel incurred by the white American missionaries on their journey to the everyday sufferings experienced within the show's projection of an imagined Africa characterized by violence, hunger, and poverty. While theatre critics adored the Tony Award winner, other reviewers rightly compared the disjunction between the effort needed for the affectionate and often, but not entirely, accurate mockery of Mormon theology and practice to the laziness in the show's Ugandan stereotypes.[11] Some of the show's overt racism in its vision of a technologically and culturally backward Africa—such as typewriters for "texting"—were removed for its return to Broadway after the COVID-19 hiatus.[12]

The number is as potentially insightful as it is undoubtedly violent. "Hasa Diga Eebowai" functions as a blasphemous protest prayer but one whose truth-value for interpreting revelation radiates only in the extra-ecclesial theological space of the Broadway stage. We learn the validity of the phrase as prayer in Act II. The words "Hasa Diga Eebowai" and tune are reworked and reprised at the finale into *thank you, God*. The musical phrase is neither an offertory hymn nor suitable for a sacred music concert. And "Hasa Diga Eebowai," however funny and provocative, surely does some harm in its depiction of human suffering for the sake of amusement and in its conscription of certain bodies to perform the jokes. Broadway spectacles that play with blasphemies often do so at great ethical risk.

But "Hasa Diga Eebowai" nonetheless presses a theological question worth asking: What blasphemies offend cultural sensibilities but do not offend God? The number runs roughshod over the niceties of north Atlantic religiosity, where cursing God's name and naming sexual violence blaspheme propriety and social niceties. Instead, "Hasa Diga Eebowai" addresses when and where choices by those in positions of comfort seek to correct the language of those living through famine, poverty, and war. I am not interested in critiquing or defending the number's ethics or the show's value, but I am interested in how the offensiveness of this number uplifts the reasonableness of a theatrical blasphemous protest prayer as the cry to God of those who are poor in the midst of rampant injustice. About three-quarters of the way through "Hasa Diga Eebowai," the African characters turn to the missionary characters and the audience to ask whether opinions about how and what is distasteful when said about God might change if one spent a few days living in their context and witnessed frequent loss of loved ones. A response to such suffering that praises God befits only Job's faithfulness or delusion. A good God of love would not delight in the suffering of God's creatures. Perhaps the blasphemies displayed in "Hasa Diga Eebowai" are material rather than verbal. This spectacle unwittingly asks if permission for social sin and the injustice of the world order blaspheme the gracious gifts of God's creation.

The Book of Mormon lampoons the angelic messenger Moroni even while replicating and laughing with the racist traditions of the American book musical. The passage of time transforms the impact of any play's play with religiosity or race. Whiteness shifts to evade responsibility for its work in the construction of others who are non-white. As David Sterling Brown shows in his study *Shakespeare's White Others*, theatre presents what he interprets to be an intraracial color line across which "whiteness polices whiteness and negotiates with itself [while] a race war rages on. The white self—the social, cultural, physical, and psychological white self that is an amalgamation of conveniently shifting ideologies of superiority—is constantly engaged in battle."[13] *The Book of Mormon* depends on that religious white other in its Mormon missionaries and frames its otherness via the battle for belief in mission territory. On one level, it is the mission territory of Disneyfied culture (be it Broadway or Orlando). On another level, it is the emancipatory message of religion as uplifting fandom proclaimed by the musical's finale.

The Book of Mormon aids theology but wounds in the process. Other shows, particularly Suzan-Lori Park's *Venus*, a retelling of the story of Saartjie Bartman, achieve a similarly liberative blasphemy with a stronger impact.[14] These spectacles call attention to suffering and linger with sin's ugliness and vulgarity. But both *Venus* and *The Book of Mormon* reveal that that which offends God is not merely crassness and sexuality, patriarchy and rapaciousness, racism and cultural supremacies but how easily humans forget humanity. Broadway provides non-ecclesial and pluralistic resources to interpret God's self-revelation in the company of blasphemies. Such a theology emerges from the experience of humans who live in a world where social sin still happens, a world characterized by the blasphemy of injustice alongside abstract speculations about angels or prophetic experiences of Moroni. But Broadway speculates about angels too.

CHAPTER FIVE

Angels and America and Apocalypse

Rather than restage Broadway's traditions of religious traditions again, this chapter notices how spectacles can stage the time of revelation via the symbol of its advent. In the context of Broadway, revelation appears most vividly in the American fascination with angels as harbingers and signs of apocalypse. *Apocalypse* denotes the end of the world as known. A great unveiling of truth lays bare that which is ultimately real. An apocalypse changes how one must live. Nothing can be the same again. Revelation refuses any option to continue life as it was before. An experience of revelation changes everything: It ends a world. And while postapocalyptic narratives are ample in fiction and film, certain Broadway shows can anticipate the end of the world as known. Time plays tricks at the edge of revelation.

What might divine revelation do to theatrical temporality? Better put, perhaps, what does sitting together in the house at the threshold of revelation do to the time of a waking dream that is a theatrical spectacle? Can theatre help theology anticipate apocalypses? An abbreviated review of the temporality of Hans Urs von Balthasar's theodramatic theology helps raise three interlocking claims that this chapter will navigate in the company of three exquisitely apocalyptic American shows and their angels.

My first claim highlights how theatrical temporality exists within a wider performance history. To look for God on Broadway means witnessing how God plays on an *American* stage in light of America's own fraught and complicated history. Broadway operates as a political and historical context for theology, and Broadway highlights theology's necessary political and historical contextualization.

As a result, and my second claim, questions about God's time can interrupt and reinvigorate theological questions just as questions about Broadway's time can interrupt and reinvigorate national questions. Such political questions may or may not be of interest for a global church and may or may not be of direct ecclesial application. As I said in the introduction, looking for God on Broadway is fragmentary, idiosyncratic, and somewhat parochial. I established in dialogue with *Fiddler* and *Doubt* that Broadway asks theological questions outside the ecclesial context. This chapter presses both of these ideas with hope to discover something about God's time via unexpected and apocalyptic American encounters.

My third claim, then, will be that God's time always breaks into the world stage and its breaking-in appears unrecognizably strange. Time at the threshold of revelation is dreamlike and about to burst. The time of revelation reminds us of an apocalypse coming. After the revelation (a revolution?), nothing can or will be the same. Time stops when history watches you because "there's no day but today," and Great Work starts with a blackout and falling curtain.

A theodramatic approach to God's time on Broadway in America, then, needs to jettison the inevitability of progress, of manifest destiny. The route to the dramatic tension between fate and freedom runs counter to confidence in human progress. And the announcement of something different from progress, an announcement of the importance of an advent-incarnational now, approaches through symbols of angels. After establishing a foundation with help from von Balthasar to think about theodramatic angels and revelation, the chapter turns to three such Broadway encounters with angels and America: the awaited Angel at the end of Tony Kushner's *Millennium Approaches*; Angel Dumott Schunard, who brings Christmas even to those who can't afford their *RENT*; and Alexander Hamilton's sister-in-law Angelica Schuyler. These angels all play with time. Each show contributes its own theodramatic understanding of time that will converge, finally, outside of history when there is only a matter of time for a saintly Eliza Hamilton's eschatological gasp.

REVELATION AND THEODRAMATIC TIME

Whether messianic or incarnational, angels reveal how God's time rushes toward the present rather than recedes or follows. A theodramatic history approaches. Angels herald a change in the movement of time. The first verse of the apocalypse of Saint John, the book of Revelation, reads, "The revelation of Jesus Christ, which God gave to him to show his servants what must happen soon. He made it known by sending his angel to his servant John." Apocalyptic revelations do something to time. The end must be soon; "the appointed time is near" (Rev 1:3). And yet that appointed time has not yet come.

Angels both *reveal* and *re-veil* time. That is, angels disclose how time operates *and* point out its strangeness. In the order of history, the impending arrival of an angel announces the end of one sort of history and the beginning of another. Angels herald apocalyptic time. Once revelation happens in time, nothing will ever be the same, especially the birth of an awaited Savior and the incarnation of the eternal God. My argument proceeds from a theologically and theatrically realist assertion that, on stage and in the world, revelation has occurred and therefore is possible.[1] That is, I am interested in working within the given circumstances of a world in which God has revealed Godself. In my view, this point becomes the same as the assertion that spectacles are performed and so revealed in the world, not confined to an ideal theatre of the mind. A term some of my actor friends use for that performed realization is *manifestation*, a word familiar to religious types and phenomenologists alike.

Revelation presumes a world. In fact, God's creation of the world is an act of God's self-revelation. Psalm 19 provides some scriptural groundwork for what came to be called *natural theology*, the idea that the world's worldliness reveals God's glory through its very existence. In fact, the psalmist's reworking of the creation story turns the world into a storyteller: "The heavens are telling the glory of God" and "Day to day pours forth speech and night to night declares knowledge" (Ps 19:1–2). But like a good piece of drama, the heavens show without telling. Speech is metaphorical: "There is no speech, nor are there words; their voice is not heard; yet their voice goes out through all the earth and their words to the end of the world" (Ps 19:3–4). Creation's wordless proclamation is God's glory, what von Balthasar understands to be the governing scriptural image for how God reveals God's beauty.[2]

Psalm 19 complicates, if not undermines, the reduction of speech to speaking. A similar complication, if not undermining, happens when theatrical texts become realized in performance, in spectacle. The speech of the play is not limited to spoken lines and sung lyrics. The play of actors—movement, touch, speed, breath—creates the "world of the play" that plays within the very world we inhabit. And the previous discussion of *Doubt, A Parable*'s "second act" emphasizes how the show does not end when the performance concludes. The falling curtain closes the world of the play, but the show continues in conversations, memories, and revivals. A world can end without stopping the show.

Broadway has intuited this particularly temporal piece of natural theology or general revelation or fundamental theology about the semantic range of the inseparable words *revelation* and *apocalypse*. Revelations are always apocalyptic: Revelations end the world as we know it. Apocalypses are always revelations: The end of our world discloses truth. Film and literature excel at depicting a world after the apocalypse, but drama can hold up a mirror to what it means to wait for apocalyptic revelation to arrive. Theatre can play with time within time. More precisely, Broadway offers dramatic resources for investigating how God reveals Godself in a world characterized by time.[3] This chapter thinks about God's time revealed in a Broadway spectacle with the help of a few angels bearing news of the end of the world and the start of another. Still, Broadway also responds directly to the flawed and faltering history of the world in which it plays, so this chapter pairs its angels with Broadway's America, captured microcosmically in Broadway's New York City, the world's greatest city, at least according to "The Schuyler Sisters."

The twentieth century is riddled with thinkers struggling to wrestle a theology of God's infinite eternity from the grips of finite temporality. Far more space, perhaps even another book, would need to be written to adequately respond to how acute the philosophical problem of time became during the same period when contemporary Broadway came into being. Martin Heidegger first published *Being and Time* in 1926, just a year before Florenz Ziegfeld produced *Show Boat* with music by Jerome Kern and lyrics and book by Oscar Hammerstein II. Correlation does not equal causation; it's hard (but not impossible) to find much *Sein und Zeit* in "Ol' Man River." Even as the river keeps rolling, Paul Robeson's baritone discloses the racialized undertones of the American Broadway show—already an amalgam of vaudeville, light opera, minstrelsy, pageantry, and European theatre.[4] Broadway's being cannot escape mixing with the flow of its nation's history, including its religious history, its liberatory history, its racist history, its violent history. Talk about the temporality of God on Broadway must also mean talk about the entanglement of Broadway time and American time in salvation history.

One approach to the temporality of God on Broadway would return to the themes of tradition and porous nostalgia from previous chapters. Broadway, like the church, carries the wounds and wounding of its tradition alongside its wonders. As Anne M. Carpenter persuasively argues, "Christian tradition is a body of action. Like all bodies, the 'action' of tradition is really many operations operating simultaneously in a system of transcending movement. Like all bodies, its 'inside' and 'outside' are self-evident only for realisms and idealisms. Something like this insight, where clean lines vanish, sustains the despair that despairs whether Christian tradition can be reformed at all, or ever. For Christian tradition is traditioned ironically, by its own sin. There is no escaping to somewhere other than where it presently is."[5]

Similarly, the achievement of the tradition of Broadway shows offers one of the distinctly *American* gifts to the history of human cultural production. Broadway cannot escape to "somewhere other than where it presently is," and it cannot escape its appropriations, its flattening of differences into stereotypes, its gestural citations of lived experience, its imperfect attempts at justice.

Theatre is an art of time and in time. Theatrical temporality is obvious from the fact that drama, when performed, unfolds in a series of events in succession. Drama happens in the middle of things. Happening in the middle implies the necessity of a beginning and an end, but the beginning and end of the *drama* are not necessarily coterminous with the beginning and the end of the *show*. Consider how many plays depend on prehistory. Oedipus must have already rescued Thebes from the sphinx in order to be considered the king who can solve the riddle of the plague. Hamlet's father must already have reigned and died in order for Claudius to ascend to rule Denmark. In fact, Hamlet himself reminds us how theatre can bend time to put it "out of joint" and tell time out of order. Sometimes the opening number is not the first moment of the story. Glinda's claim that "No One Mourns the Wicked" demands that the supposedly wicked already be departed and dead. Drama works by throwing us into a river of story that keeps on rolling and so carries us along with it.

The structure of a performed play presents the movement of history as the medium for storytelling. Whether ritual or opera or integrated musical or play, drama and music fit together so well because they are both temporal arts. Any tidy classification system to separate Broadway musicals from operas from plays always fails because all these genres of dramatic storytelling rely on the same foundational medium: time. Spectacles are temporary rearrangements of the meanings of stuff. Flashy lights are flashy because they flash. Constant illumination ceases to be the same sort of spectacle because drama remains, ultimately, about change. And changes require time.

For Christian theology, herein lies the great paradox of the Incarnation and the question of this world's temporal relationship to God's triune life. The infinite God, who is eternal and ever-living, enters into the history of the very world God has loved into being. But, to borrow a memorable question from von Balthasar, "how can an infinite Word be said in a finite way without losing its sense?"[6] Drama offers a route toward one resolution of this paradox. Theatre demonstrates how the infinite reservoir of meaning contained in a dramatic script—that is, a script as a text that can be interpreted and reinterpreted and re-reinterpreted *ad infinitum*—must be made manifest via the finitude of a particular performance. Each and every performance of a piece of theatre is its own singular event in history: No ensemble or audience or historical context will ever perfectly match so as to re-create that historical co-interpretation again.[7] Certainly, the cast of a given production shares their common interpretation of a play with a multitude of different audiences, but the show tonight will not be the exact same as the show yesterday or the show tomorrow. We admit as much in the allure of the "original cast" or the disappointment of a surprise understudy for the role of the star. Swapping out the actors does not mean we saw a different production, but we did see a different instantiation of the show.

Drama describes a singular and consequential event in time, and so drama becomes the metaphorical vehicle for von Balthasar's Christology. God enters onto the world stage as the main character in the love story of salvation history in the person of Jesus the Christ. The world becomes a part of the eternal "play" of God's triune love.[8] The temporal structure of drama makes further sense of the theodramatic analogy when applied to the Christ: The story of God's love for the world begins before the curtain rises on the Gospel account of the Christ event and continues after its conclusion. The infancy narratives make clear that Jesus arrives as part of a larger story that reaches back, at least according to Matthew's genealogy (Matt 1:1–17), to the beginning of God's covenant with Israel; the Acts of the Apostles and Christian history continue the story through the life of the church that is a "prolongation of Christ's mediatory nature," primarily through the sacraments (more on these in the next chapter) and communion of saints, always looking forward to the eschatological revelation of the Christ's return.[9]

A problem, of course, arises when Christian history and its temporality appear to be some inevitable unfolding of the providential script as *predicted* in the book of Revelation. Apocalyptic imagery becomes coded instructions for how the script will unfold. Spectacle raises questions about the reality of any revelatory vision. There are no quick propositional answers to the conundrum between the *appearance* and *actuality* of freedom and potential loss in a history always flowing toward God's ultimate eschatological victory: "So we must also hold fast to this tension: on the one hand, the Lamb is and has always been victorious—the Lord appears to the seer in majesty, with all the emblems of triumph—and yet a struggle is going on (and actually intensifying) in which everything is at stake. The author of the Book of Revelation . . . is not a dramatist but someone commissioned to write down objectively the events shown to him."[10] Even the life of Jesus in the Gospels can appear fated rather than free, a series of obediential responses to the Christ's divine Father that seem to lack the reality of human self-determination.

For von Balthasar, drama, again, provides an analogy for making sense of the confrontation between the infinite freedom of God and the finite freedom of God's creatures.[11] Rather than articulate a tight philosophical-theological solution, drama presents an alternative framework that holds fate and freedom in the dramatic tension of providential love. The confrontation between fate and freedom happens in God's action toward and for the world.[12] God's action expresses the good;[13] "revelation comes from God."[14] Goodness could only be fulfilled in that which truly reaches out and takes humanity by the hand.

Performance clarifies von Balthasar's point. Action also requires temporality to make any sense to human creatures because all human action in the world *does*. Actors act by making choices, and choices enact change over time.[15] God's action makes history. Once witnessed as an element of salvation history, God's particular action becomes legible via analogy as God's performance on the world stage. Drama returns to make sense of the eternal (pure) activity of God translated into temporal performance. When God makes Godself known through action, God reveals Godself to the world. Incarnation is the premier mode of God's self-revelation because God makes Godself known as human and in a human way. Put another way, God takes the stage in the same revelatory mode as any other character that steps out from behind the curtain, a symbolic and literal veil of invisibility, into the world shared by actors and audience. Consequently, God's pure act that is triune life distills into discrete performances on the world stage and so takes on the temporality of worldliness.

Theo-Drama directly addresses the question of divine temporality: "God intends not to dominate creaturely time from above but to embed it, with all its created reality, in his eternal time."[16] Creaturely time moves toward an apocalypse, a time at the end of time when all will be made known. This eschatological orientation tends to be one that delays revelation, that locates heaven after the world, be it the end of the earthly pilgrimage home to God in individual death or the conclusion of the world's history.

But are all temporal movements toward the end also necessarily movements toward the good? As it says in *Theo-Drama*'s fourth volume on *The Action*, "The entire modern ideology of progress, even where it wears a religious mask, represents a history of the relationship between earth and heaven that has been tipped up so that heaven is 'in the future.' Today it has been turned into a naked power-struggle between superpowers using naked technological means of annihilation; this is the completely logical conclusion where something intended as an instrument in the service of man has been made into an absolute."[17] Von Balthasar refers here in his critique of inevitable progress in time to nuclear weapons but speaks as readily to what Pope Francis calls the "technocratic paradigm" in response to climate crisis in *Laudato Si'* or the technological determinism at play in many contemporary discussions about generative artificial intelligence or prolonging human life for the sake of maximizing its duration.

Three Broadway angels from *Angels in America*, *RENT*, and *Hamilton* announce and enact a different sense of God's temporality from the ideology of inevitable progress. All three shows premiered after von Balthasar's death and focus on pressing questions of American identity at the end of a world. Far more can and should be said about these shows in a theological register, especially about how they complicate simplistic political theologies of gender, sexuality, and race. But time is of the essence for the sake of this chapter.

ADVENT: *MILLENNIUM APPROACHES*

Broadway spectacle carries the capacity to symbolize adventual anticipations. This is particularly true for Tony Kushner's angel and the other bits of stage magic that make manifest its subtitle, "A Gay Fantasia on National Themes." *Angels in America* works precisely because of its religio-magical realism where the spectacle of the stage symbolizes a world where transcendence appears wherever and however it wants.

I am not interested, here, in theorizing or theologizing about the obvious religious and apocalyptic elements of *Millennium Approaches*'s sequel,

Perestroika—its sublime angelology and its fiery depiction of divine ennui. Nor will I comment extensively on the importance of *Angels in America* as it recirculates through other references like in *The Laramie Project* or in subcultures both queer and theatrical. I am more interested in what I might see by viewing time spent waiting for the living God through the spectacular lens of *Millennium Approaches*. The play's American civil, Jewish, Mormon, ecological, and Marxist theologies swirl and blend and play out in their own drag. *Perestroika* answers some of the spiritual questions that *Millennium Approaches* raises, but I wonder if there may also be theological rather than theatrical answers to those questions. It seems necessary to arrest the forward momentum of the plot of the duology to allow an angel to crash through the roof of theological dramatic theory's well-made play.

Millennium Approaches points out theology's problem of expectations. Drama presents the paradox of the incarnate human condition between body and spirit, contemporary practicalities and meaningful history, mundane mortality and eternal destiny. This paradox is not unique to Christianity or Christian drama; von Balthasar identifies how Judaism also presents how "man is 'here below', whereas God is 'yonder';' man stands forth in all his paradoxes, almost more defenseless and full of riddles than the hero of a Greek tragedy. How, given his absolute mortality, can he have dealings with and share a covenant with, the God who is absolutely 'the living God'?"[18] For Kushner, absolute mortality manifests in the symbol of AIDS. Absolute mortality appears, too, in *Angels*'s play with embodiment and sexualities, with climate change and substance abuse, with religion and politics, with power and vulnerability. Where von Balthasar places the idea of the living God, Kushner offers us the unseen, until revealed in the end, angelic messenger.

But revelations occur throughout the play. During *Millennium Approaches*, spectacle is transcendence. Material in its materiality can show forth something beyond the material. Kushner describes an aesthetic for the staging in a prefatory note about a Brechtian balance between "pared-down style" in this "actor-driven event" and the play's need for grand spectacle "to be fully realized, as bits of wonderful *theatrical* illusion—which means it's OK if the wires show, and maybe it's good that they do, but the magic should at the same time be thoroughly amazing."[19] Spectacle can present simultaneous theatricality and revelation (I discuss this at length in the next chapter's meditation on theatrical sacraments).

The awaited arrival of the angel begins in an end. The play rushes headlong toward its final sentence: "Greetings, Prophet; The Great Work begins: The Messenger has arrived."[20] The play works because each end is a beginning; history is circular. Once linked to its sequel, *Millennium Approaches* functions as anticipatory prologue. But, if vivified so that the first play's Old Testament quality ceases to replicate a benign supersessionism, *Millennium Approaches* displays an integrity from which much can be learned. Kushner signals the dramatic role of spectacular revelations in their guise as an apocalypse. A prophet can be an apocalyptic visionary of end-times: Ezekiel, Daniel, John of Patmos, Prior Walter. But apocalypse may also be the great realignment of ongoing values and concerns. After the revelation—of death, of love, of illness, of electoral will, of betrayal, of identity—nothing remains the same. Apocalyptic visions need not be limited to the fall of civilization or images of terrible monsters rising from a foaming sea. The writing on the wall says many things.

The approach of the millennium—be it the second coming, Y2K, or that new dawning age of revolution or apocalypse—is a journey, a movement through time and space. Harper identifies that "maybe Christ will come again" during her discussion with Mr. Lies about travel to Antarctica to witness the hole in the ozone layer that responds to apocalypses unfolding in her marriage as well as for the planet.[21] The rabbi's monologue with which Kushner opens *Angels in America* is a meditation on the same religious "crossing and dwelling,"[22] voyage and emigration imagery that connects the immigrant communities explored in *Fiddler* or *Doubt*. The play's image of Mormonism becomes a counterpoint: a Christianity born and bred in America. Kushner treats the Latter-Day Saints differently from *The Book of Mormon* but no less as a composite symbol of the religious politics of American Christianity, exemplified in invocations of Ronald Reagan's "Truth exists and can be spoken proudly."[23] Kushner's prophets ask if there can still be room for robust pluralism in the midst of proudly singular Truth.

There is also that theoretically prior Walter, who inspires the character-prophet's name. As many commentators note, Walter Benjamin consciously hovers like an ozone layer above the action of *Angels in America*. Benjamin's theory of history waits in the wings of this play and sustains its sense of (queer, messianic) history-remaking.[24] One image comes from Benjamin's short reflection, the ninth of his "Theses on the Philosophy of History," on an angel of history inspired by the *Angelus Novus* painting by Paul Klee.

For Benjamin's angel, the past is but "one single catastrophe." As much as the angel would like "to stay, to awaken the dead, and make whole what is smashed," his wings are caught in the winds of a storm, originating in paradise, blowing the angel toward the future. His back remains turned against what will come; all the angel can see is the wreckage created by the catastrophe of history's chain of events. Benjamin writes, "This storm is what we call progress."[25] The angel can only watch the disaster of the world's history from the perspective of an apocalyptic now (*Jetztzeit*) that ruptures the ideology of historical continuity.

Critic David Savan writes, "Benjamin's allegory of history is, in many respects, the primary generative fiction for *Angels in America*. [...] And the play's conceptualizations of the past, of catastrophe, and of utopia are clearly inflected by Benjamin's 'Theses,' as is its linkage between historical materialism and theology."[26] The apocalyptic revelation of the Angel is an event that announces a new dramatic time: the coming of the prophet, the arrival of the "great work" that only *now* begins. Ethel Rosenberg's ghost echoes Walter Benjamin: "History is about to crack wide open. Millennium approaches."[27] The plot moves forward in time toward the moment of spectacular angelic descent, but apocalypse appears through angelic presence earlier in the "wine-dark kiss of the angel of death" manifested in the lesions on Prior's skin.[28] Kushner plays with a messianic awaiting that disrupts and rearranges temporality while nonetheless still waiting for the apocalyptic revelation that gives history its ultimate meaning. In other words, *Millennium Approaches* is both a Benjamin-infused re-narrating of American religious and sexual mythologies and a meditation on waiting during history's devastations and impending dooms.

But Kushner's show also engages with another of Benjamin's essays, "The Work of Art in the Age of Mechanical Reproduction," though less explicitly. Here, Benjamin identifies the loss of what he calls "aura," that special element of an original communicable only through its "presence in time and space, its unique existence at the place where it happens to be."[29] Once a work of art is mechanically copied and mass-produced, that sense of aura fades because a mass-produced work of art functions like any other commodity in its extraction from cultural or ritual contexts: "The technique of reproduction detaches the reproduced object from the domain of tradition. By making reproductions it substitutes a plurality of copies for a unique existence."[30] Critics debate how much irony to locate in Benjamin's discussion of an original artwork's "aura" (it seems strange for a Marxist to endow a painting with a spiritual surplus value), but Benjamin's essay turns from the diminishment of aura in mass factory reproductions of painting and photography to a surprising reflection on close-up shots in film compared to the sense of aura maintained by theatre:[31] "In the theater one is well aware of the place from which the play cannot immediately be detected as illusionary."[32] Theatre maintains the capacity to be mistaken as "real" because there is an immediacy to its presence. But there is no such place for film. The show is projected, and Benjamin highlights how the material conditions of reception are different.[33] Cinema's artistic innovations belong to the camera. The close-up allows access to a world ordinarily unseen, from an actor's emotion or a focus on an object or the capacity to witness ordinarily unseeable smallness in the natural world. So, too, the montage and the use of slow motion.[34] Most critically, Benjamin identifies cutting—the ability to splice different moments of time together. Sound from one scene can overlap with the imagery of another, like the way weeks of Rocky's training can be collapsed into a series of moments. And insofar as film can aesthetically slow down and speed up time thanks to changes in the frame rate, movies can literally manipulate duration in addition to perspective. Theatre remains a temporal art caught in time and space. Theatre depends on its placement in tradition and the presence of the audience, so it holds on to aura in a way film's reliance on the camera cannot.

Theatre can only happen now, in Benjamin's *Jetztzeit* (though musicals often feature montage-like developments and passages of time in a single number, as in *Legally Blonde: The Musical*'s "What You Want" or how *Rocky the Musical* cites the famous training montage through its use of the same music). Kushner plays with theatrical temporality in ways that recall the intercutting of film. So much of our communication continues to be mechanically reproduced and fragmented. A powerful symbol of American capitalist simultaneity remains Roy Cohn's "I wish I was an octopus" sequence, where he juggles multiple phone calls at once.[35] One conversation includes securing a client tickets for *Cats*, still running two blocks away when *Millennium Approaches* premiered on Broadway in 1993.[36] Cohn, who fancies himself the agent of his own history, can only exist in so many timelines because he makes his interlocutors wait on hold. But the phone does not require copresence. Events only *appear* simultaneous on stage, but time is most certainly shared. Throughout *Angels in America*, scenes are intercut as in film as if to restore the aura of strangeness to the time humans share. In many scenes, the audience sees two different spaces spliced together simultaneously on stage, their ongoing action flowing in and out of focus.[37]

The waking dream of a play happens in a shared time of waiting. *Millennium Approaches* works so well to stage adventual anticipation because it contextualizes how frequent and mundane apocalyptic reckonings can be. Act I, scene 7 presents a "mutual dream scene." Prior's supernatural visions—the aforementioned stage magic where it's perhaps good for the wires to show—offer a campy exaggeration of revelation analogous to the campy exaggerations of his drag performance at the top of the dream/hallucination meeting. Harper's experience at the "threshold of revelation"—learning a shocking fact about her husband—is perhaps more relatable to most audiences than the voice that commands Prior to look up at the scene's end. Harper's theology of revelation is explicit: "Nothing unknown is knowable."[38] Harper has never met Prior before, so knowledge shared via hallucination/dream must be given from beyond, a "blue streak of recognition."[39] Revelation cannot be imagined or anticipated; revelation comes from outside the possibilities expectable in the world.[40] So, too, revelation's temporality is its awaited but unexpected approach from the future rather than the inevitable end of a timeline.

That the Angel ultimately crashes from the heavens onto the stage to conclude the play literalizes the conversations of the mutual dream scene. Apocalypse arrives in its own time, *toward* the present, without regard for what Benjamin called the "chain of events" that preceded the moment of in-breaking. The whole of the Kushner's play has been waiting at the same "threshold of revelation" we see thanks to shared dreams of Prior's drag and Harper's drugs. The time of apocalyptic reckoning—after which nothing can be the same—is a now spent waiting. Such a revelation comes in Prior's mode of prophesying truths about hidden sexual identities and coming sexy angels. But it might also be Harper's threshold of revelation testament to incorruptible human dignity: "Deep inside you, there's a part of you, the inner part, entirely free of disease. I can see that."[41] As revelation, this seeing happens spontaneously. God's time, the temporality heralded by angels, *arrives* and cannot be magically conjured or mechanically reproduced at the end of a human process.

CHRISTMAS: "TODAY 4 U"

Apocalyptic revelations change what is to be expected about God. As easily as one can point to the triumphant Lamb that is slain who becomes the light of the world in the book of Revelation, one can also point to the paradox of the God-human born to a virgin and her betrothed in a city so full of tourists they cannot afford a room. If Joseph and Mary were to go in search of a free manger in New York City on Christmas Eve in 1991, perhaps they could find a room to rent, or squat, in Alphabet City.

RENT is at least partially a Christmas story, the kind of Christmas story where the celebration of the Christ's birth might be marked by a funeral celebration of a dog's short life that raises a glass to "La Vie Bohème." Jonathan Larson does not appear to have more at stake in setting *RENT* as two different temporal circulations in the orbit of Christmas Eve other than the source material, Puccini's *La Bohème*. Act I takes place entirely on Christmas Eve and arrives at a midnight liturgy. Act II examines the subsequent year in the life of those friends. Religiously, *RENT* plays with symbols and ideas of multireligious and post-religious identities. Mark's experience of Jewishness, for instance, figures prominently in his film's self-narration.

There exist manifold Christian interpretations of the character of Angel as a Christ figure who reveals a queer God in radical solidarity with the poor, marginalized, and suffering people of the play. These readings make sense. Most stagings of the Act I showstopper "La Vie Bohème" construct an overt visual tableau reminiscent of da Vinci's *Last Supper*; at the very least, the number features a table for a Christ figure and twelve disciple figures (requiring thirteen separate orders of French fries in addition to wine and wheat in the form of beer). Angel saves the fallen, gathers together a community, offers gifts, dies, "rises" from the dead, and appears to Mimi before she returns from the brink of the otherworld during her near-death experience. In Act II, a priest refuses to celebrate Angel's funeral and hurls the epithet "queer" as a slur. Angel appears as the one Godforsaken in death. Simultaneously, Angel's Christmas Santa drag inverts consumerism into a kenotic act of abundant gift-giving. (I bracket, here, that the bonus for decorating merely adds to the larger payment for drumming an annoying dog into oblivion.) But I think the imperfection of the canine hit money that funds the Christmas Eve celebration only adds to Angel's proclamation of a counter-revelation. Angel subverts any clear and angelomorphic Christ-figure reading. Instead, I think Angel pronounces how apocalyptic time might be joyful, anticipated in an experience of love rather than dread.

Angel dies of AIDS. Angel is the only character for whom rent on a body runs out during the duration of the story. *RENT*'s plot happens "under the sign of apocalypse."[42] Most of the characters have, and all of the characters love someone with, a disease. Death stays. Illness need not be the only symbol of an approaching end, but AIDS is the horizon against which the suffering of these New York bohemians plays out. Life appears to happen between an uncertain number of AZT breaks. But Angel introduces the alternative theodramatic temporalities of the show: exemplified in two themes, "No Day But Today" and "Seasons of Love." Angel points toward a Christian theory of counter-exchange where vulnerability and gift beget more giving. Those gifts include the capacity for a kind of radical integrity. Angel demonstrates a performance of self that confounds the symbols of gendered expectations, particularly in response to hate; as Mimi eulogizes in the funeral scene. Angel's drag invites questions about the ways angels and humans *perform* gender like the way Kushner's second play, *Perestroika*, explains that angels feature male and female body parts. Gender expectations for the ways bodies act, move, and love are culturally and historically contingent; what it means to be man or women *rents* rather than *owns*.

Further, Angel helps frame a response to sickness and suffering that resists the choice of fear. Angel participates in the "Life Support" community that challenges assumptions of medical diagnoses as death sentences by demonstrating the necessary compatibility of faith with reason. A minor character named Gordon explains his ordinarily reliance on intellect; Roger responds with reason's argument that he should already be dead. The capacity to choose against fear that Angel and the Life Support community promise requires openness to gratuity, an act of faith that life consists in something more than measurable materiality like a T-cell count. In some cast recordings, we hear someone, perhaps Collins, respond to this theological moment with an audible amen.[43]

A Broadway spectacle presents the strange temporality of faith's interplay with reason. God's self-revelation refuses to be an event fixed in time around which time flows unaffected. Instead, God's revelation opens creaturely temporality to God's eternity. Fixed stories of past and future limit revelation to a time already gone in histories or a time not yet manifest in prophetic predictions. Angels, including *RENT*'s, announce a liberated temporality where "the kingdom of heaven is at hand" right now. Von Balthasar identifies a structural parallel for understanding the Christ as a revelation of God. He writes,

> The only way to grasp the "figure" of Jesus, the central actor of the theo-drama, is by *not grasping* it and by allowing it to take its place in the "ungraspable" context of the mystery of the Trinity. This grasping by "letting go" is what we mean by faith, and it probably requires more letting go than is prepared for; fortunately, however, what it tries to hold on to will ultimately be wrested from it anyway.

> Mystery does not begin at the point where reason, having taken many rational steps, does not know how to proceed: mystery begins right in the middle of the Prologue.[44]

The angels announce God's reign already present. *RENT*'s play with the time of faith rectifies the confusion often brought about by metaphors for knowledge limited to images of hands and holding.

Rather than read Angel as a Christ figure, I find it far more instructive to take Angel's name seriously as a symbol of the angelic. The infancy narratives in the Gospels and Christmas hymnody both identify how angels herald the revelation of the living God in an infant named Jesus. The shepherds only learn about the birth of the Christ child due to a chorus of angels (Luke 2:8–15). Joseph can only recognize his adopted son, Jesus, as the Christ conceived from the Holy Spirit because an angel appears to him in a dream (Matt 1:20–21). Even the total self-revelation of God in the Christ requires angelic explanation to be understood as God's self-revelation. Angels link prophesied history to the present. Angels make the anticipations of script(ure)s present now, and *RENT* is a musical where the Christmas angel reveals the fullness of time in and through love. Angel anchors the time of the musical in both acts. On Christmas Eve, it is Angel's generosity that creates the conditions for bohemian possibility.

RENT asks questions about how to view time under the conditions of American capitalism and impending apocalypse, concretized most obviously in Roger and Mark answering the questions of "Rent" in "What You Own." At first blush, *RENT*'s reception history suggests its solution to the problem of money-time-meaning in its primary hymn, "Seasons of Love"—the tear-jerking reunion anthem for a whole generation of high school theatre kids, surpassed in the new millennium only by *Wicked*'s "For Good." "Seasons of Love" argues that the measurement of one year—525,600 minutes—makes more sense according to shifting and transitory moments of beauty, connection, travel, delight, and struggle as seasons of love. Act II opens as a bit of a commentary on how to view the events of the second act as these seasons of love, but the tune also appears as the underscore to the orations at Angel's funeral.

Much of the original merchandise and even the tagline for the musical ultimately taught lessons about the greater reality of the now: There's no day but today. Angel reveals the alternative to rented time, one that views the encroaching apocalypse of nightmarish lost dignity and loneliness as foreclosure. Angel refuses to limit finitude's meaning to an inevitably rescinded rental of healthy bodies, relationships, wealth, or artistic inspiration. In truth, both past and future are illusory; there is no time but now. That is, Angel reveals the divine gift of today to be *for you*, recognized and realized, in the end, as giving in to love so as not to live according to fear. Indeed, the second finale becomes an ostinato oscillation on reflections about dying without you and today as the only day. The surrender to love welcomes the possibility of eternity as a now filled with love.

A WINTER'S BALL: ANGELICA'S REWIND

If Broadway angels symbolize theodramatic time because the arrival of angels changes temporality, then one angel of history in Lin-Manuel Miranda's *Hamilton* must be Angelica Schuyler. Her Act I number "Satisfied" not only presents an Augustinian sense of insatiable desire and drive but also breaks the rules of American history's forward temporal motion. Her showstopping number offers a rewind to reimagine the previous scene, her sister's first meeting and eventual marriage to Alexander Hamilton, from another perspective. Angelica raps at a speed that demonstrates her own intellectual acuity, enough to weave memories that literally turn back time to that night.

Other characters beyond Angelica have names that carry some trace of the religious. The play's recasting of the pantheon of revolutionary patriots depends on the well-known American civil religious tendency to divinize its presidents and founding fathers.[45] *Hamilton* interprets the failures of the American experiment in freedom in eschatological terms that rhyme with theology's. I am less interested in *Hamilton*'s casting and use of musical styles to democratize the whiteness of the American founding as an attempt to rewrite national mythologies like *Angels in America*. Surely 2009's *Bloody Bloody Andrew Jackson* offers more political resonance for the post-Obama moment with its rallying cry, "Populism, Yea, Yea!" As *Hamilton*'s brand of American politics appears increasingly dated once historicized, I find it becomes easier and more interesting to interrogate the musical's other themes. Some of the most obvious religious-political references in the play tend to circle Washington, who spends an entire number quite literally quoting scripture. Perhaps that is why Barack Obama's recorded version of "One Last Time" on *The Hamilton Mixtape* works so effectively.

Plays that stage history in the present also face the theatrical temporal dilemma. Part of what makes *Hamilton* interesting for a theodramatic reading is its reflections on time. Angelica is, of course, not the only character who calls into question the physics of temporal entropy. Aaron Burr, the show's narrator and a literal descendant of the fire and brimstone sermonizer Jonathan Edwards, demonstrates *already* what it means to "Wait for It" when there are things preaching and hymnody cannot teach. Burr insists that, in his apparent hesitations, he is not frozen but waiting to pounce. Waiting only appears to be something outside of the flow of time; to wait is always an action and a choice. Pauses move in time, so even revelations of revolutionary victory can be delayed and deferred until later. In the call to revolutionary action now, "My Shot," John Lawrence educates that to be really free demands extending the rights to all those in bondage. The God-the-Fatherlike George Washington issues a divine command that forestalls the cause of emancipation and renders what Lawrence explicitly identifies as true freedom into an eschatologically receding horizon, a not yet.

Thoughts of impending death also pause, but not arrest, the play's time. Alexander Hamilton stops the plot whenever he imagines death. The staging during Angelica's "Satisfied" contains moments when her own realizations of threefold simultaneous truths echo Alexander's tendency to occupy center stage in a singular white down spot. During his moments of introspection, Alexander pauses the action on stage into an aside, a confession from the calm of the still-swirling storm. Hamilton's "Hurricane" cites similar winds of progress to those billowing the wings of Benjamin's angel of history. The attempt to write his own way out of devastation only compounds it. But the eye of Hamilton's hurricane is not outside history's forces, only a break within it. To pause time—to rest, in musical terms—still signals forward movement in time that moves "Non-Stop."

This is not to say that God's eternal grace never breaks into time and works *through* a pause. Moments of quiet are usually where musical mercy is likely to live. Perhaps that is what Alexander fails to understand in his own insatiable need to write like his time is running out. God, unlike a revolution driven by human agents, has infinite time for mercy. *Hamilton* expresses this theological theme twice. Both are opportunities to think theodramatically about a love from eternity transforming temporality. Both also feature heavenly sisters, one an "angel" and another perhaps a "saint," reinterpreting history. The show becomes an image of what the church does in its actions of storytelling: "So it is that all subjective efforts within the Church share in the same life, which is the transition from earth to heaven."[46] Angelica describes the work of grace in interpersonal (perhaps even sacramental) forgiveness. Eliza's redemptive storytelling extends divine grace to tell the story of the founders after Hamilton's death. Telling a story marks a transition from earth to heaven. Telling that story in the action of tradition becomes an image of the time of the world's transition heavenward. History's redemption becomes a matter of time.

Angelica narrates "It's Quiet Uptown," a number that reiterates an operatic tradition exemplified in Mozart's *Marriage of Figaro*. Famously, a finale request for forgiveness—"Contessa, perdona"—lapses into the uniquely musical sound of silence during the time between other sounds. Forgiveness happens *during* that moment of musical silence. Miranda, similarly, places divine grace familiar to any married couple wherein the aesthetics of forgiveness take the musical shape of a fermata over a rest. We do not witness any conversation where Eliza formally and firmly absolves Alexander of his sins against God and against her. We never see Alexander's selfless rather than ego-serving confession in words. Instead, the Hamiltons' shared grief includes an action that is properly unimaginable because certain reconciliations demand a mercy that can be imagined only in light of God's revealed will to make all things one in Godself. The grace of this moment has a power beyond words that could name it.[47] Angelica interprets what we see and hear as forgiveness, but the stage directions and lyrics are simply descriptive. The Hamiltons hold hands, and Eliza echoes Alexander's observation of uptown quiet. Angelica plays the role of an angel announcing that this moment is the kind of reconciliation that confounds vocabulary. The stage direction echoes the arrival of Kushner's angel; the moment of forgiveness is an in-breaking that will shatter Alexander.[48] "It's Quiet Uptown" places the unimaginable spectacle of forgiveness into quiet that is no less musical.

EPIPHANY: ELIZA'S GASP

Eliza does not absolve Alexander during their lifetime as seen in the world of the play. The dead, *Our Town*-like Eliza who speaks *sub specie aeternitatis* in the play's finale is decidedly *not* an angel.[49] For Christians, dead humans do not transfigure species into angels on their arrival in heaven no matter how wonderful their lives. But Eliza may well be a symbol of a saint, one who enjoys the presence of God in eternity. And it is the show's theodramatic eschatology evident in a finale that makes its strongest theological argument about time.

The finale harmonizes time, history, and storytelling. Eliza returns herself to the narrative and extends the very time that Hamilton always seems to be running out of. Time comes to be an explicitly divine gift that disrupts the rush of revolutionary progress. It is not Washington who delays the inevitable, but Eliza identifies it is God who kindly grants saving time.[50] The play ends with the leitmotif about living, dying, and telling stories over a repeated and melodic invocation of the word *time*. The history that has its eyes on the actions of America's founders shifts from what might be interpreted as a kind of ancient fate into a distinctly free action: Who tells your story? By extension, whose story do you tell? To *perform* the story before the eyes of history redeems and extends the narrative. Where Washington understands the eyes of history to be the judgment of fate or descendants, Eliza theologically nuances the redemptive work of history—symbolized in the reunion of loved ones in heaven—into a matter only of time. That is, it is not *what* has occurred in history but rather *who* tells its story and *how*. The finale borders on a kind of Roman quest for enduring glory except for its promise of eschatological reunification. Eliza seems to argue that stories can be told from the perspective of eternity. Drama instantiates that perspective *in* the time of performance.

Thinking about time in the context of eternity is admittedly a bit of a wonky idea—so wonky, in fact, that von Balthasar takes to calling God's eternal becoming an event in "supertime."[51] But imagine how meaningful creaturely time must be for God if God not only acts during the showtime of history on the world stage in order to save a human plot *but also* takes up creaturely time into the eternal dynamism of God's own life. For God, there will always be the possibility of more time. For von Balthasar, eternity is not merely timelessness; eternity can hold creaturely time in its fullness of meaning. He claims that creation's time matters so much that God is willing to bring and envelop creaturely time in eternity without absorbing it. Time does not pass away into its own death. Time does not erase or disperse or fade into a silent void. The drama of God's life enfolds, enriches, and enlivens time itself. There will always be more to enjoy in the unending and surprising drama of God's eternal life.

Balthasarian theopoetics, like the sudden eschatological vision of Eliza's return to redeem a burned narrative, might border on the verge of the nonsensical for those who are not already fans of the Swiss theologian's production style. "Supertime" raises more questions than it answers. How can time be enfolded in eternity? A Balthasarian theory promises some access to the idea of an everlasting now: time remembered as a creature with all its creaturely integrity but without that pesky tendency to be dismissed, to be forgotten, to be ignored. For von Balthasar, creaturely time operates analogically for eternity, and the *Theo-Drama* is a place for analogies to play. Theatre likewise provides a ready-made image to bring von Balthasar's eschatological time into clearer view as consequential for human experience in the present. The apocalyptic becomes a glimpse of eternity, a vision of the world illuminated by the light of the Lamb that spotlights the meaning and significance of love in the present. The apocalyptic precisely reveals that there is no day but God's today.

So given this theatrical view of God and time, how are we humans to play our part to keep the drama of creation interesting? The freedom and responsibility for *acting* creation is in human hands. Actors know that the work of theatre-making comes from their choices about verbs. Any introduction to acting or improvisation course reminds novice actors to *do* stuff in order to tell their version of the story. Actions bring the story to life. Guided by directors, actors must discern what desires motivate their characters' activity, what physicality to bring to any given scene, and how to signal subtleties in relationships and emotion. Actors do not explicate or describe these interpretive choices as an abstract theory; actors *perform* interpretive choices in time. Theatre gives meaning to the present because it emphasizes actions that can really be done. Doing happens in the present tense, and theatre presents human doing as artwork.

Theatrical drama thus enlivens history by showing how our stories matter in two ways: First, theatre points our attention to missed moments of importance, and second, theatre materializes new possibilities for stories in embodied space and time. *Hamilton* argues that time's meaning derives from our decisions and our verbs, that is, our *actions*. When we speak history—a narrative that builds our interpretation of the past by reassembling its bits and pieces in the present—we tell stories of actions done to and with one another. Theatre reinterprets reality and, in doing so, stages a new possibility for sharing time. *Hamilton* constantly circles themes of telling stories.

Multiple characters in Miranda's *Hamilton* assert, "History Has Its Eyes on You" because humans cannot control who survives or who writes the history.

George Washington first intones these ideas to raise the stakes on the choices of military and political leaders. The same words return to close this fictionalized version of real history; the play constantly cites both time and story as the dramatic stakes of action. Music signals the transition from the present of decision toward the dramatic memory of history. Harmonic themes for revolution "rise up" to resound similarly between Hamilton's dogged drive in "My Shot" and Washington's attentiveness to the ways that choices matter for others in "History Has Its Eyes on You." Action is revolutionary and consequential. The juxtaposition of these musical ideas echoes, yet again, to mark victory at the Battle of Yorktown when "The World Turned Upside Down." Indeed, the finale of Miranda's blockbuster demonstrates how the meaningfulness of our choices unfolds beyond our own time. Eliza, the other titular Hamilton, tells stories and transfigures the haunting and energetic melody into her eschatological benediction. The stories we choose to tell in the present remember the people and things we loved in the past and shape the direction of shared futures.

Theatrical drama distills meaning for time and represents it for us now—one way in which all kinds of drama can illustrate time's potential. Drama sparks interest, focuses attention, and names what refuses to be boring. *Theodrama* is von Balthasar's term for thinking theologically in the midst of the world's dramatic tensions, but it is also possible to imagine how theodramatics illustrate time's meaning in a peculiar way. The world waits for its end, when our ordinary performance choices will be placed in the context of the much larger and longer drama of salvation history.

It can be easy to forget that history has its eyes on us because we cannot know what consequences flow from our verbs or which stories the future will choose to tell about us and our actions. All we can know is that our time must be important. Theatre's greatest theological insight, perhaps, is that the present is a matter of what we do with our presence together. Relationships, after all, must be built over time. God promises to remember time for us even after the world stage's showtime runs its course; there will still be more story to tell after this world's curtain call.

The printed version of *Hamilton*'s script does not include any reference to a choice by actress Phillipa Soo immortalized by the filmed version of the show that was released to the streaming service Disney+ during the COVID-19 pandemic. At the very end of the play, Soo's Eliza looks over the audience and gasps. The spectacle is ambiguous: Is this Eliza's own death;

her shocked realization of all that she has accomplished in her life's time; or a fourth-wall break where Eliza sees *this* audience watching a Broadway show about *Hamilton* (now streaming to millions of viewers) that directly extends her telling of the story for a length of time she could never have dreamt?

The moment is also theologically rich. Perhaps Eliza's gasp shows redemptive storytelling in a simultaneous beatific vision of God and a recognition of God's presence in a gathered audience. History certainly has its eyes on her, eyes enfleshed in those present in the auditorium and beyond. The fact that the gasp was recorded on film and streamed to the world makes the temporality of this moment significant.[52] The gasp is, was, and ever shall be *live*. Time, so loved by God, does not pass away into lost history. Rather, God fills time with surprising possibilities from a future not yet realized. God's time rushes toward the present. Perhaps the only reasonable response to such a revelation is a gasp. Maybe Eliza's gasp is more universal than Soo anticipated. The spectacle of a human gasp at the moment of revelation might be what prompts angels to begin their messages with a reminder: "Be not afraid."

CHAPTER SIX

Staging Sacramental Spectacles

Broadway stages religious "stuff." There are as many different approaches to God and to writing as there are different ways that God plays on Broadway. This chapter gives the lead to the 2015 Deaf West Theatre revival of *Spring Awakening* that was nominated for three Tony Awards. Deaf West's *Spring Awakening* brings together many of the themes that organize the preceding chapters: revelation as God's show business, spectacular attention as a mode of prayerful interpretation, theatrical materiality as that which remembers God, God played by an audience, the porous nostalgia of tradition, and the time of God announced to be waiting in the wings of history. These modes of analysis converge on *Spring Awakening* as a theological text. I look to two sequences of this Broadway show that made a theological argument by staging a sacramental spectacle. At the end of the first act of the 2015 Deaf West revival, "I Believe" became a complex layering of theatrical, erotic, religious, and embodied meanings. At the end of the second act, shared silence created community and crossed through a veil between this world and an accessible otherwise future.

REVIVALS, TRANSLATIONS, AND TRANSUBSTANTIATIONS

Every work of theatre has the capacity to be reinterpreted. Theatrical texts hold a near-infinite reservoir of what the interpretation theorist Paul Ricoeur calls "surplus meaning."[1] As discussed in terms of a pandemic-era *Godspell*, plays and musicals can be restaged to rediscover how surplus meaning adds to surplus meaning via theatrical interpretive work. One set of surplus meanings arises from performances of Frank Wedekind's 1891 *Frühlings Erwachen*. Another collection of surplus meanings arises from Steven Slater and Duncan Sheik's 2006 adaptation into *Spring Awakening*, a Broadway rock musical. Still more surplus meanings arise from Deaf West's revival of the 2006 musical in 2015 directed by Michael Arden.

North Hollywood's Deaf West Theatre Company makes theatre for both Deaf and hearing audiences.[2] The model aims for theatrical credibility in the form of accessibility and inclusion. The Deaf West revival directed by Arden took a bilingual approach, performing this musical for both Deaf and hearing audiences with a mix of spoken and written English and American Sign Language (ASL). This included doubling some characters so they were played by both hearing and Deaf performers. Theatrical doubling calls attention to the both/and of embodied performance, but Deaf West's staging choices consistently bring our attention to another sort of theatrical doubling. Bilingualism invites hospitality for two cultures, two languages, two sorts of musicality. Inclusion need not compromise aesthetic concerns or theatrical virtuosity, and the proof happens in the public testament of the transfer of the show to a successful run on Broadway.

Deaf West's revival awakened a multidirectional invitation to see differences between interpretations of a shared world. The plot's questions about differences in sexual embodiment and the differences between knowledge that is young and old opened toward Deaf and hearing interpretations of the world. Theatrical seeing becomes choreography that "sings" to those fluent in ASL and yet recalls the gestural abstractions of Bill T. Jones's movement work for the original production of *Spring Awakening*. The 2015 revival came quickly on the heels of *Spring Awakening*'s 2006 premiere. Many of Deaf West's design choices paid homage to the first production's scenography. The 2006 version symbolized an analogy between the experience of nineteenth-century German youth and twenty-first-century US teenagers, using music as an expression of interiority and subtext. The musical numbers sit alongside the plot; as composer Steven Slater writes, "I wanted a sharp and clear distinction between the world of the spoken and the world of the sung."[3] Clues in self-referential set pieces (e.g., a classroom chalkboard listing the show's musical numbers) and the presence of handheld microphones and lyric anachronisms like references to a stereo link historical and contemporary experience.

The plot of *Spring Awakening* follows a group of middle-class German students at the turn of the twentieth century as they experience social and sexual enlightenment to the often violent alarm of the adults (all collapsed into roles for two adult actors). The drama's vignettes match ordinarily unspoken tragedies of childhood with the misunderstanding or abuse of adults. Wedekind called his version *Eine Kindertragodie*, a children's tragedy.[4] The 2015 Deaf West production, however, emphasized the encounter with and fear of difference that undergirds the show's depictions of social and sexual violence. Unlike the original production, Deaf West foregrounded differences in ability as a feature of the plot and the staging. In the 2015 staging, we now find interiority physicalized in the doubling of certain characters. Wendla and Moritz (among others) as well as the Adult Man and Adult Woman were doubled with a Deaf character, played by a Deaf actor, who interacted with others in the world of the play and that character's Voice, played by a hearing actor.[5]

Visually, this choice underscores how ASL and written/spoken English are two distinct languages. So, too, sign languages and oral/written languages reflect two distinct theatre cultures: English speakers and the Deaf community. The choice, and the show's prevalent classroom themes, permitted Deaf West's production to point surplus meaning in the direction of educating its audiences. Mortiz's inability to succeed at school now reflects as much the struggles of an individual student and a system unwilling to make pedagogical accessibility accommodations. While the fundamental cognitive proficiencies for ASL and English are related and so support inclusive classroom models, many studies have affirmed key cultural and linguistic differences between ASL acquisition and acquiring spoken/written English.[6] Bilingualism twins cultures; it does not simply add captions.

This production is not the first to make meaning from the theatrical realization of interiority. Brian Friel's 1965 meditation on emigration from Ireland, *Philadelphia, Here I Come!*, similarly presents two versions of its protagonist that allow the audience to see both Public and Private Gar's experiences. While film can feature a disembodied voiceover and a novel can narrate a character's thoughts, theatre poses the problem of the directly incommunicable quality of an invisible inner life. The original musical presented the tragedies of childhood interiority through commentaries via contemporary music. The accidents of historical context change, but there is a shared struggle to learn what it means to be human in all its sexual and social complexity. Struggles of interiority can only be symbolized, but staging can confront a character with their own inner disagreements and affective struggles. Staging can also preserve tension and ambiguity. Inner conflict need not be resolved. The Deaf West production of *Spring Awakening* extends the original show's commentary via microphones into real-time doubling. That is, emotional responses can conflict, and neither Body nor Voice necessarily has a more authentic reaction. Bilingual staging uplifts how invisible interiority must be *translated* into visible performance.

Bodies and their differences are central to the Deaf West revival, both in the shift to the Moritz plot and in the technical complexities required to make a musical with hearing and non-hearing performers. Casting a Broadway actor who uses a wheelchair, Ali Stroker, broadened the scope of the play's inclusivity. Deafness need not disable musicals any more than Stroker's wheelchair disqualifies her from a Broadway role. Stroker went on to win a Tony Award for her performance as Ado Annie in the 2019 Broadway revival of *Oklahoma!*. Borrowing language from Alison Kafer, Deaf West's staging imagines an "accessible future" for theatre-making beyond the industry's compulsory able-bodiedness.[7] Not only does this show display an inclusive spectacle; Deaf West's performance practice also displays the political and social construction of disabling spaces. That is, the capacity for particular bodies to participate in social life redounds not to individuals but to choices about social scenography.

Gestures of stylized choreography and ASL perform side by side in a paradoxical undoing of the exclusion of Deafness precisely by sharing a character between both a hearing and a non-hearing actor. Doubling Wendla, Moritz, and the adult characters performs the gap between Deaf and hearing experiences. By naming that difference, *Spring Awakening* proceeds to transcend it by making the play accessible (but not *identical*) to hearing and non-hearing audiences. Distances between the audience and the stage, between adulthood and childhood, between sexed bodies and social locations, between God and world found symbolic undercutting by the original production's placement of audience members on the stage with chorus members in street clothes who sang along with real microphones. Deaf West staged a visual undoing of a supposed gap between bodies on Broadway and its audiences. This undoing came not in rewriting the lyrics or text but through redirecting the stage spectacle to generate whole new surplus meaning. Nothing about the play's words or the music's notes changed for the Deaf West performance. The production *added*, and those theatrical additions produced new meanings.

CREEDS AND COMMUNIONS

Two moments bear on the discussion of God in Deaf West's *Spring Awakening* revival: the Act I finale, "I Believe," and the play's final moment. The surplus meaning of the performance foregrounded a fusion of Christian theology, sexuality, and ability in scenes showing the "adult world's" wrongful forced separation of transcendence, pleasure, and embodiment. At the same time, Deaf West's spectacle cited and critiqued a hayloft scene's portrayal of sexual violence. Deaf West's spectacle presented its own erotic theology of a Christian communion ritual in ways that recast the connection between passivity and silence in von Balthasar's theodramatics. The spectacle of communion on stage also prompts new consideration for what might count as a "theatrical sacrament."

Spring Awakening's first act concludes with Wendla and Melchior's first sexual experience.[8] During a rainstorm, the two find themselves alone in the hayloft of a secluded barn while the rest of the town rehearses music at church. Wendla and Melchior's conversation leads to kissing, embrace, and, ultimately, sexual intercourse. Throughout the scene, the cast sings a simple chorale of their own about belief, heaven, love, and forgiveness. "I Believe" translates the first words of the creedal statements for the Christians in the play: *Credo in unum deum*. "I believe in One God." If the song is to be taken as a liturgical placeholder, then this moment visually connects sexual bliss and heavenly bliss, erotic transgression and ultimate forgiveness. The chorus prays a version of Melchior and Wendla's faith in desire to feel something, an inherent goodness at once wise, peaceful, harmonious, and joyful. The moment also inaugurates the plot of youth forsaken by adults in the second act.

The 2006 musical version of *Spring Awakening* made a significant change to the hayloft scene from Wedekind's original. Wedekind shows Melchior ignore Wendla's protest in rapacious violation in the middle of the second act, pronouncing the absence of love from sex over Wendla's objections.[9] The 2006 musical plays out this erotic expression as a fully consensual and mutually pleasurable embrace as a finale for Act I.[10] The Deaf West revival took a third option made possible through its doubled characters and visualized the ambiguities of sex, bodies, and belief. While Wendla embraces Melchior with enthusiasm, Wendla's Voice appears visibly hesitant, if not concerned. The two actresses share a look, performing a moment of active decision rather than gendered passivity.[11] Wendla's Voice turns her back on Wendla, who, in turn, chooses to lie down on the hay. Eventually, Wendla's Voice returns to witness this moment of erotic communion. Rather than validate this scene's origin in nonconsensual sexual violence or override it into one of uncomplicated consensual enthusiasm, doubling Wendla's character shows forth a more complex approach to both sex and spirituality.

Deaf West's spectacle confirmed and pressed a theological reading. While Melchior and Wendla ascend the hay, two lit candles flanked the implication of the hay bales as an altar. The cast circled behind singing and signing the *Spring Awakening* creed. At the same time, two members of the cast, costumed in Christian liturgical clothing of cassock and surplice, walked down the aisles of the Brooks Atkinson theater swinging lit incense in thuribles. Dressed in ritual garb as readily found in churches of the nineteenth century as it could be today, the musical made present the sights, sounds, and smells of Christian ritual. Behind the hay, members of the cast knelt before the Adult Men dressed in preaching tabs, who mimed the placement of a communion wafer into the cast's mouths.

The *credo* "I believe" could also be a loose translation of the Hebrew word *amen*. The word, of Hebrew origin, can literally translate to *so be it, truly,* or *verily,* sometimes even *I believe*.[12] Many Christians utter "amen" at the moment of communion, a ritual act believed to unify the believer with the real presence of Christ in a foretaste of the experience of God in heaven.[13] To utter "amen" in the presence of the consecrated bread—body of Christ—attests to the reality of this spiritual presence. Despite profound and significant differences in theology and terminology, Orthodox, Catholic, Lutheran, and Anglican Christians will mostly agree to a theology that supports some presence of the Christ in the Eucharist. The practices of the Eucharist are the sacramental making-present of God in the world by means of the performance of bread and wine. The Deaf West staging enacts a theological *tour de force*. The physical erotics of eucharistic reception—kneeling, feeding, taking Christ's body onto the tongue—occupy the same visual field as the moment of sexual communion.

Rather than merely function as a theatrical warning against conservative prudishness, Deaf West's *Spring Awakening* does theology and sexuality at once. Word becomes flesh in the movement of creed into ASL choreography; no bodies are ineligible for communicating as the word of the Christ's body.[14] This spectacle of enfleshed multiplicity in unity repairs the abusive sermons of silent obedience preached by pastors and parents throughout the second act.

Belief that everyone and everything will be forgiven, however, now includes *all* of that which seems unforgivable and forsaken, all that appears too bodily.

THEATRICAL SACRAMENTS

All sorts of theophanic spectacles might be said to share a kind of public interpretability with sacraments. Theophanies and sacraments both manifest the presence of God through discernible and universal phenomenality: discernible because theophanies and sacraments both can become subject to description, universal because theophanies and sacraments—unlike private mystical experiences—occur in straightforwardly phenomenal ways. Theophanies and sacraments can be *witnessed as a performance on the world stage*. In other words, both theophanies and sacraments can appear as a spectacle. What sharply differentiates sacraments from theophanies, however, will be the lack of any coterminous divine self-confirmation. The great biblical theophanies discussed in chapter 2, the burning bush and the speaking storm, both include the content of God's revelation through a speech act in addition to the spectacle.[15] The special effects also have divine dialogue. Sacraments, by contrast, do not self-confirm with such a clearly objective form of revelation.[16] Only Jesus's baptism in the Jordan concludes with the heavens opening to announce a child with whom God is well-pleased; ordinary sacramental baptisms do not feature such astonishing clarity about ontological change. Instead, sacraments offer themselves to private scrutiny and to the questions of a community of faith as to whether the activity named as a sacrament revealed something of or from God.

If a play mediates a religious experience, the performance of an actor might be said to reveal theatrically what the performance of a minister—paradigmatically God's priest—ordinarily reveals sacramentally. But should stage depictions of spiritual realities be considered properly revelatory phenomena? Or are the religious experiences occasioned by stage spectacles of sentimentalized "religious feeling" always automatically suspect? The world of Deaf West's *Spring Awakening* certainly seems at home with the great heights of emotionalist pietism. The staging of "I Believe"—it's blue-and-white-hued lighting, its incense, its creedal lyrics—calls to mind all sorts of contemporary Christian worship. The stage picture of cassock and surplice and kneeling communicants may very well evoke a kind of spiritual communion. The designers, actors, writers, and directors surely do not intend to do what the church does, but the aesthetics of the scene surely do intend to look like what the church does. Could valid prayers arise from such a sacramental spectacle?

I call such moments *theatrical sacraments* to underscore a risky comparison to the religious performance of sacramental sacraments. The patristic concern about theatricality returns, however, when such a spectacle calls into question the veracity of ritual actions to be what they present themselves to be. There are differences in *intent* between a Christian ritual in a religious context and spectacles of religiosity for the sake of theatrical entertainment. Catholic doctrine from the time of the Council of Trent, for example, demands the clear announcement "I do not intend to consecrate" before a priest rehearses the ritual actions of the mass.[17] So, too, differences in *context*.[18] A couple that joins hands and says special words during a wedding scene does something distinct from a couple doing the same actions during a marriage rite (even if the very same people perform the same performative speech acts in both cases).[19] One common solution appears according to locational context and expressed intent: Theaters present "fake" revelation in their profane citation of religion, and churches and other holy events signal "real" revelation in their performances of sacred truth. Context and intent matter for religious practice, but such an easy solution for religious spectacles become ultimately unsatisfying when it relegates the standard for "real revelation" to the physical and social location of the event. The standard by which Christians should judge the really real belongs only to God. We know that a "real" religious ritual can occur because a religious community happened to gather and celebrate their rites on a theater's stage; we know that a "fake" religious ritual can occur in a church.

A stronger line of analysis considers the situation according to experience. What of the spectator in the audience/congregation? If we bracket the intent of the actors and knowledge of the context, there seems to be little left to distinguish theatrical spectacles from religious ones in the *experience* of an observer. The truth of the play appears in its performance *for* the audience as manifestation, not in the interior life of the artist. So, too, I argue, insofar as revelation (in Christian understanding) always functions as revelation *for* a receiver because God reveals Godself for and to the world. Spectacles exist in their performance. Is there any meaningful distinction between the experience of what might be revealed by stage spectacles and the revelation accessed via a more straightforwardly religious performance of a sacrament?

On one level, *theatrical sacrament* could describe any moment in a play that so successfully cites the phenomenological experience of a religious ritual as to be momentarily indistinguishable from it. Some examples readily flood to mind, though they apply the term *sacrament* analogously: sung prayers in *Sister Act* or *Come from Away* or Father Flynn's opening sermon from *Doubt, A Parable* or "Sabbath Prayer" or the wedding sequence during "Sunrise, Sunset" from *Fiddler on the Roof* or "Helpless" from *Hamilton* provide potent examples for generically religious theatrical "sacraments." But the *Spring Awakening* staging for "I Believe" offers a *sacramental* theatrical sacrament in its depiction of the communion ritual. Few audience members would mistake the background communion imagery for a "real" religious ritual, but theatrical sacraments do not need to trade on obfuscatory verisimilitude. A theatrical sacrament functions religiously by sufficiently becoming the visible sign of an invisible reality to prompt prayerful attention. The real presence of Christ's body, blood, soul, and divinity cannot be found on the *Spring Awakening* stage in the eucharistic species, but a theatrical sacrament might nonetheless give rise to an experience of (ecumenical) *spiritual* communion.

On another level, *theatrical sacrament* functions as a term for when spectacle becomes revelatory. The Deaf West *Spring Awakening* merely plays with the most direct possible citation of a theatrical sacrament in its staging of a communion ritual. As such, a theatrical sacrament calls into question easy reliance on the sacred/profane dialectic for dramatic revelation. If revelation is God's prerogative rather than a human achievement, even a sacrilegious performance should be reasonably able to prompt a religious experience. Phenomenological attention restores the more ancient understanding of spectacle as always and already potentially theatrical *and* religious.[20] The category of revelation, reserved to God, secures the theological meanings a theatrical sacrament gives phenomenally as spectacle.

I will focus on the problem of a theatrical sacrament according to a Catholic-Christian framework (sometimes invoked as a "sacramental imagination"), but a phenomenological approach to stage revelations remains fundamentally open to other religious ways of knowing. The situation in *Spring Awakening* is already ecumenical. Evidence in the show indicates that the characters are more Lutheran than Catholic; Act II begins with a patriarchal motto beloved of Martin Luther. Theatre's necessarily pluralistic audiences anticipate and perhaps require an *ecumenical* theology open to a wider world of differences.[21] Broadway's stages are spaces that are public and religiously pluralistic. Interpretations of theatrical sacraments will present a better avenue for making theological meaning of God on Broadway than scrying for religious intent on the part of artists or context. Revelation approaches from God's future, after all; a theatrical sacrament can be a site for revelation anytime God wishes to make Godself known.

Theatrical sacraments remain open to interpretation like any other object on stage. Theatrical sacraments include depictions of religious rites and ideas on stage or the use of "real" hymns and prayers, as in the compilation of actual prayers and religious songs in *Come from Away*'s number "Prayer." Theatrical sacraments give themselves in a threefold way: in their ordinary phenomenality, in their role in the play, and as (potentially) revelatory. Here, I understand "revelatory potential" to be the capacity for a phenomenon to serve as a site for an experience of God's self-revelation in excess of that phenomenon's own manifestation without placing a requirement on God's action. Just as God's time approaches creaturely time and will not be inevitably achieved through human effort or progress, so, too, are sacraments—even theatrical sacraments—reliant on God's activity.

There remains, however, an important distinction between theatrical sacraments and their religious namesake. From a Christian perspective, theatrical sacraments do not trustworthily confer grace like religious sacraments do. The latter category—churchy sacraments—requires both religious intentionality and religious contexts, but theatrical sacraments are often reported as occasions for religious experiences.[22] Could that which is revealed to experience via theatrical sacraments be credible *as* revelation? Or are theatrical sacraments simply a citation or simulation of the religiously revealed? Theatrical sacraments also might identify when any spectacle becomes a "religious experience," itself a thorny category, regardless as to whether the spectacle cites a "real" religious phenomenon.

An approach that begins from experience can say more about theatrical sacraments than other modes of analysis because it avoids the pitfalls of filtering the meaning of religious phenomena through intent, context, or the faithful (or methodologically atheist) interpretations of the observer. As in other types of fiction, it might make sense as to how spectacle reveals truth through fantasy or myth. Actors may not really be praying and the objects on stage not really sacred things, but a properly religious experience of a play can and should be rightfully considered a religious experience. A phenomenological approach to a theatrical sacrament underscores that it does not really matter for the sake of phenomenological analysis, if the performers or the playwrights hold any particular belief about God. Drama functions akin to how Kevin Hart describes reading poetry: "Whether God exists, or exists as the poet thinks, is beside the point when it comes to reading a poem."[23] Spectacles are situations where the reception of surfaces and their impact matter more than their success as translated interior intentionalities. On stage, it matters little what the actor was going for; significance lies in what the audience sees and receives. Theatrical and sacramental meaning emerges *ex opere operato*, from the work worked, in analogous ways.

If spectacle can be shown to be revelatory, then it is the spectacle that carries God's self-revelation. So even flashy, commercial, and patently illusory theatrical sacraments may nevertheless disclose revelation (i.e., become revelatory) akin to intentionally religious spectacles (i.e., ritual or liturgy). Attention to theatrical sacraments shows how theological questions can and must operate outside the contextual boundaries erected by measurable criteria like intent, material, location, or preexisting faith. The Deaf West *Spring Awakening* cast may have been full of Christians hoping to trigger an experience of God, or the cast may have been non-Christian or agnostic or even opposed to God's reality. It is the *stuff* on stage that creates the possibility for spectacle to become a theatrical sacrament, a site for a revelatory religious experience ready to be interpreted theologically.

This is not to claim boundaries that separate church and stage are immaterial. Religious intentionality and religious contexts are precisely the grounds of differentiation between performances that are religious spectacles and other theatrical phenomena. Instead, theatrical sacraments indicate how revelation may appear even in nonreligious or so-called secular contexts. Theatrical sacraments give themselves for religious attention because they become transparent to a truth that reveals itself. Given the ubiquity of "performance" as a category for making sense of the event character of human social life and God's dramatic intervention in salvation history, theatrical sacraments provide a salient locus to investigate what criteria might make other phenomena credible as revelatory.

HUSHED WONDER

It is easy to notice how the citation of the communion ritual in the Deaf West production functions as a theatrical sacrament. It is a case of apples to apples (or wafers to wafers). But the bodies of actors in the presence of audiences become their own kind of theatrical sacrament. Theatrical performance, as von Balthasar and countless Christian theologians attest, always recalls the logic of incarnation. Structurally, actors visibly enflesh the word of an invisible playwright. The theodramatic analogy for the trinitarian persons builds on the fundamental structure of an invisible author-Father whose will is perfectly expressed on stage by a visible actor-Son. A Spirit-director ensures the actor-Son's perfect expression the author-Father's will for the character.[24] For von Balthasar, Jesus the Christ is the concrete analogy of being that reveals the love of God for the world and makes credible theology's testimony to the loving relationship between God and the world.[25] It is the Christ, the visible Son of the invisible Father also one with the Father in the Spirit, who performs the meaningfulness of the world to God and the meaning of God for the world. Making a Balthasarian modification to a phrase from Brecht: Christ is the visible truth of God, and the truth is concrete. God's love begins to be known from being itself. Balthasarian emphasis on the *analogia entis*, the analogy of being, is an analogy of the excessive meaning of being to God because God creates and loves the being of the world.

God takes the world stage in the enfleshed body of Jesus the Christ.[26] The Son becomes a visible sign of the invisible Father. So, too, Deaf West's doubling of characters between a Deaf actor and a hearing Voice translates invisible interiority into a visible theatrical symbol. In Deaf West's production, however, attention to the body as potentially revelatory meant ensuring that Deaf actors played Deaf characters. The choice might be read simplistically as liberatory representation: This story about marginalized communities makes Broadway accessible to those very communities. Theatrical sacraments are spectacles worth taking seriously for their theological, not simply sociological, argument. This bit of secular theatre, in the world beyond an ecclesial context, offers theological surplus meaning. Deaf West's choices do theological work precisely in the bilingual idioms of musical theatre and Christian ritual enacted through the revival's spectacle. Performance's permeable barrier flows in many directions.[27] Deaf West's spirituality of sexual complexity and its theatrical liturgy arrive at the image of an accessible future in a comingling of differences. Its communion eschatology happened through a spectacle for an active audience participating by means of copresence, making meaning by being present together. Act I ends with a theatrical sacrament of a liturgical communion; Act II concludes with a theatrical sacrament of a communion liturgy.

The last number in *Spring Awakening*, "The Song of Purple Summer," offers a kind of epilogue. Melchior's wish that everyone will know one day receives an echo: All shall know wonder. The cast assembled in matching white night-dress costumes and brought out a ghost light, symbolizing a time outside the time of the show.[28] The company sang and signed the tune in place until its final repeated refrain. As the accompaniment fell away, an illuminated portal opened into a woodland. The adult characters watched in silhouette as the youth processed out through the door into a bright, green future outside the world the adults had made and enforced. As the actors left the stage, their voices fell away, too, until the whole of the theater—cast, crew, and audience—shared common silence. The end of the show became a theatrical sacrament of spiritual communion.

In this way, Deaf West's revival of *Spring Awakening* corrected a theatrical theology that imagines its audiences as passive object rather than co-participant. On Broadway—operating within what I called the LuPone paradigm in the introduction—crafting silence requires work from the audience. Silence is not some default absence of sound. Wailing sirens, beeping phones, whispering patrons, and crinkling candy wrappers all compete against the hush necessary for silent wonder on Broadway. Indeed, silence can be deadly for theatre; actors, comedians, radio hosts, and seminar professors fear that awkward quiet looming as "dead air." Sometimes the liveness of the play dies into silence. Other times, the room works together to share a hushed wonder.

Theodramatic theology often treats dramatic silence exclusively as a symbol of death. The Son of God dies on the cross, and the dramatic performance of the Incarnation is met with forsaking silence. The idea of the silence of an audience that does not applaud is, in itself, a certain symbol of forsakenness. But for what audience does a drama of crucifixion and forsakenness play if *everyone* is involved in the action of the world's drama? The silence of the Father's non-responsiveness to the Son's cry of dereliction on the cross raises questions about the passivity of any audience invited to try on God's role as spect-actors. Silence might be forsakenness, and von Balthasar argues the Son experiences the silence of the Father as an active rejection. In the words of another writer, Maurice Blanchot, "Solitude as the world understands it is a hurt which requires no further comment here."[29] Silences can be lonely. But the implication of some experience of loneliness intrinsic to God's triune life due to the cross risks a theological mistake because of a theatrical mistake.

Drama resists a reduction to solitary loneliness because theatre's essence subsists in being present together, yet von Balthasar seems insistent on God's loneliness as an element of an eternal mystery. He writes, "The mystery of Good Friday and Holy Saturday is thus a mystery of the loneliness of love between Father and Son in the Spirit, so much so that the outcome of these events (in their reunion, in the Resurrection) which is a 'mystery of eternal life', can take place only in 'full loneliness.'"[30] Von Balthasar is right insofar as God alone is uniquely God. Further, only the triune God could undergo such an experience of lonely rejection in unity as happens on Good Friday and Holy Saturday. The structure of the theatre suggests that von Balthasar might be wrong insofar as he has implied that God's singularity constitutes a radical abandonment into the *affective* "loneliness" of "solitude" (his German here is *"Einsamkeit"* rather than *"Alleinsein"*)[31] like the feeling of some lack of community due to being the "only one like this in the world" for all eternity.[32] The trinitarian God made known in the Christ is dynamic relationality, not dynamic solitude and affective loneliness. The shared silence of bodies might be a theatrical sacrament for divine copresence, the capacity to be unified *in* difference.

Broadway thus offers a corrective to any understanding of the audience as a passive recipient to the drama. Spectacles are not done *to* audiences but rather enacted *with* them. The boards of stages are properly passive to the actors who tread on them, but the performance of a show requires active cooperation. Audiences, even theatre critics, only remain "external" to the event of a show if one assumes reality to be *limited* to the poetic world of the play opened on stage by performance. A spectacle like a Broadway show is always also the shared reality of the performance event.

Silence returns in *Spring Awakening*'s own theatrical eschatology. At the end, the play's final moments show differently abled bodies of the cast—a theatrical sacrament revealing the absolute difference among all human bodies[33]—assisting one another through the portal that has opened into a colorful outside. Perhaps, eventually, all shall know the wonder in the dawn of a newly verdant garden seen through this crack in the grayscale set. Music faded into silence as the cast continued to help one another and sign the lyrics. "All shall know the wonder" promised by the finale's sustained moment of shared, sacramental, fully bilingual silence. Far from an expression of passivity, silence became a gift of copresence. The final lines of *Theo-Drama* imply the surplus meaning of worldly performance to be a gift returned freely to God: "What does God gain from the world? An additional gift, given to the Son by the Father, but equally a gift made by the Son to the Father, and by the Spirit to both. It is a gift because, through the distinct operations of each of the three Persons, the world acquires an inward share in the divine exchange of life; as a result the world is able to take the divine things it has received from God, together with the gift of being created, and return them to God as a divine gift."[34]

Spring Awakening dramatizes this notion of gift returned unto gift. Yet, for von Balthasar and Catholic-Christian theology, God must always be understood to be *more dissimilar* than that which is "like God" in any theological analogy. Analogies illustrate similarity despite significant differences. Studies of the theory of analogy in von Balthasar frequently cite his reliance on an axiom of the Fourth Lateran Council's condemnation of Joachim of Fiore (1215): "For between Creator and creature no similitude can be expressed without implying a greater dissimilitude" (*quia inter creatorem et creaturam not potest tanta similitudo notari, quin inter eos maior sit dissimilitudo notanda*).[35] I prefer to think of the *maior dissimilitudo* qualification as an "irreducible difference."[36] That which is compared by analogy cannot be the same and co-identical. Analogy exposes similarities that depend on greater dissimilarity. The major dissimilarity in analogies must be real; otherwise, there can be no analogical third term to compare these different entities. The structure of analogy without irreducible difference is tautology ("The sun is like the sun"); the structure of analogy without any apparent comparison to a third term is predication ("The sun is warm"). Theological speech has its own set of unique problems because all finite speech acts about the infinite must be, by definition, analogies. Even a concept of "the infinite" appears finite when symbolized with a definition, the definite article, and a singular word. A poetic language often speaks God better than predication. *Spring Awakening* suggests an embodied experience of shared silence that offers a theatrical sacrament better than words for provoking wonder.

Communion in the broken body of Christ does not immediately and irrevocably heal the brokenness of the world. The Creator's difference from creation reigns theologically supreme, so the gift-giving of the world back to God in and through the offering of the Christ remains ultimately more different from the self-donating exchange of trinitarian persons. The world's gift back to God remains an analogy in terms of understanding the drama of God's love for the world God has loved into being.

The theatrical sacrament at the end of Deaf West's *Spring Awakening* prompts an anthropological rejoinder. The opening to the outside symbolizes something like an accessible eschatology. Perhaps, in witnessing what *Hadestown* calls a crack in the wall or catching sight of what causes Eliza Hamilton's gasp, audiences can begin to all wonder, together, about a world where social life is constructed to be shared. The Deaf West revival anticipates something of an everlasting spring's awakening in resurrection-as-revival. Outside of the world stage as we know it subsists a resurrected and revived version of *this* world given as surprising gift back to God, what Saint Paul calls the *new creation*. It appears in the green of spring's return. Yet this final tableau for *Spring Awakening* also mirrors something back as a gift to this world. The finale, in silence, allows all to know the wonder of this in-breaking of communion in bodily copresence. The last actor walking through an open door into verdant light signs "The Song of Purple Summer," where all know shared wonder in a shared silence. Perhaps, refracted through a theatrical sacrament, theodramatic anthropology gains its own incarnational dictum. Awash in a spectacular silence of shared wonder, Broadway offered an argument for why humanity must be theologically interpreted to be *more similar* than we are dissimilar.

CHAPTER SEVEN

Variations on a Theme

At the beginning of this book, I asked the reader to trust, or at least withhold judgment of, the idiosyncrasies of this writer's preferences in hopes that theologians and theatre lovers alike would be able to play along. The book tried to interpret revelation in and through commercial spectacles. Plays and musicals offered moments for asking questions while sitting in the theatrical house trusting that theology can benefit from encounters beyond expected ecclesial contexts and expected religious references.

The book had two major Christian spiritual guides: Augustine and von Balthasar. Their influences appear in ways analogous to the balance between the onstage and backstage artists who create Broadway spectacles eight shows a week. Citations to Hans Urs von Balthasar starred in both leading and supporting roles throughout the book. *God on Broadway* continued studies of drama in the style of von Balthasar's *Prolegomena* to develop dramatic resources for interpreting God's self-revelation with the help of a theodramatic analogy. Where von Balthasar surveyed the history of European theatre to focus on the themes of the world stage (*theatrum mundi*) and the transition from role to mission, this book uplifted popular and commercial entertainments to ask even more theodramatic questions. Broadway situates theological inquiry amid the "joys and hopes, griefs and anxieties" of the modern world, outside the exclusive confines of the ecclesial community, ready to grapple with contemporary life's "dramatic characteristics."[1] This book aimed to play Broadway shows in a recognizably Balthasarian way in order to prove the ongoing usefulness of theodramatic theologies but also theology's readiness to engage with theatrics meaningful to many in the anglophone world. *God on Broadway* could have starred a different guide as well as different scripts, but its aim remained to surface how Broadway shows help further conversations about spectacle, liveness, memory, tradition, temporality, and stuff in an idiom that remains open to the God who may yet surprise, delight, and bring together.

Balthasarian theodramatics returned, time and again, to help us notice how God reveals who God is in the Christ who joins the play of the world's show. Drama, including Broadway spectacle, focuses attention on and through what theologians call the "second person" of the Holy Trinity, the Son who is Jesus the Christ, making known God's love for the world. For Christians (particularly Catholic-Christians after the Second Vatican Council), any conversation about God finds sense in the words of an ongoing conversation about the One whose Love the Christ fully and tangibly reveals. Von Balthasar's theodramatic approach recognizes that talking about God occurs within a world where the Christ takes the stage alongside other creatures. In the Christ, Christians recognize that God's heart beats as an incarnate, human heart. The Love that the Christ shows us of God is a Love we recognize in a sacred heart like our human hearts.[2] The audience sitting in the house watching and thinking and reflecting and interpreting is a part of the show and move toward the wider show of the world. In other words, theological interpretations of drama are, themselves, dramatic. He writes, "For theology is not an adjunct to the drama itself: if it understands itself correctly, [theology] is an aspect of it and thus has an inner participation in the nature of the drama (where content and form are inseparable). Secondly, theology has at its disposal various degrees of intensity of such participation as well as various literary themes and patterns, enabling it to represent revelation's dramatic character, and each of these embraces one aspect of the unique, archetypal, and inexhaustible drama."[3]

Like von Balthasar, I know that any theological interpretation of popular spectacle will remain ultimately unsatisfactory to both the theatre lovers and theologians I invited to play along; I echo his apologies for "grievously trying the patience" of the specialists and the dabblers alike.[4] The upshot, with hope, has been to follow von Balthasar's inspiration to find new angles from which to watch, marvel, and question God's action and our own. To that end, the show cannot be limited to the spectacle as performed. The reception history to *Godspell* and the copresence of shared quiet at the end of Deaf West's *Spring Awakening* make the point in a provocative way: Curtain calls are not a symbol of death and end but a symbol of a community that awaits with joyful hope for an arrival, a messianic coming Savior.[5]

Saint Augustine of Hippo, also a theatre kid, served as a stage manager. Augustine's influence is less visible in the footlights of footnotes but no less important for this show to go on. Some people love spectacles; I'm certainly one of them. Spectacles carry the power to distract and disclose all the while ordering collective attention and forming desire. That is, while Augustine adopted an ascetic avoidance of Rome's spectacular culture in order to more closely follow the Christ, Augustinian confidence in spectacle's ability to reveal the unseen calls the cues for this book. Theatre anticipates sacraments. Broadway spectacles might be used as an escape from the depth of the world, or spectacles might be enjoyed as one route to more fully realizing the mystery of Love at the heart of creation. An Augustinian spirituality holds open a capacity for the world *both* to perform and to distract from the reality of God's love. No wonder so many mystics and visionaries wrote their experience of the Lord as an expression of their own restless heart. Augustine's stage management helps make spectacle, even Broadway, a worthwhile place to go chasing after a closer knowledge of God. So, too, Augustinian spiritual stage management professionally adheres to Equity rules and actor and audience safety concerns.[6] Lovers of spectacle can easily mistake the heightened emotional experience of delightful aesthetics for revelation.[7] Spectacle open to the accessibility of the widest possible public will always risk a merely general sense of the numinous. That general sense—that warm and teary feeling—may flood with an interpreter's own malformed desires and opinions. Spectacle can be turned toward the self in interpretation (Augustine's concern about sin as a curving into self). Theological interpretations of spectacle would then become about who we think God should be rather than respond to the Love God reveals that God is.

Perhaps beloved popular spectacles remain too dangerous to be a theological resource, but giving in to anxiety artificially limits an arena of ordinary life where questions about God are alive. Theology, like any interpretive act, is a human endeavor. Theology, more than other interpretive acts, must emerge from a personal experience because God's revelation is not the same as the revealing of a thing among things. So rather than quest after some pure "objectivity," as impossible for theatre as it is for theology, an Augustinian sensibility always seeks God in community with others. His great narration of personal interiority in the *Confessions* constantly names friends, family, teachers, rivals, and visions. So, too, his own relationship with God.

Augustine's own script interlaces with scripture, but Augustine speaks his life's narrative into the second person. "Great are you, Lord, and worthy to be praised" opens the *Confessions*. Augustine speaks himself in direct address to God; centuries of readers overhear the conversation. Overhearing, though, is certainly part of Augustine's purpose. His *Confessions* are made public, not kept to the privacy of the mind or under the secrecy of what later comes to be codified as a sacramental confessor's seal.

Throughout Augustine's book, the second-person address of the *Confessions* provides an inverted model for the ways in which Broadway spectacle might be overheard as prayerful theology. That is, the *Confessions* are a prayer that can be treated without reference to the reality of God, that can be read by countless undergraduates in countless universities as a late antique autobiography and spectacular display of Latin rhetorical mastery. The *Confessions* make a great book, in the fullest sense of the contested term, but a reader can overhear Augustine's prayer without making it their own thanksgiving and second-person praise of God. Broadway shows do it backward. Broadway-style shows are entertaining spectacles where God can be overheard revealing something about God. Overhearing risks misinterpretation and instrumentalization, but overhearing—even wrongly—can also provide theological inspiration.

"YOU WILL BE FOUND"

Long before seeing the musical on Broadway myself, I once had a great conversation with a future Christian minister about how "seen" they felt by *Dear Evan Hansen*. I did not know the show at the time. More than a few Christians and non-Christians and anti-Christians have found comfort and inspiration in Benj Pasek's and Justin Paul's music and Steven Levenson's book from *Dear Evan Hansen*. But the soundtrack resounds with themes that sound theological or, at the very least, "spiritual": falling, finding, community, dawn, discovery, self-worth, expression, love, family, death, value, memory, singing requiem. The plot does not eschew religion, particularly the strongly implied Jewishness of Jared's sexual escapades at camp or the heart-wrenching image of a tie for Bar Mitzvah season that never received an invitation to be used. Neither the Murphy nor the Hansen family makes appeals to religious knowledge beyond exasperated invocations of Jesus Christ. Divinity remains conspicuously absent from much of the plot.

Such absence might well be a mode of God's presence in the midst of the show's concentric tragedies and flawed redemptions. *Dear Evan Hansen* arrests the attention of believers and nonbelievers alike precisely for the depth of its plot's humanity and the perceived beauty of its musical score. Like all shows, others find the musical trite and overwrought. Over time, the show appears more and more obviously dated. Humanity and beauty are both ironically filtered by and played out in the (literal) light of social media. At times, humanity and beauty interrupt the endless scroll of posts and likes, alternatively treating a cacophony of online voices from "the community" as an inspiring or damning chorus. If silence—even a pause or rest in music—manifests a mode of God's presence through absence on Broadway, then the show's interruptions to the fast-paced improvisation of digital life might suggest something analogous to God's grace at work in repairing the world or, at the very least, in turning our attention to what it means to share bodies in space and time despite ever-increasing screen time, digital mediation, large language models, and ecclesial-political polarization.

To build such an idea about apophatic theology from the material that is *Dear Evan Hansen* unashamedly reads *into* the show. Reading into Broadway has been the gambit of this entire book. Interpreting interrupted improvisation as grace undoubtedly proceeds "in front of the text"[8] in line with the Ricoeurian homiletical theory of James Henry Harris. Harris argues that preachers—particularly in the tradition of the Black church—need to locate their preaching in the world opened in front, rather than behind, the scriptural text. The same might be said for theological interpretations of God's self-revelation that rely on spectacles. Theology gets in front of the "text" of the spectacle to speak from a position that sits in the house. *Dear Evan Hansen* offers plenty of necessary symbolic tools for making Christian meaning: Trees result in falls, broken relationships can be healed, all are shown to matter through the memory of the death of one, hope emerges in the promise that all will be made new.

The central conceit of the plot proposes an epistolary narrative self. Evan (with the help of Jared) writes the story of a graced relationship with Connor that, in fact, never existed. The musical proposes modulating the idea of a person as the author of their own story. Rather than the image of an individual and isolated novelist composing a life, *Dear Evan Hansen* shows us a messy editorial writers' room and the making of meaning through interpretation. A scene of composition, the number "Sincerely Me" blends Evan, Jared, and the projected "memory" of Connor.[9] The work of "The Connor Project" argues that no person should be forgotten. But does the memory of a person's influence on history need to be historically accurate in order to be true, good, or beautiful? The show opens that question without offering a moralistic answer (perhaps one of the show's greatest strengths). Is Connor a symbol for how an ancient community might have told Jesus's story? The Connor Project might be thus easily framed as a stand-in for contemporary Christian worship, an online "church" community that does its work—for good and for cancellation-as-excommunication ill—in dangerous remembrance of Connor Murphy. "You Will Be Found" and its reprise would not merely recall the sound world aesthetics of contemporary praise and worship music but could also function as a diegetic hymn.

But, in light of the work done in *God on Broadway*, my goal has been to encourage theological interpretations of theatrical spectacle that press beyond the classic religion and literature quest to locate figural representations of religious themes.[10] In fact, something of *Dear Evan Hansen* would be lost if its theological contribution could be reduced to Christ figures and churchy aesthetics. I am far from the first interpreter to notice the resonances between "You Will Be Found" and Christian theological and musical themes. The show offers a striking opportunity to make specifically Christian theological meaning in a world characterized by religious pluralism. It is possible to interpret a revelation of the God revealed in and through Jesus the Christ without reducing the presence of non-Christian religious traditions to generic symbols of transcendence or accidents of culture devoid of their own religious specificity.

Instead, I want to suggest that *Dear Evan Hansen*'s "You Will Be Found" stages interruptions of grace as a *dark* that crashes through into the world of the play. The possibility of God's presence can become most noticeable in moments of humanity twinned with music that present the impossible spectacle of God's absence: "You Will Be Found." That is, the phenomenality of God's absence *remains* a mode of God's presence: You are not alone. The show's hope perhaps consists in its confidence that falling is inevitable, but someone will run to help get you home. A cavalcade of thanks, indexed to names and places across a continent, sings promises that will rise up again. A litany of voices asserts over and over and over how you are not left by yourself.

Symbols of resurrection life linger, in both the music and the staging. The music slowly builds. We see images of Evan's speech at a school memorial service for Connor Murphy, but we hear the content of the speech in the musical number. Evan intones both melody and his speech's message—"You Will Be Found"—and, like a speech posted to the internet that goes viral, the tempo, the orchestration, and the melodic complexity swirl, swell, and build. The number's hope that none of us are alone depicts how many hear truth in Evan's message. In the final swell of the chorus, the staging depicts Connor's father finally collapsing in mourning. The song interweaves a theologically rich language of brokenness and newness, emptiness and community, feeling lost and being found.

The argument of the lyrics seems deceptively simple even if addressed to an undefined "you": look around and be found. But this turning to look around could be a *metanoia*. The turn to look toward others that recognizes you are not alone is, always and already, a turn outward away from the anxiety of felt abandonment and loneliness. Noticing that you are not alone carries hope, consolation, and responsibility. Noticing that you are not alone introduces hope that shatters the ideology of isolated suffering: "To stand under the burden of suffering always means to become more and more isolated. Greek tragedy depicts this process by which relationships dissolve one after the other until the individual is finally alone."[11] *Dear Evan Hansen* inverts this tragic process. By noticing suffering as a shared reality, community gathers: "The way leads out of isolated suffering through communication (by lament) to the solidarity in which change occurs."[12] Consolation is in the realization that others not only share the experience of apparent Godforsaken brokenness but are also willing to reach out in action. Responsibility is in becoming the friend who runs toward another who has fallen. To say "You are not alone" proclaims both solidarity and the need to be *for others*.

When I saw the Broadway version, I was struck by staging choices that rendered this number both quasi-religious in its lighting and staging and hymnic repetition but also its depictions of grieving parents falling to their knees or the creation of a community bonded through reimagined loss.

The titular pronoun works ambiguously in this rocking theatrical theological anthem. Who is the "You" who will be found? Those (perhaps all) in the audience feeling lost and broken? A preferential option for the one who suffers? An open signifier of deferral in perpetual ethical search of those not yet brought into community? Or, perhaps, the pronoun inaugurates a shift into the second person of theological reflection. In the experience of God's absence—precisely out of shadows and interruptive *dark*—God reveals Godself as the One who wills to find and be found. Ambiguity stands in wonderment at a God who, in God's apparent absence, is excessive enough to be a Love that never leaves (even fallen) creation alone.

Pressed just a bit further, the song's exclamations that You are not alone offer words of praise that define the God of ever-circulating, tripersonal love. In the incarnation, God binds Godself and the story of God's life to creation in such a way that God's creatures can find God. God did not need to create out of love in order to be God. God does not need the world. God *could have been* alone. But, articulated like a reverie of praise and thanksgiving, the song's chorus echoes. Indeed, God is not alone because God has not willed to be apart from the world God continually loves into being. Precisely in God's understanding and participation in human brokenness and Godforsakenness with a promise that with morning all becomes new, God chooses to be the sort of God who will be found.

The song suggests an apophatic theology that speaks with confident hope.[13] God may elude recognition in ordinary experience, but You will be found. Sometimes through speculations on a Broadway spectacle.

FINALE ULTIMO

No play says everything about God, and no book can say everything about God or about Broadway.[14] Much remains missing from my attempt to interpret revelation through commercial spectacles and theatrical sacraments. A Broadway show can trigger a change in perception: the newness of the world revealed in the spectacle of the fact that the show is still happening. You are not alone is a fact. Theatre is always a gathering of humans doing human things in community. The work of a book about God on Broadway remains inviting prayerful attention toward what might be missed, skipped, covered, or elided by spectacle.

Theatrical phenomena are spectacular, and Broadway shows and megamusicals make spectacle central to their being and establish an imagined "standard" for theatrical art. Broadway shows grab attention; they elicit emotion; they prompt reflection. Searching for God on Broadway makes the mirror of theatre into a recognition that human life is full of attending, remembering, instrumentalizing, traditioning, blaspheming, waiting, watching, ritualizing, singing, dancing, and storytelling. Humans *perform* for each other on the stage of the world, and sometimes we render that spectacle into a show worthy of our paying attention. Sitting in the house, at the end of any show, we are confronted yet again with what it means to live together. In a beloved phrase from Stephen Sondheim and James Lapine's *Into the Woods*, "No One Is Alone."

Looking for God on Broadway, as demonstrated throughout this book, breaks the theatrical fourth wall in ways beyond simply direct address to the audience. A "you" crosses the aesthetic distance between audience in the house and performers on stage and backstage crew and all the many humans moving in and around a bustling city outside. Spectacle happens between performer and witness, but a performance requires *both* actor and audience to be a spectacle.

Theatre's "you" always invokes a register incarnational and prayerful and social and in the world; the "you" identifies a crowd of witnesses and an opportunity to recognize God's possibility anew in the ordinary space between human beings. Searching for God on Broadway is as much a route to theologizing spectacle as it is a spectacular recognition of the God encountered on the countless broadways journeyed outside a theater in performances of everyday life. Broadway spectacle gestures toward what it means to encounter and know the God who enters into dramas, stories, and even popular lyrics of the human community.

An audience, on so many occasions, plays a role like what we imagine to be God's. Revelation, then, appears as readily in the friends, lovers, strangers, and fellow tourist pilgrims with whom we shuffle off to continue the play of conversation. Departing from a revelatory spectacle carries a similar injunction like the one received at the liturgy. God's show continues in the work done by those who dangerously remember God and tradition (hand on) God's love in the world by performing the Christ for others. Broadway discloses how theologians cannot limit God's spectacular appearance to what happens during the length of the show. God's time is still approaching, and sitting in the house describes only one scene in an entire life's drama.

So where do you find God on Broadway after the show ends, when the house is emptied save for a ghost light? Do you hear the people sing? If so, it will be the humming of a tune on the street bringing the spectacle outside. The final word for a book about God on Broadway, then, will also need to be how Fantine and the voice of a bishop end *Les Misérables*: "To love another person is to see the face of God."

Acknowledgments
Curtain Call

At the end of any Broadway show, the cast turns to the audience and reverences its presence with a bow. The audience, in turn, applauds and maybe even cheers. The curtain call and its obligatory ovations mark the transition from spectacle back to everyday life. Curtain calls manifest actors and characters in Victor Turner's liminal space: The audience celebrates the actor by means of the costumed image of their character.[1] In some shows, a bow may reflect something of the character's character rather than the actor's. The one playing the villain in a children's show will be celebrated best with a chorus of boos. The current industry standard for a curtain call often demands some gesture, open palmed and gracious, toward the lighting booth or the orchestra pit. This moment orients the thanks of everyone in the house—performers and spect-actors of the audience—to those backstage who make the show happen.

First, then, a bow of reverence to you. And thank you for reading.

Second, a request for your indulgence. I have been chasing the ideas in this book for most of my life. I doubt I am done with them. But this project has interlocking origin stories before its first scene played out on a pandemic era Zoom call with friends that resulted in a book proposal. One origin gives thanks to my grandparents, who both inspired my faith and built me a stage in a suburban basement. Thanks to all my extended family for playing along. Another origin is my first real theatre teacher, Ms. Leta Strain, who cast me in *Peter Pan* in sixth grade, and my time acting and directing with the Seven Mile Island Stars (thanks to many mermaids, especially my first producer in my directing work, Kelly Dansky). Thanks to all the casts and crews and to all the Broadway shows. My high school mentors and teachers at Bishop Eustace fostered my love of big questions and drama. I remain grateful to Ms. Joan Cecil and Mr. Jim Brady, and especially the late Mr. Joseph Marquart, for providing me such a strong foundation. So, too, the many holy and good priests who talked theology with me in the sacristy before serving mass. Another origin is the lifelong encouragement and mentorship for thinking about art and culture provided by Joseph Neubauer and Jeanette Lerman-Neubauer.

Another story of origin gives thanks to the professors who trained me to think theologically and theatrically. That story opens with the conversation about *Les Misérables* I had with Kevin Hughes in a library lounge during college and his responsibility for first assigning me to do a project on Hans Urs von Balthasar. Jesse Coenhoven; Paul Danove; Tony Godzieba; John Immerwahr; Valerie Joyce; Rev. Martin Laird, OSA; Gene McCarraher; Heidi Rose; Tom Smith; and Michael and Helena Tomko will find their impact on me throughout this book. The Villanova origin story continues through writing a senior thesis on von Balthasar guided by D. C. Schindler and Rev. David Cregan, OSA, while helping Fr. David produce a version of *Godspell* staged in actual sanctuaries. Thanks, too, to many friends from Villanova and beyond who thought these and related questions alongside me, especially Rev. Bryan Kerns, OSA; Anthony and Anu Cetta; Andrew Clare; Cayce Farina; Miguel Gutierrez and Rachel Conley; Andrew Lavadera and Melissa Nally; Shashika and Emily Stanislaus; Mark and Cait Versella; and those for whom the symbols of VSMT, Singers, and Pastoral Musicians make shared meaning.

Another origin of this project is my time at Yale Divinity School and Institute of Sacred Music, where Peter S. Hawkins taught me how to write, to pray joyfully, and to love scripture and ensured I would never stop doing or thinking about theatre. Thanks, as well, for courses with Rev. Maggi Dawn, Junius Johnson, Aaron Rosen, Linn Marie Tonstad, Andre Willis, and many others that helped frame my understanding of the questions in this book. I am a better theatre-maker and human because of Nathaniel Dolquist. So, too, Sean McAvoy, L. Patrick Burrows, Jewelle Bickel, Rev. Portia Corbin and Rev. Chris Corbin, Rev. Rebecca and Alex Floyd Marshall, Craig Ford, E. S. Kempson, and Kelly Stewart. This book emerges from theatrical theological collaborators, especially Rev. Justin Crisp and Justin Kosec. Sections of this book were first presented at parishes and the Association for Theatre in Higher Education alongside them. At the invitation of Rev. John Tirro, Justin Crisp and I held a liturgical drama workshop at Tyson House at the University of Tennessee at Knoxville, where I first gave a talk about Broadway's commercial theology. Misty Anderson later, in Manhattan, directly asked me, "When are you going to grapple with Kushner?" God's grace and providence ensures that Justin, Jewelle, Valkyrie, and now Beatrice continue to add so much to my family's life, my thinking, and my writing.

ACKNOWLEDGMENTS

Another moment of origin is the request, first intoned by Jennifer Geddes at my dissertation defense, for me to write a different book about my theology with and through shows I love rather than instrumentalize theatre to talk about von Balthasar. Further, I could not be who I am today, nor this book make any sense, without the guidance and lessons of my *Doktorvater* and friend Kevin Hart. He directed me to learn about revelation, and he continues to be the one to whom I flee to renew confidence in my vocation as a teacher and scholar and for unwavering support for my career. Many of the ideas in this book also bear the mark of conversations with my teachers and friends Nichole Flores and Rev. Gerald Fogarty, SJ. My ideas were refined and enhanced through ongoing discussions with William Boyce, Lucila Crena, Brandy Daniels, Ashleigh Elser and Matt Elia, Rebecca Epstein Levi, Jeremy Fisher, Peggy Galloway, Daryn Henry, Rev. James Henry Harris, Paul Dafydd Jones, Chuck Mathewes, Christina McRorie, Rachel and Jonathan Teubner, Rev. Heather Warren, Rev. Joseph Walker-Lenow, and Daniel and Rev. Leah Wise. Thanks, too, to Joe (and his dad) for facilitating an invitation to offer the Dillard Forum at Trinity United Methodist Church in Richmond, Virginia, on "Theology and Theater" that sketched some of this book for the first time.

But any Broadway script reflects an event. This book's first through fifth drafts were performed while teaching. First, as a student alongside my own Teacher and Jedi master, Larry D. Bouchard. Larry graciously invited me to colead a seminar on "Religion and Modern Theatre" as a graduate student, and it was in teaching with Larry that I first juxtaposed *Fiddler on the Roof* with *Doubt, A Parable*. Reading Larry's scholarship inspires my own, including our work together to coedit a special issue of *Religions*. Every conversation with Larry opens a world and reconfirms my hope, and Larry continues to read my writing, compare notes on good shows, comment on absurdities, and sharpen my thinking with wit and laughter.

At Sacred Heart University, I have been blessed to offer an undergraduate course with the title "God on Broadway." SHU values a culture where I can connect research and teaching. My students became real coconspirators in thinking through the arguments present in this book. As promised, my note of thanks (alphabetically by class): Juliana Balzano, Jenna Chernick, Jack Damato, Chris Fusina, Gabrielle Gottschall, Mairead Kearns, Allyson Lombardo, Madison McCall, Destiny Sanchez, Lexi Yost, Rina Damon, Nicky Duca, Mariella Esperti, Taylor Gibbs, Bella Gongora, Aliza Leander, Ava Manzo, Connor Nelson, Linsey Palma, Amanda Pizzi, David Robillard, Lucia Silva, Delaney Smith, Michael Castellano, Matthew Damon, Elena Fourounjian, Helena Mitchell, Alexandra

ACKNOWLEDGMENTS

Parsons, Camille Vail, Kat Barry, Allie Cimaglia, Emma Cruess, Kaylie Mallegol, Victoria Rinaldi, Angelica Zacarola, Erica Allocca, Juliana Agostini, Connor Cunha, Emma Drzewiecki, Michael Gordon, Jenna Lee, Leanne Suazo, Matthew Carrara, Sarah Margerison, Grace Walker, Jack Ferreira, Elizabeth Kalfayan, Tara Keating, Ronald Petrillo, Olivia Saraceno, Kathleen Sullivan, Celia Brnetic, Frank Celli, Leslie Duda, L, Brooke Manna, Michael Morelli, Emma Riccardi, Sarah Batho, Carlie Buono, Jacqueline Champoux, Morgan Fitzpatrick, Ellen Micallef, Nan Payton, Christopher Seebode. Thanks also to Elizabeth Turello and my many, many other students.

To write this book, I depended on the support of my colleagues and cherished friends at Sacred Heart University. Thank you to my Department of Catholic Studies—Michelle Loris, Dan Rober, Brent Little, Jillian Plummer, Chelsea Jordan King, and Callie Tabor—for many, many conversations. A writing group with Jillian, Chelsea, and Callie supported me and vastly improved multiple chapters of this book. I could not have done this without them. Abundant thanks, as well, to ongoing conversations and encouragement from Funda Alp, Mark Beekey, Abby Bender, Lori Bindig Yousman, Robin Cautin, June-Ann Greeley, Michael W. Higgins, Michael Iannazzi, Annie Johnson, Jennifer McLaughlin, Chrystal Lewis, Elizabeth Luoma, Amanda Moras, Ami Neville, Francis Origanti, John Petillo, Bill Yousman, Darcy Ronan, John Roney, Peter Sinclair, Matthew Shields, and Brian Stiltner. Special thanks for the opportunity to think about theatre alongside my research collaborators in the Dramatic Humanities, Emily Bryan and Rachel Bauer. And much gratitude to Amie Reilly and Dave Thomson who, in different ways, got this book and me back on track more times than I can count. I am also thankful to learn in my work with the whole of Project Untitled, especially Keith Hamilton Cobb and Jessica Burr. I benefit immensely from the constant encouragement of folks across the university, especially my friends and colleagues in the Office of Mission and Culture, who enrich our community and constantly boost me. And there are many others at Sacred Heart and beyond, including Valerie Kisselback and Glenn Sauer and the wonderful humans who cared for my daughter at Bright Horizons.

Versions of the arguments in this book were presented at many scholarly conferences: the American Academy of Religion; the Association for Theatre in Higher Education; the Catholic Theological Society of America, especially my dear friends in the Hans Urs von Balthasar Consultation; the Catholic Studies Consortium; the College Theology Society; the International Federation for Theatre Research; the International Society for Religion, Literature, and Culture; and the International Conference for Collaborative Philosophy, Theology,

ACKNOWLEDGMENTS

and Ministry. I am grateful for the insight and encouragement I received as a member of these communities and for friendships too numerous to name. Thanks are due to Crina Gschwandtner, Thomas Schärtl-Trendel, Neal DeRoo, Tamsin Jones, Jeffrey Bloechl, and my fellow participants in the Phenomenology and Revelation seminar who helped me refine the argument at the heart of this book. I was fortunate to workshop parts of chapter 3 at Boston College with the Northeast Philosophy of Religion Colloquium with thanks to Rev. Bill Woody, SJ, for his hospitality and friendship. A special word of thanks to Anne Carpenter and Jennifer Newsome Martin for supporting me and encouraging my work in so many ways.

An invitation to visit the University of St. Thomas in St. Paul confirmed the course of this project. My friendship with Erika Kidd and John Boyle sustained and encouraged me throughout this writing. Thanks to all the students and faculty in the Department of Catholic Studies and beyond at St. Thomas for talking with me about chapter 1 and *Hadestown*.

Portions of chapters 2 and 6 appeared previously in *Münchener Theologische Zeitschrift*. A section of chapter 5 previously appeared in the *Other Journal*. My thanks to Thomas Schärtl-Trendel and Zac Settle.

The incredible Ryan Hemmer not only edited this book and helped to shape my thinking and writing but also once met me to talk in person in a hotel lobby until the wee hours of the morning. His unrivaled friendship and confidence in me were essential to beginning and ending this project. My further thanks to Chantelle Gibbs and everyone at Fortress Press for their belief in this project and help to make it happen. I add that all the good that is in this book comes from what I have learned in conversation with so many, including those I may have failed adequately to name and those who disagree with me. Thank you. But the errors and mistakes are all mine.

A final set of deepest thanks. My parents, Charlie and Cathy Gillespie; and my brother, Jamie, have always been proud of me. My mom and dad always nurtured my love of Broadway and performing, from asking about the endless rehearsal days, helping with sets and makeup, or always making the trip to see me in a show. Jamie demanded pages; here they are. I am lucky to have their love and support to pursue my vocation. Thank you, thank you, thank you.

And to my scene partners Tara Powers and Rosie. You are my "wonder of wonders, miracle of miracles." There are not enough words to acknowledge what you have given me or how much I love you. Thanks to you, "now my life is rosy." This book is for you.

Bibliography

Alonso, Antonio Eduardo. *Commodified Communion: Eucharist, Consumer Culture, and the Practice of Everyday Life*. Fordham, 2021.
Aronson-Lehavi, Sharon. *Performing Religion on the Secular Stage*. Routledge, 2023.
Althaus-Reid, Marcella. *Indecent Theology: Theological Perversions in Sex, Gender and Politics*. Routledge, 2000.
Anselm. *Proslogion*. In *Basic Writings*, edited and translated by Thomas Williams. Hackett, 2007.
Arrandale, Rick. "Artaud and the Concept of Drama in Theology." *New Blackfriars* 88, no. 1013 (January 2007): 100–112.
Artaud, Antonin. *The Theater and Its Double*. Translated by Mary Caroline Richards. Grove, 1958.
Auerbach, Erich. *Mimesis: The Representation of Reality in Western Literature*. Princeton University Press, 1953.
Augustine. *City of God*. Translated by Henry Bettenson. Penguin, 1995.
———. *Confessions*. Translated by Henry Chadwick. Oxford University Press, 1991.
Austin, J. L. *How to Do Things with Words*. Harvard, 1962.
Balthasar, Hans Urs von. *Convergences: To the Source of the Christian Mystery*. Ignatius, 1983.
———. *Epilogue*. Translated by Edward T. Oaks, SJ. Ignatius, 1991.
———. *Explorations in Theology, Volume IV: Spirit and Institution*. Translated by Edward T. Oaks, SJ. Ignatius, 1994.
———. *Explorations in Theology, Volume III: Creator Spirit*. Translated by Brian McNeil, CRV. Ignatius, 1993.
———. *The Glory of the Lord: A Theological Aesthetics*, Vol. 1, *Seeing the Form*, edited by Joseph Fessio, SJ, and John Riches. Ignatius, 1982.
———. *Love Alone Is Credible*. Translated by D. C. Schindler. Ignatius, 2005.
———. *Mysterium Paschale: The Mystery of Easter*. Translated by Aidan Nichols, OP. Ignatius, 1990.
———. *Razing the Bastions: On the Church in This Age*. Translated by Brian McNeil, CRV. Ignatius, 1993.
———. *Theo-Drama I: Prolegomena*. Translated by Graham Harrison. Ignatius, 1988.
———. *Theo-Drama II: Dramatis Personae: Man in God*. Translated by Graham Harrison. Ignatius, 1990.
———. *Theo-Drama III: Dramatis Personae: Persons in Christ*. Translated by Graham Harrison. Ignatius, 1992.
———. *Theo-Drama IV: The Action*. Translated by Graham Harrison. Ignatius, 1994.

———. *Theo-Drama V: The Last Act*. Translated by Graham Harrison. Ignatius, 1998.
———. *Theodramatik I: Prolegomena*. Johannes Verlag, 1973.
———. *Theodramatik II/1: Die Personen Des Spiels Teil I: Der Mensch in Gott*. Johannes Verlag, 1976.
———. *Theodramatik II/2: Die Personen Des Spiels Teil II: Die Personen in Christus*. Johannes Verlag, 1978.
———. *Theodramatik III: Die Handlung*. Johannes Verlag, 1980.
———. *Theodramatic IV: Das Endspiel*. Johannes Verlag, 1983.
———. *Theo-Logic: Theological Logical Theory*, Vol. 1, *The Truth of the World*. Translated by Adrian J. Walker. Ignatius, 2000.
———. *Truth Is Symphonic: Aspects of Christian Pluralism*. Ignatius, 1987.
Barnett, David. *A History of the Berliner Ensemble*. Cambridge University Press, 2015.
Barish, Jonas. *The Antitheatrical Prejudice*. University of California Press, 1981.
Barth, Karl. *Church Dogmatics*, edited by G. W. Bromiley and Thomas F. Torrance. T&T Clark, 1956–1969.
———. *The Word of God and Theology*. Translated by Amy Marga. T&T Clark, 2011.
Begbie, Jeremy S. *Voicing Creation's Praise: Towards a Theology of the Arts*. T&T Clark, 1991.
Bell, Catherine. *Ritual Theory, Ritual Practice*. Oxford University Press, 2009.
Benjamin, Walter. *Illuminations*, edited by Hannah Arendt. Translated by Harry Zohn. Schocken, 1969.
Beattie, Tina. *New Catholic Feminism: Theology and Theory*. Routledge, 2006.
Beyt, Adam. "'Beautiful and New': The Logic of Complementarity in *Hedwig and the Angry Inch*." *Religions* 10, no. 11 (2019): 620.
Bial, Henry. *Acting Jewish: Negotiating Ethnicity on the American Stage and Screen*. University of Michigan Press, 2005.
———. *Playing God: The Bible on the Broadway Stage*. University of Michigan Press, 2015.
Blanchot, Maurice. *The Space of Literature*. Translated by Ann Smock. University of Nebraska Press, 1982.
———. *The Writing of the Disaster*. Translated by Ann Smock. University of Nebraska Press, 1995.
Boal, Augusto. *Theatre of the Oppressed*. Theatre Communications Group, 1985.
Bord, Guy du. *The Society of the Spectacle*. Translated by Ken Knabb. Bureau of Public Secrets, 2014.
Bouchard, Larry D. "Religion and the Limits of Metatheatre in *Our Town* and *Sunday in the Park with George*." *Religions* 11, no. 2 (2020): 94.
———. *Theater and Integrity: Emptying Selves in Drama, Ethics, and Religion*. Northwestern University Press, 2011.
———. *Tragic Method and Tragic Theology: Evil in Contemporary Drama and Religious Thought*. Penn State University Press, 1989.
Brecht, Bertolt. *Brecht on Theatre: The Development of an Aesthetic*, edited by John Willet. Hill and Wang, 1992.
Brook, Peter. *The Empty Space*. Repr. ed. Scribner, 1995.
Brown, David Sterling. *Shakespeare's White Others*. Cambridge University Press, 2023.
Brown, Frank Burch. *Good Taste, Bad Taste, Christian Taste: Aesthetics in Religious Life*. Oxford University Press, 2000.
Butler, Judith. *Bodies That Matter: On the Discursive Limits of Sex*. Routledge, 1993.
———. *Gender Trouble: Feminism and the Subversion of Identity*. Routledge, 1990.

———. *Excitable Speech: A Politics of the Performative*. Routledge, 1997.
———. *Notes Toward a Performative Theory of Assembly*. Harvard University Press, 2015.
Burrows, L. Patrick. "Theology in Place: Religion, Geography, and the American South." Diss., Harvard Divinity School, 2021.
Calvin, John. *Institutes of the Christian Religion*. 2 vols., edited by John T. McNeill. Westminster John Knox, 2011.
Carlson, Marvin. *The Haunted Stage: The Theatre as Memory Machine*. University of Michigan Press, 2003.
Carpenter, Anne M. *Nothing Gained Is Eternal*. Fortress, 2022.
———. *Theo-poetics: Hans Urs von Balthasar and the Risk of Art and Being*. Notre Dame Press, 2015.
Cavanaugh, William T. *Being Consumed: Economics and Christian Desire*. Eerdmans, 2008.
Chambers, Claire Maria. *Performance Studies and Negative Epistemology: Performance Apophatics*. Palgrave Macmillan, 2017.
Cornille, Catherine. *Meaning and Method in Comparative Theology*. Wiley Blackwell, 2020.
Csikzentmihaly, Mihaly, and Jeanne Nakamura. "Effortless Attention in Everyday Life: A Systematic Phenomenology." In *Effortless Attention: A New Perspective in the Cognitive Science of Attention and Action*, edited by Brian Bruya. MIT Press, 2010.
Cusack, Carol M. *Invented Religions: Imagination, Fiction, Faith*. Routledge, 2010.
Denzinger, Heinrich. *Enchiridion symbolorum defeinitionum et declarationum de rebus fidei et morum*. 43rd ed., edited by Peter Hünerman; Latin-English ed., edited by Robert Fastiggi and Anne Englund Nash. Ignatius, 2012.
Derrida, Jacques. *Specters of Marx: The State of the Debt, the Work of Mourning, and the New International*. Translated by Peggy Kamuf. Routledge, 1994.
Durkheim, Émile. *The Elementary Forms of Religious Life*. Translated by Joseph Ward Swain. George Allen, 1915.
Douglas, Mary. *Purity and Danger: An Analysis of Concepts of Pollution and Taboo*. Praeger, 1966.
Dox, Donalee. *Reckoning with the Spirit in the Paradigm of Performance*. University of Michigan Press, 2016.
Ellacuría, Ignacio. "The Crucified People: An Essay in Historical Soteriology." In *Ignacio Ellacuría: Essays on History, Liberation, and Salvation*, edited by Michael E. Lee. Orbis Books, 2013.
Francis, Pope. *Dilexit Nos*, 2024. https://www.vatican.va/content/francesco/en/encyclicals/documents/20241024-enciclica-dilexit-nos.html.
Flannery, OP, Austin, ed. *Vatican Council II, Vol 1: The Conciliar and Postconciliar Documents*. Costello, 1996.
Flores, Nichole M. *The Aesthetics of Solidarity: Our Lady of Guadalupe and American Democracy*. Georgetown University Press, 2021.
Flower, Harriet I. "Spectacle and Political Culture in the Roman Republic." In *The Cambridge Companion to the Roman Republic*, edited by Harriet I. Flower. Cambridge University Press, 2014.
Gadamer, Hans-Georg. *Truth and Method*. Rev. ed. Translated by Joel Weinsheimer and Donald G. Marshal. Continuum, 1989.
García-Rivera, Alejandro. *The Community of the Beautiful: A Theological Aesthetics*. Liturgical Press, 1999.

Gardner, Lucy, David Moss, Ben Quash, and Graham Ward. *Balthasar at the End of Modernity*. T&T Clark, 1999.
Gillespie, Charles A. "Imagining the Unseen in Catholic Studies: Complexities of Encounter, Credibility, and *Oedipus*." *Logos: A Journal of Catholic Thought and Culture* 26, no. 3 (Summer 2023): 138–149.
———. "Sustainable Canons: Gadamer's Hermeneutics and Theatre." *Labyrinth: An International Journal for Philosophy, Value Theory and Sociocultural Hermeneutics* 24, no. 2 (Winter 2022): 150–175.
———. "Theodramatic Themes and Showtime in Nassim Soleimanpour's *White Rabbit Red Rabbit*." *Religions* 11, no. 10 (2020): 499.
Gillespie, Charles A., and Larry D. Bouchard, eds. *Religion and Theatrical Drama*. MDPI, 2022.
Gillespie, Charles A., Justin Kosec, and Kate Stratton. "Treasure in Clay Jars: Christian Liturgical Drama in Theory and Praxis." In *Theatre Symposium: Ritual Religion and Theatre*. Vol. 21. University of Alabama Press, 2013.
Goehr, Lydia. *The Imaginary Museum of Musical Works: An Essay on the Philosophy of Music*. Clarendon Press, 1992.
Goffman, Erving. *The Presentation of Self in Everyday Life*. Doubleday, 1959.
Goizueta, Roberto S. *Christ Our Companion: Toward a Theological Aesthetics of Liberation*. Orbis, 2009.
Gonzalez, Michelle A. *Sor Juana: Beauty and Justice in the Americas*. Orbis, 2003.
González-Andrieu, Cecilia. *Bridge to Wonder: Art as a Gospel of Beauty*. Baylor University Press, 2012.
Gschwandtner, Christina M. *Reading Religious Ritual with Ricoeur: Between Fragility and Hope*. Roman and Littlefield, 2021.
Habermas, Jürgen. *The Theory of Communicative Action*. 2 vols. Translated by Thomas McCarthy. Beacon, 1985.
Hans Urs von Balthasar: His Life and Work, edited by D. L. Schindler. Ignatius, 1991.
Harris, James Henry. *Beyond the Tyranny of the Text: Preaching in Front of the Bible to Create a New World*. Fortress, 2019.
Hart, Kevin. *Kingdoms of God*. Indiana University Press, 2014.
Henerson, Evan. "'The Word of Your Body' Is Reborn in Deaf West's *Spring Awakening*." *Playbill*, September 8, 2014.
Horkheimer, Max, and Theodor W. Adorno. "The Culture Industry: Enlightenment as Mass Deception." In *Dialectic of Enlightenment*, edited by Gunzelin Schmid Noerr. Translated by Edmund Jephcott. Stanford University Press, 2002.
Hoffman, Warren. *The Great White Way: Race and the Broadway Musical*. Rutgers, 2014.
Huizinga, Johan. *Homo Ludens: A Study of the Play-Element in Culture*. Beacon, 1955.
Husserl, Edmund. *Ideas: General Introduction to Pure Phenomenology*. Routledge, 2004.
———. *Phantasy, Image Consciousness, and Memory (1898–1925)*. Translated by John B. Brough. Springer, 2005.
Jennings, Willie James. *After Whiteness: An Education in Belonging*. Eerdmans. 2020.
———. *The Christian Imagination: Theology and the Origins of Race*. Yale University Press, 2010.
Johnson, Elizabeth. *She Who Is*, ann. ed. Crossroad, 2012.
Johnson, Junius. *Christ and Analogy: The Christocentric Metaphysics of Hans Urs von Balthasar*. Fortress Press, 2013.
Johnson, Todd E., and Dale Savidge. *Performing the Sacred*. Baker Academic, 2009.

Julian of Norwich. *Revelations of Divine Love*, edited by A. C. Spearing. Penguin, 1998.
Kant, Immanuel. *Critique of Judgment*. Translated by Werner S. Pluhar. Hackett, 1987.
———. *Foundations of the Metaphysics of Morals: And What Is Enlightenment?* Translated by Lewis White Beck. Macmillan, 1959.
Kafer, Alison. *Feminist, Queer, Crip.* Indiana University Press, 2013.
Kilby, Karen. *Balthasar: A (Very) Critical Introduction.* Eerdmans, 2012.
Knapp, Jeffrey. *Shakespeare's Tribe: Church, Nation, and Theater in Renaissance England.* University of Chicago Press, 2002.
Knight, Mark. "Wirkunggeschichte, Reception History, Reception Theory." *Journal for the Study of the New Testament* 33, no. 2 (2010): 137–146.
Krieger, Marilyn. "The O Antiphons." *Cistercian Studies Quarterly* 51, no. 4 (2016): 475–482.
Kushner, Tony. *Angels in America.* Theatre Communications Group, 2003.
Lacoste, Jean-Yves. *Experience and the Absolute.* Translated by Mark Raftery. Fordham, 2004.
———. *From Theology to Theological Thinking.* Translated by W. Chris Hackett. University of Virginia Press, 2014.
Lane, Belden C. *Ravished by Beauty: The Surprising Legacy of Reformed Spirituality.* Oxford University Press, 2011.
Larson, Jonathan. *Rent.* Applause, 2008.
Laycock, Joseph P. *Speak of the Devil: How the Satanic Temple Is Changing the Way We Talk About Religion.* Oxford University Press, 2017.
Levinas, Emmanuel. *Collected Philosophical Papers.* Translated by Alphonso Lingis. Nijhoff, 1987.
———. *Entre Nous: On Thinking-of-the-Other.* Translated by Michael B. Smith and Barbara Harshav. Columbia University Press, 1998.
Leyerle, Blake. *Theatrical Shows and Ascetic Lives: John Chrysostom's Attack on Spiritual Marriage.* University of California Press, 2001.
Lipshitz, Yair. *Theatre and Judaism.* Red Globe, 2019.
Little, Brent. *Acts of Faith and Imagination: Theological Patterns in Catholic Fiction.* Catholic University of America Press, 2023.
Lonergan, Bernard. *Early Latin Theology.* Collected Works of Bernard Lonergan. Vol. 19, edited by Robert M. Doran and H. Daniel Monsour. Translated by Michael G. Shields. University of Toronto Press, 2011.
———. *Insight: A Study of Human Understanding.* Philosophical Library, 1958.
Lubac, Henri de. *The Drama of Atheist Humanism.* Ignatius, 1995.
———. *The Mystery of the Supernatural.* Translated by Rosemary Sheed. Crossroad, 1998.
Luckhurst, Mary. *Dramaturgy: A Revolution in Theatre.* Cambridge University Press, 2006.
MacIntyre, Alasdair C. *After Virtue: A Study in Moral Theory.* University of Notre Dame Press, 1981.
Marion, Jean-Luc. *Revelation and Givenness.* Translated by Stephen E. Lewis. Oxford University Press, 2016.
———. *In the Self's Place: The Approach of Saint Augustine.* Stanford University Press, 2012.
———. *The Essential Writings*, edited by Kevin Hart. Fordham University Press, 2013.
Martin, Jennifer Newsome. "Balthasar *avec* Kristeva: On the Recovery of a Baroque Teresa of Avila." *Modern Theology* 37, no. 1 (January 2021): 23–43.
———. *Hans Urs von Balthasar and the Critical Appropriation of Russian Religious Thought.* Notre Dame University Press, 2016.

———. "The 'Whence' and the 'Whither' of Balthasar's Gendered Theology: Rehabilitating Kenosis for Feminist Theology." *Modern Theology* 31, no. 2 (April 2015): 211–234.
Marschark, Marc, Gladys Tang, and Harry Knoors, eds. *Bilingualism and Bilingual Deaf Education*. Oxford University Press, 2014.
Mason, David V. *The Performative Ground of Religion and Theatre*. Routledge, 2019.
Mathewes, Charles T. "Augustinian Anthropology: Interior intimo meo." *Journal of Religious Ethics* 27, no. 2 (1999): 195–221.
McCarraher, Eugene. *The Enchantments of Mammon: How Capitalism Became the Religion of Modernity*. Belknap, 2019.
Metz, Johann Baptist. *Faith in History and Society*. Translated by J. Matthew Ashley. PublishDrive, 2007.
Miller, Arthur. *Death of a Salesman*. In *The Portable Arthur Miller*, edited by Christopher Bigsby. Penguin, 2003.
Miller, Vincent J. *Consuming Religion: Christian Faith and Practice in a Consumer Culture*. Bloomsbury, 2003.
Miranda, Lin-Manuel, and Jeremy McCarter. *Hamilton: The Revolution*. Little Brown, 2016.
Mitchell, Anaïs. *Hadestown*. Concord Theatricals, 2021.
Moriarty, John. *Turtle Was Gone a Long Time, Volume 1: Crossing the Kedron*. Lilliput, 1996.
Morrill, Bruce T. *Anamnesis as Dangerous Memory: Political and Liturgical Theology in Dialogue*. Liturgical Press, 2000.
Muñoz, José Esteban. *Disidentifications: Queers of Color and the Performance of Politics*. University of Minnesota Press, 1999.
Nichols, OP, Aidan. *No Bloodless Myth: A Guide Through Balthasar's Dramatics*. Catholic University of America Press, 2000.
Plato. *Plato: Complete Works*, edited by John M. Cooper and D. S. Hutchinson. Hackett, 1997.
O'Malley, John W. *What Happened at Vatican II?* Harvard, 2008.
O'Regan, Cyril. *The Anatomy of Misremembering: Von Balthasar's Response to Philosophical Modernity*. Crossroad, 2014.
Phelan, Peggy. *Unmarked: the Politics of Performance*. Routledge, 1993.
Prevot, Andrew. *Thinking Prayer: Theology and Spirituality amid the Crises of Modernity*. University of Notre Dame Press, 2015.
Quash, Ben. "Ignatian Dramatics: First Glance at the Spirituality of Hans Urs von Balthasar." *The Way* 38 (January 1998): 77–86.
———. *Theology and the Drama of History*. Cambridge University Press, 2005.
Rahner, Karl. *Foundations of Christian Faith: An Introduction to the Idea of Christianity*. Seabury Press, 1978.
Ratzinger, Joseph (Pope Benedict XVI). *Caritas in Veritate*, 2009. https://www.vatican.va/content/benedict-xvi/en/encyclicals/documents/hf_ben-xvi_enc_20090629_caritas-in-veritate.html.
———. "Concerning the Notion of Person in Theology." *Communio* 17, no. 3 (Fall, 1990): 439–454.
———. *Jesus of Nazareth*. Doubleday, 2007.
Ricouer, Paul. *Hermeneutics and the Human Sciences*. Cambridge University Press, 1981.
———. *Interpretation Theory: Discourse and the Surplus of Meaning*. Texas Christian University Press, 1976.
———. *The Symbolism of Evil*. Translated by Emerson Buchanan. Beacon, 1967.

———. *Time and Narrative*, edited by Kathleen McLaughlin and David Pellauer. 3 vols. University of Chicago Press, 1984–1988.
Rozik, Eli. *The Roots of Theatre: Rethinking Ritual and Other Theories of Origin*. University of Iowa Press, 2002.
Russell, Letty M. *Just Hospitality: God's Welcome in a World of Difference*, edited by J. Shannon Clarkson and Kate M. Ott. Westminster John Knox Press, 2009.
Sautter, Cia. *The Performance of Religion: Seeing the Sacred in the Theatre*. Routledge, 2018.
Sartre, Jean-Paul. *No Exit*. Translated by S. Gilbert. Vintage, 1989.
Schechner, Richard. *Between Theater and Anthropology*. University of Pennsylvania Press, 1985.
———. *Essays on Performance Theory, 1970–1976*. Drama Book Specialists, 1977.
Schindler, D. C. "Notes Toward the Definition of Memory." *Communio: International Catholic Review* L, no. 2 (Summer 2023): 218–254.
Schleiermacher, Friedrich. *Christmas Eve Celebration: A Dialogue*. Translated by Terrence N. Tice. Cascade, 2010.
———. *Hermeneutics and Criticism*, edited by Andrew Bowie. Cambridge, 1998.
———. *On Religion: Speeches to Its Cultured Despisers*, edited by Richard Crouter Cambridge University Press, 1996.
Schneider, Rebecca. *Performing Remains: Art and War in Times of Theatrical Reenactment*. Routledge, 2011.
———. *Theatre and History*. Springer, 2016.
Shakespeare, William. *As You Like It*, edited by Juliet Dusinberre. Arden Shakespeare Third Series, 2006.
———. *Hamlet*, edited by Ann Thompson and Neil Taylor. Arden Shakespeare Third Series, 2006.
Shanley, John Patrick. *Doubt*. Theatre Communications Group, 2005.
Smith, Christian. *Soul Searching: The Religious and Spiritual Lives of American Teenagers*. Oxford University Press, 2005.
Solle, Dorothee. *Suffering*. Fortress, 1975.
Solomon, Alisa. *Wonder of Wonders: A Cultural History of Fiddler on the Roof*. Metropolitan, 2013.
Sontag, Susan. *Under the Sign of Saturn*. Farrar, Straus & Giroux, 1980.
States, Bert O. *Great Reckonings in Little Rooms: On the Phenomenology of Theater*. University of California Press, 1987.
Stein, Joseph, Jerry Bock, and Sheldon Harnick. *Fiddler on the Roof*. Limelight, 1964.
Stempel, Larry. *Showtime: A History of the Broadway Musical Theater*. Norton, 2010.
Stewart, Zachary. "Reviews: 'An Act of God.'" *Theatermania.com*, June 6, 2016. https://www.theatermania.com/broadway/news/an-act-of-god_77357.html/
Strand, Emily. "Sankofa: Reaching Back for Father Clarence Joseph Rivers." *American Catholic Studies* 135, no. 2 (Summer 2024): 91–110.
Taylor, Charles. *A Secular Age*. Belknap, 2007.
Tertullian. *de Spectaculis*. Translated by S. Thelwall. In *Anti-Nicene Fathers, Volume III: Latin Christianity: Its Founder, Tertullian*, edited by Alexander Roberts and James Donaldson; American ed., edited by A. Cleveland Coxe. Scribner, 1905.
Tillich, Paul. *Systematic Theology*. 3 vols. University of Chicago Press, 1951, 1967, 1971.
———. *Theology of Culture*. Oxford University Press, 1964.
Tonstad, Linn Marie. *God and Difference: The Trinity, Sexuality, and the Transformation of Finitude*. Routledge, 2016.

Townes, Emilie M. *Womanist Ethics and the Cultural Production of Evil*. Palgrave Macmillan, 2006.

Turner, Victor. *Dramas, Fields, and Metaphors: Symbolic Action in Human Society*. Cornell University Press, 1974.

———. *The Forest of Symbols: Aspects of Ndembu Ritual*. Cornell University Press, 1970.

Tweed, Thomas A. *Crossing and Dwelling: A Theory of Religio*. Harvard University Press, 2008.

Vander Lugt, Wesley. *Living Theodrama: Reimagining Theological Ethics*. Ashgate, 2014.

Vander Lugt, Wesley, and Trevor Hart, eds. *Theatrical Theology: Explorations in Performing the Faith*. Lutterworth Press, 2015.

Vanhoozer, Kevin. *Faith Speaking Understanding: Performing the Drama of Doctrine*. Westminster John Knox Press, 2014.

———. *The Drama of Doctrine: A Canonical-Linguistic Approach to Christian Theology*. Westminster John Knox Press, 2005.

von Balthasar, Hans Urs. *Theo-Drama: Theological Dramatic Theory*, 5 vols., trans. Graham Harrison. Ignatius, 1988–1998.

Vasko, Elizabeth T. "The Difference Gender Makes: Nuptiality, Analogy, and the Limits of Appropriating Hans Urs von Balthasar's Theology in the Context of Sexual Violence." *Journal of Religion* 94 (2014): 504–528.

Walatka, Todd. *Von Balthasar and the Option for the Poor: Theodramatics in the Light of Liberation Theology*. The Catholic University of America Press, 2017.

Waller, Alexis G. "Violent Spectacles and Public Feelings." *Biblical Interpretation* 22, no. 4/5 (2014): 450–472.

Wedekind, Frank. *Frühlings Erwachen*. In *Werke*, edited by Erhard Weindl. Artemis and Winkler Verlag, 1994.

Weil, Simone. *Gravity and Grace*. Translated by Arthur Wills. University of Nebraska Press, 1997.

———. *Waiting for God*. Translated by Emma Craufurd. Harper Perennial, 1973.

Williams, Shannen Dee. *Subversive Habits: Black Catholic Nuns in the Long African American Freedom Struggle*. Duke University Press, 2022.

Williams, Tennessee. *The Glass Menagerie*. 1945. New Directions New Classics Edition. New Directions, 1949.

Wolf, Stacy. *Beyond Broadway: The Pleasure and Promise of Musical Theatre Across America*. Oxford University Press, 2019.

Wojtyła, Karol (Pope John Paul II). *The Acting Person*, edited by Anna-Teresa Tymieniecka. Translated by Andrzej Potocki. R. Reidel, 1979.

———. *The Collected Plays and Writings on Theater*. Translated by Boleslaw Taborski. University of California Press, 1987.

Zeitz, James V. "Przywara and von Balthasar on Analogy." *Thomist: A Speculative Quarterly Review* 52, no. 3 (1988): 473–498.

Zuboff, Shoshana. *The Age of Surveillance Capitalism*. Profile Books, 2019.

Notes

INTRODUCTION

1 Whether the proper spelling uses *-re* or *-er* for *theatre/theater* is hotly and exhaustingly debated. I will follow theatre studies conventions that reserve the *-er* for a physical auditorium (e.g., a lecture theater) and the *-re* for the art, practice, and study of drama and performance (e.g., musical theatre). My convention will bring about sentences such as "I went to the downtown theater to see my friend from the theatre department make their musical theatre debut." I will break my own rules in the case of a proper name (e.g., London's Olivier Theatre), and I will not change quotations. Similarly, though I will argue that theatre is a place to play with fixed gendered meanings and analogies, my preferred pronoun for God in English will be *God*. I will not change direct quotations.
2 The stage as mirror for the drama of human existence appears in countless theatrical and theological theories, but Hamlet's speech on good acting phrases it poetically and best: "The purpose of playing, whose end, both at the first and now, was and is to hold as'twere the mirror up to Nature" (*Hamlet*, III.2.21–24).
3 Hans Urs von Balthasar, *Theo-Drama: Theological Dramatic Theory*, 5 vols., trans. Graham Harrison (Ignatius, 1988–1998). Hereafter the volumes of Graham Harrison's English language translation are abbreviated in notes as follows: TD 1 = Volume 1: *Prolegomena* (1988); TD 2 = Volume 2: *The Dramatis Personae: Man in God* (1990); TD 3 = Volume 3: *The Dramatis Personae: Persons in Christ* (1992); TD 4 = Volume 4: *The Action* (1994); TD 5 = Volume 5: *The Last Act*, (1998). For von Balthasar's discussions of drama as a theological mode, see the discussion of dramatics between aesthetics and logic in TD 1 and the discussion of drama between epic and lyric modes of theology in TD 2: "We shall not get beyond the alternatives of 'lyrical' and 'epic', spirituality (prayer and personal involvement) and theology (the objective discussion of facts), so long as we fail to include the dramatic dimension of revelation, in which alone they can discover their unity" (TD 2, 57).
4 I am grateful for Larry D. Bouchard for first pointing out to me the way preshow announcements are also rites of initiation.
5 See Lydia Goehr, *The Imaginary Museum of Musical Works: An Essay In the Philosophy of Music* (Clarendon Press, 1992), esp. 236–239.
6 Patti LuPone recounted the moment during an ABC News segment on July 10, 2015. Available online at https://www.youtube.com/watch?v=43mB4QuXGTE, accessed December 4, 2020.

NOTES

7. The audio of the exchange is available online, https://www.youtube.com/watch?v=WruzPfJ9Rys, accessed December 4, 2020.
8. Mary Douglas, *Purity and Danger: An Analysis of Concepts of Pollution and Taboo* (Praeger, 1966).
9. Cia Sautter, *The Performance of Religion: Seeing the Sacred in the Theatre* (Routledge, 2018), 15.
10. "There is something performative in religion and theatre. What is *performative* lies in a singular, poetic impulse to bring self into being and manifests in *acting*—a phenomenon that we construe variably. In some cases, we call acting *religion*, in other cases, *theatre*" (David V. Mason, *The Performative Ground of Religion and Theatre* [Routledge, 2019], 9). Both activities respond to the same "poetic impulse" that grounds creativity: "In theatre, ritual, storytelling, dance, theology, the hundred forms of performing, *poesis*, not *mimesis*, spreads through a group, whose actors mutually coordinate and mutually constitute each other as collaborators with existence's essential and ongoing undoneness" (Mason, *The Performative Ground of Religion and Theatre*, 156, emphasis original).
11. One can frame the "text" of the show to be its script or when the performance is "read like a text" through acts of interpretation.
12. Henry Bial, *Playing God: The Bible on the Broadway Stage* (University of Michigan Press, 2015).
13. These religious references often become productive for theological discussion. See, for example, Adam Beyt, "'Beautiful and New': The Logic of Complementarity in *Hedwig and the Angry Inch*," *Religions* 10, no. 11 (2019): 620.
14. TD 1, 9.
15. "Today's polemics against the middle-class, commercial theatre shows that people still expect the theatre to be a genuine laying-bare of existence. The fact that this is expected of the *theatre*, with its aspects of play and illusion . . . manifests the theatre's intrinsic function, namely, to be a place where man can look in a mirror in order to recollect himself and remember who he is" (TD 1, 86, emphasis original).
16. TD 1, 125.
17. See Kevin Vanhoozer, *The Drama of Doctrine: A Canonical-Linguistic Approach to Christian Theology* (Westminster John Knox Press, 2005), and its companion, *Faith Speaking Understanding: Performing the Drama of Doctrine* (Westminster John Knox Press, 2005).
18. Shannon Craigo-Snell, *The Empty Church: Theatre, Theology, and Bodily Hope* (Oxford University Press, 2016).
19. See Larry D. Bocuhard, *Tragic Method and Tragic Theology: Evil in Contemporary Drama and Religious Thought* (Penn State University Press, 1989), and *Theater and Integrity: Emptying Selves in Drama, Ethics, and Religion* (Northwestern University Press, 2011).
20. Ben Quash, *Theology and the Drama of History* (Cambridge University Press, 2005).
21. See Todd Walatka, *Von Balthasar and the Option for the Poor: Theodramatics in the Light of Liberation Theology* (The Catholic University of America Press, 2017), and Roberto S. Goizueta, "Theo-Drama as Liberative Praxis," *CrossCurrents* 63, no. 1 (March 2013): 62–76.
22. Wesley Vander Lugt and Trevor Hart, *Theatrical Theology: Explorations in Performing the Faith* (Cascade, 2014).
23. Vander Lugt and Hart, *Theatrical Theology*, xiii.

24 Vander Lugt and Hart, *Theatrical Theology*, xiv. They argue that "theatrical theology" will further "orient theology toward its performance, particularly its realization through various forms of life and liturgy" (xv).
25 Contrary to the anti-theatrical bias that understands performativity as "fakery," playing roles may actualize integrity. See Bouchard, *Theater and Integrity*.
26 John Calvin, *Institutes of the Christian Religion*, 2 vols., ed. John T. McNeill (Westminster John Knox, 2011). For a discussion of the *theatrum mundi* theme in Calvin, see Belden C. Lane, *Ravished by Beauty: The Surprising Legacy of Reformed Spirituality* (Oxford University Press, 2011): "The church, as the 'orchestra' in the theater of God's glory, has to assume a leading role in this work. Yet Calvin goes on to affirm the role of the rest of the cosmic order in offering world-changing praise as well" (82). The *theatrum mundi*, theatre of the world, theme is not unique to the discussion of creation: "The word *theatrum* itself appears at least seven times in the *Institutes* and dozens of times in Calvin's sermons and biblical commentaries, especially in his commentaries on Genesis, Isaiah, and the Psalms" (60).
27 Jeremy S. Begbie, *Voicing Creation's Praise: Towards a Theology of the Arts* (T&T Clark, 1991), 99.
28 This is my translation for the German that reads: "*Was hier interessiert, ist der ganze Theater Komplex: dass es so etwas gibt, wie es als Vorgang (als Aufführung) strukturiert ist, und schließlich: was gespielt wird. Das Ganze soll auf Theologie hin transparent, alle seine Elemente auf sie hin brauchbar gemacht warden*" (*Theodramatik* I, 9).
29 *Theo-Drama* opens with a twofold "apologia" for trying the patience of theologians for its lengthy assembly of resources without yet actually doing the work of theology and "men of letters" for its idiosyncratic selection of plays and its lack of "formal aesthetic evaluation; the dramatists and works referred to are accepted as having literary significance; I make no attempt critically to justify it" (TD 1, 9).
30 TD 1, 11.
31 Lack is a point of fact, not necessarily a failure. This book also lacks things that I notice and that I do not, including much of the scholarly discussion about von Balthasar's theodramatics and its implications (especially around gender roles and sexuality) or from theatre studies about the many shows I cite. While I have a keen interest in many of the playwrights von Balthasar studies at length—especially Shakespeare, Brecht, and Beckett—I will need to save them for a later project. Some of my preliminary writing on these themes can be found in my dissertation. The goal here is to prioritize, as much as possible, how to theologically interpret spectacle via Broadway shows. As a result of that focus, I also avoid extensive commentary on my practical work with experimental theatre like my collaborations with the *Untitled Othello* Project (https://untitledothello.com/). For an introduction to that work in a theological key, see Charles A. Gillespie, Emily Bryan, and Rachel E. Bauer, "Table Work as Anti-Racist Spirituality: Reflections on *Untitled Othello*, Embodied Pedagogy, and Spiritual Productivity" in *"Why We Can't Wait": Racism and the Church*, ed. Catherine Punsalan-Manlimos, Elisabeth T. Vasko, and Tracy Sayuki Tiemeier (Orbis, 2023), 65–79.
32 Rebecca Schneider, *Theatre and History* (Springer, 2019), 1.
33 For a lengthier discussion of those boundaries, see Larry D. Bouchard and Charles A. Gillespie, "Religion and Theatrical Drama, an Introduction," *Religions* 12, no. 4 (2021): 257.

NOTES

34 Broadway is but one place for Christian theology. See L. Patrick Burrows, "Theology in Place: Religion, Geography, and the American South," (diss., Harvard Divinity School, 2021).
35 Sharon Aronson-Lehavi, *Performing Religion on the Secular Stage* (Routledge, 2023), 2.
36 Elizabeth Johnson convincingly argues how the "symbol of God functions" in *She Who Is*, ann. ed. (Crossroad, 2012).
37 Stacy Wolf, *Beyond Broadway: The Pleasure and Promise of Musical Theatre Across America* (Oxford University Press, 2019), 4.
38 Catherine Cornille, *Meaning and Method in Comparative Theology* (Wiley Blackwell, 2020), 158.
39 TD I, 9.
40 Willie James Jennings, *After Whiteness: An Education in Belonging* (Eerdmans, 2020), 45.
41 Zachary Stewart, "Reviews: 'An Act of God,'" June 6, 2016, https://www.theatermania.com/, accessed January 2, 2024.

CHAPTER 1: BROADWAY'S COMMERCIAL THEOLOGY

1 For this reason, and throughout the book, I will only cite a printed version of a script if I intend to do extensive work with it as a source text. Stylistically, this is to let those lines and lyrics float in the text as they do in memory, juxtaposing allusions to Broadway scripts with the theologian's saturation in scriptural and liturgical allusions. If I hazard this strategy and misquote a show, that is perhaps all the better. I have also relied on a variety of scriptural translations, primarily the New Revised Standard Version and the New American Bible.
2 Official State Song. 25 Okla. State § 94.1-3 (1953).
3 The entirety of Jacques's metatheatrical speech develops an account of life's many changes in role as a performance on the world stage. See William Shakespeare, *As You Like It* (Arden Shakespeare Third Series, 2006), II.7.136–166.
4 For a discussion of this theme in *Oedipus Rex* in the context of Catholic studies, see Charles A. Gillespie, "Imagining the Unseen in Catholic Studies: Complexities of Encounter, Credibility, and *Oedipus*," *Logos: A Journal of Catholic Thought and Culture* 26, no. 3 (Summer 2023): 140–141.
5 Augusto Boal, *Theatre of the Oppressed* (Theatre Communications Group, 1985).
6 But, crucially for me, not all performances are shows. The increasing use of *performative* to mean *fake and showy* muddies the usefulness of performativity as an analytical category to signal that which exists during its doing.
7 See, among many examples, Larry Stempel, *Showtime: A History of the Broadway Musical Theater* (Norton, 2010).
8 See Eugene McCarraher, *The Enchantments of Mammon: How Capitalism Became the Religion of Modernity* (Belknap, 2019).
9 See Jonas Barrish, *The Antitheatrical Prejudice* (University of California Press, 1985).
10 The *Phaedrus* myth describes the soul's encounter with the forms using explicitly visual language, particularly insofar as the soul "remembers" perfection most directly in shimmering glimpses of the beautiful. See, among other examples, Plato, "Phaedrus 250c," in *Plato: Complete Works*, ed. John M. Cooper and D. S. Hutchinson (Hackett, 1997), 528.

Hereafter *Plato: Complete Works* is abbreviated as CW. An explicit reference to the stage appears at *Phadrus* 258b, CW 534. My thanks to Ryan Brown for pointing this out.
11 Plato, *Republic* II.392b, CW 1030.
12 Plato, *Republic* II.395a, CW 1032.
13 Plato, *Republic* 7.514b, CW 1132.
14 Susan Sontag, "Fascinating Fascism," in *Under the Sign of Saturn* (Farrar, Straus & Giroux, 1980).
15 The conclusion of the first act of *Cabaret* features a rousing chorus of what operates in the show as a nationalistic anthem. The number juxtaposes Nazi symbolism, an interrupted engagement party, and a palpable shift from subtle to overt antisemitism.
16 Tertullian, *de Spectaculis*, in *Anti-Nicene Fathers*, vol. 3, trans. S. Thelwall (Scribner, 1905), 79–91, ch. III.
17 Tertullian, *de Spectaculis*, ch. XXV.
18 Tertullian, *de Spectaculis*, ch. XXIII.5.
19 "Condemning, therefore, as He does hypocrisy in every form, He never will approve any putting on of voice, or sex, or age; He never will approve pretended loves, and wraths, and groans, and tears. Then, too, as in His law it is declared that the man is cursed who attires himself in female garments, what must be His judgment of the pantomime, who is even brought up to play the woman!" (Tertullian, *de Spectaculis*, ch. XXIII.6).
20 Harriet I. Flower, "Spectacle and Political Culture in the Roman Republic," in *The Cambridge Companion to the Roman Republic*, ed. Harriet I. Flower (Cambridge University Press, 2014).
21 Blake Leyerle, *Theatrical Shows and Ascetic Lives: John Chrysostom's Attack on Spiritual Marriage* (University of California Press, 2001), 66, with internal references to Chrysostom's, *Homiliae in Matt* 17.6 (Patrologia Graeca 57.264) and *Adversus Judaeos* 7.6 (Patrologia Graeca 48.925).
22 Augustine, *City of God*, trans. Henry Bettenson (Penguin, 1995), II.29, 87.
23 Augustine, *City of God*, VII.28.
24 "A member of the audience is not excited to offer help, but invited only to grieve. The greater [the spectator's] pain, the greater [the spectator's] approval of the actor in these representations." Augustine, *Confessions*, III.ii.2 (Oxford University Press, 1991), (Chadwick, 36).
25 Erich Auerbach, *Mimesis: The Representation of Reality in Western Literature* (Princeton University Press, 1953), 71.
26 Auerbach, *Mimesis*, 69.
27 Chadwick, *Confessions*, IV.viii.13, 100–101.
28 Auerbach, *Mimesis*, 69.
29 Auerbach, *Mimesis*, 71.
30 Auerbach, *Mimesis*, 70. Augustine's Latin reads, "*Spectavit, clamavit, exarsit, abstulit inde secum insaniam*" (*Conf.* VI.viii).
31 Chadwick, *Confessions*, VIII.xii.29, 152.
32 Chadwick, *Confessions*, VIII.xi.29, 153, citing Rom 13:13–14.
33 Julian of Norwich, *Revelations of Divine Love*, ed. A. C. Spearing (Penguin, 1998).
34 TD 1, 20. Though this is not my translation, I have added a note about von Balthasar's use of "*ganz-anderes*" to describe God's "wholly other" or "totally other" play. The idea of world history as a play within a play operates under von Balthasar's Barthian-inflected sense of analogy. God's play is fully different from the play of creatures.

NOTES

35 Joseph Ratzinger, "Concerning the Notion of Person in Theology," *Communio* 17, no. 3 (Fall 1990): 439–454.
36 "In all of its particular manifestations—news, propaganda, advertising, entertainment—the spectacle is the model of the prevailing way of life." Guy du Bord, *The Society of the Spectacle*, trans. Ken Knabb (Bureau of Public Secrets, 2014), 3.
37 Shoshana Zuboff, *The Age of Surveillance Capitalism* (Profile Books, 2019).
38 See, among many, Antonio Eduardo Alonso, *Commodified Communion: Eucharist, Consumer Culture, and the Practice of Everyday Life* (Fordham, 2021); William T. Cavanaugh, *Being Consumed: Economics and Christian Desire* (Eerdmans, 2008); Vincent J. Miller, *Consuming Religion: Christian Faith and Practice in a Consumer Culture* (Bloomsbury, 2003).

CHAPTER 2: PAYING ATTENTION TO SPECTACLE AND REVELATION

1 The opening sequence has always carried something like a ritual invocation. The original staging by Hal Prince evoked social commentary by setting the story within the misery of a Victorian factory, complete with a shift change whistle to mark scenes breaks. Some productions, like the Live at Lincoln Center concert version, embrace this opening number as a conjuring. What begins in concert formal wear erupts into a frenzy of concert hall desecrations. The show is rife with religious allusions. Later in the play, Sweeney's "Epiphany" will equate "salvation" with "vengeance." Some of the delight in the show's sacrilegious play with Christianity derives from its subversions, literalized in Mrs. Lovett's human-meat pies. Eating "a little priest" functions akin to eucharistic cannibalism, all become one in the mutual feeding of the body. The setup obliquely recalls Jesus's great reversal at table where last shall be first, here kneaded into the class logic of "upstairs, downstairs" and the scenographic architecture of the demon barber's chair atop the pie shop: "Those above serve those below."
2 Dei Verbum 2, https://www.vatican.va/archive/hist_councils/ii_vatican_council/documents/vat-ii_const_19651118_dei-verbum_en.html.
3 The theme of the Christ expressing God's heart is as much a general reference to the incarnation as it is the Catholic devotion to the Sacred Heart of Jesus. Pope Francis emphasized the theme of the heart in his encyclical *Dilexit Nos*, 2024, https://www.vatican.va/content/francesco/en/encyclicals/documents/20241024-enciclica-dilexit-nos.html.
4 Dei Verbum 12.
5 Karl Barth, "The Strange New World of the Bible" in *The Word of God and Theology*, trans. Amy Marga (Bloomsbury, 2011), See also Karl Barth's, *Church Dogmatics*, ed. G. W. Bromiley and Thomas F. Torrance (T&T Clark, 1956–1969).
6 Dei Verbum 10.
7 Dei Verbum 7.
8 Juan Luis Segundo, "Revelation, Faith, Signs of the Times," in *Mysterium Liberationis*, ed. Ignacio Ellacuria and Jon Sobrino (Orbis, 1993), 332.
9 The logic of Matthew 25, where corporal merciful action to respond to human suffering is a response of ministry and service to the Christ, undergirds Joseph Ratzinger / Pope Benedict XVI's social teaching. See Joseph Ratzinger, *Jesus of Nazareth* (Doubleday, 2007) and his encyclical Pope Benedict XVI, *Caritas in Veritate*, 2009, https://www.vatican.va/content/benedict-xvi/en/encyclicals/documents/hf_ben-xvi_enc_20090629_caritas-in-veritate.html.

10 See Ignacio Ellacuría, "The Crucified People: An Essay in Historical Soteriology," in *Ignacio Ellacuría: Essays on History, Liberation, and Salvation*, ed. Michael E. Lee (Orbis Books, 2013).

11 God remains "ever greater" even than the knowledge about God derived from revelation: "But even when God goes on to give his creature a new, deeper knowledge and participation, such revelation only causes the Revealer's freedom to shine forth even more brightly; it makes it impossible for man to turn this gift he has received into a possession of his own, impossible for him to dissolve the faith which trusts (and the insight which he gains *within* such faith) into some kind of autonomous knowledge" (TD 2, 119, emphasis original).

12 On the doctrine of analogy, see Thomas Aquinas, *The Summa Theologiae of St. Thomas Aquinas*, 2nd ed., trans. Fathers of the English Dominican Province (1920), ed. Kevin Knight (2017), I.13, https://www.newadvent.org/. Hereafter *Summa Theologiae* is abbreviated to ST.

13 Hans-Georg Gadamer, *Truth and Method*, 2nd and rev. ed., trans. Joel Weinsheimer and Donald G. Marshall (Continuum, 2004), 290–291.

14 Paul Ricoeur, "Existence and Hermeneutics," in *The Conflict of Interpretations: Essays in Hermeneutics*, trans. Kathleen McLaughlin, ed. Don Ihde (Northwestern University Press, 1974), 4.

15 TD 2, 91. This striking assertion by von Balthasar that all theology is an act of interpretation also appears in the original German: "*Sofern alle Theologie Auslegung der göttlichen Offenbarung ist, kann sie als ganze nur Hermeneutik sein. Sofern aber auch die Offenbarung Gottes in Jesus Christus Selbstauslegung Gottes ist—worin zudem Gottes eigene Deutung seines Weltplans im ganzen und im einzelnen enthalten sein muß—, ist auch sie Hermeneutik*" (*Theodramatik* II/1, 81). The theme of God's interpretation of Godself and its influence on theological logic takes pride of place in von Balthasar's, *Theo-Logic: Theological Logical Theory*, vol. 1, *The Truth of the World*, trans. Adrian J. Walker (Ignatius, 2000).

16 "Interpretation, philosophically understood, is nothing else than an attempt to make estrangement and distanciation productive" (Paul Ricoeur, *Interpretation Theory: Discourse and the Surplus of Meaning*, trans. Ted Klein [TCU Press, 1976], 44).

17 The Christian tradition understands God to be eternally relating (triune), so God is constant in dynamic fidelity. There is not some moment in history when God "evolved" into someone other than who God is. Great debate exists about how to interpret God's becoming. One response that I take up in a later chapter of this book regards how Broadway can help reframe the ways Christians interpret God's time.

18 Anne M. Carpenter, *Theo-Poetics: Hans Urs von Balthasar and the Risk of Art and Being* (Notre Dame Press, 2015), 134, citing *Theo-Logic* I, 77–178.

19 Jean-Luc Marion, *Revelation and Givenness*, trans. Stephen E. Lewis (Oxford University Press, 2016), 5.

20 See Paul Tillich, *Theology of Culture* (Oxford University Press, 1964) and Tillich, *Systematic Theology*, 3 vols. (University of Chicago Press, 1951, 1967, 1971).

21 As an example of the influence of Augustine's definition, see Aquinas's reliance on it in ST III.Q60.1.

22 The language, here, is an oblique reference to Hans-Georg Gadamer's hermeneutic theory in *Truth and Method*. Gadamer builds on Johan Huizing, *Homo Ludens: A Study of the Play-Element in Culture* (Beacon, 1955) to ground hermeneutics (particularly the interpretation of the arts) in an autotelic self-presentation of meaning

NOTES

that occurs in the event of play. See Gadamer, *Truth and Method*, especially the section called "Play as a Clue to the Ontology of a Work of Art," 101–134. For a more explicit study of Gadamer's writing as it applies to theatre, see my "Sustainable Canons: Gadamer's Hermeneutics and Theatre," *Labyrinth: An International Journal for Philosophy, Value Theory and Sociocultural Hermeneutics* 24, no. 2 (Winter 2022): 150–175.

23 Émile Durkheim, *The Elementary Forms of Religious Life*, trans. Joseph Ward Swain (George Allen, 1915).

24 This framework helps also avoid the pitfalls of determining theatre according to the attitude or physical location of its audience. As such, it follows the notion of performativity developed in response to J. L. Austin. Performatives are speech acts that do what the words describe in a given context. Classic examples of a performative utterance include "Class dismissed," "I accept your apology," and "I do" (in the context of a wedding ceremony). See the discussion of performatives throughout J. L. Austin, *How to Do Things with Words* (Harvard, 1962). Most recent scholarship on performativity follows how Judith Butler expands performativity to be an ontological category, one that identifies the reality of socially constructed phenomena in bodily doing rather than idealized or essential being. Butler has developed her notion of performativity across multiple projects. See especially *Gender Trouble: Feminism and the Subversion of Identity* (Routledge, 1990); *Bodies That Matter: On the Discursive Limits of Sex* (Routledge, 1993); *Excitable Speech: A Politics of the Performative* (Routledge, 1997); *Notes Toward a Performative Theory of Assembly* (Harvard University Press, 2015). For an account of the ways performativity migrates disciplinary locations, see Jill Dolan, *Geographies of Learning: Theory and Practice, Activism and Performance* (Wesleyan University Press, 2001). For performativity in the context of religion, see Sautter, *Performance of Religion*, and Mason, *The Performative Ground of Religion and Theatre*.

25 See Mihaly Csikzentmihaly and Jeanne Nakamura, "Effortless Attention in Everyday Life: A Systematic Phenomenology," in *Effortless Attention: A New Perspective in the Cognitive Science of Attention and Action*, ed. Brian Bruya (MIT Press, 2010), 182.

26 A stage need not be the proscenium arch of a neoclassical opera house or Dionysius's amphitheater carved into the side of a hill. Peter Brook's, *The Empty Space*, reprint ed. (Scribner, 1995) defines a stage as any "empty space" across which an actor might walk. This might be framed even more loosely, following Huizinga's philosophy of play, to understand a stage as any demarcated place of play where the rules of ordinary life are suspended for a given time.

27 Simone Weil, *Gravity and Grace*, trans. Arthur Wills (University of Nebraska Press, 1997), 170. See also her essay "Reflections on the Right Use of School Studies with a View to the Love of God," in *Waiting for God*, trans. Emma Craufurd (Harper Perennial, 1973), 57–65. Weil also raises the many connections between the themes of attention, attending, and waiting for God between her work and Samuel Beckett's play *Waiting for Godot* (Grove Press, 1994). In French, both of their titles include versions of the French word for waiting, *attendre*.

28 On the natural attitude and its distinctness from the phenomenological attitude, see Edmund Husserl, "Pure Phenomenology, Its Method, and Its Field of Investigation," in *The Phenomenology Reader*, ed. Dermot Moran and Timothy Mooney (Routledge, 2002), 128.

29 Here, I distinguish prayer from one of its species in speech acts directed to God. Certainly, words directed to God are prayers. Words directed to God are often the normative example for praying. My expansive account of prayer only comes in analogy to prayer as directed attention of consciousness for communication with God. My point about prayer and attention simply means to underscore how prayer need not be only linguistic or cognitive or contemplative.
30 Weil, "Reflections on the Right Use of School Studies," 57.
31 Everything visible on the stage presents both itself *and* its role in the *mise-en-scène*. I refer to this dual signification as "dramatic doubling" following the title of the collection of essays by Antonin Artaud, *The Theater and Its Double*, trans. Mary Caroline Richards (Grove, 1958). For Artaud, "the theater is identical with its possibilities for realization when the most extreme poetic results are derived from them; the possibilities for realization in the theater relate entirely to the *mise en scène* considered as a language in space and in movement" (45).
32 Artaud, *Theater and Its Double*, 59, emphasis original.
33 Bert O. States, *Great Reckonings in Little Rooms: on the Phenomenology of Theater* (University of California Press, 1987).
34 States, *Great Reckonings in Little Rooms*, 45.
35 See States, *Great Reckonings in Little Rooms*, 30ff.
36 The line in context: "I don't say he's a great man. Willy Loman never made a lot of money. His name was never in the paper. He's not the finest character that ever lived. But he's a human being, and a terrible thing is happening to him. So attention must be paid. He's not to be allowed to fold into his grave like an old dog" (Arthur Miller, *Death of a Salesman*, Act I, in *The Portable Arthur Miller*, ed. Christopher Bigsby [Penguin, 2003], 60).
37 See Nichole M. Flores, *The Aesthetics of Solidarity: Our Lady of Guadalupe and American Democracy* (Georgetown University Press, 2021).
38 The bishop's kenotic gift to Valjean not only provides the explicit theological frame for the plot of *Les Misérables*, including the conflict between Valjean's experience of God's mercy and Javert's idolatrous obsession with the law rather than justice, but this moment also reflects a musical theme of emptying and sacrifice. The melody for the bishop's speech to Valjean is the same leitmotif as the elegiac "Empty Chairs at Empty Tables" reflection on the sacrifice and loss of comrades in arms.

CHAPTER 3: PLAYING WITH DANGEROUS MEMORIES

1 My thanks to Emily Bryan for this question.
2 *Cats* reunion livestream, Stars in the House, on YouTube (June 12, 2020). Betty Buckley @ 49:20: "Like one thing I remember that's really cool that Ken and I did . . . We're together on the tire and then I step up onto the cherry picker crane as it goes out to the ceiling, and they built this room at the top of the Winter Garden just for us, for this crane to go through. And so, we worked this thing out where when I get on the – I'm really nervous about getting on - in real life I was also . . . no wires or anything to secure you in case you fell and it was a really small thing. So Ken is assisting me as I get up there and so we touch each other's hands like this as we pull away. It was like Michelangelo's - that beautiful Sistine Chapel . . . we stole that image, and it's been in all the productions with the machine like that since. And I'm really proud of

NOTES

that contribution we made." Ken Page: "They used it as the button on one of the commercials . . . but I always felt like that was our major contribution above everything else we did."

3 References to the Heaviside Layer function as a symbol of the afterlife in T. S. Eliot's play *The Family Reunion*, but it is also a physical phenomenon used for relaying early radio signals. See Elizabeth Bruton, "Cats and the Heaviside Layer," *Science Museum Blog*, December 20, 2019, https://blog.sciencemuseum.org.uk/cats-and-the-heaviside-layer/#:~:text=TLDR%3A%20The%20Heaviside%20layer%20is,used%20to%20bounce%20radio%20waves.&text=O'Connor%2C%20J.J.%20and%20E.F.,Heaviside%20(1850%2D1925).

4 "The endeavor to understand the Scriptures as a whole in terms of the concept of 'art' (and, therefore, of human proportions) may be given a pride of place within intellectual history almost *a priori*," Hans urs von Balthasar, *The Glory of the Lord: A Theological Aesthetics, Vol. 1, Seeing the Form*, ed.S. J. Joseph Fessio and John Riches (Ignatius, 1982), 77. Hereafter, *The Glory of the Lord* is abbreviated GL.

5 GL 1, 78.
6 GL 1, 114.
7 See Christian Smith, *Soul Searching: The Religious and Spiritual Lives of American Teenagers* (Oxford University Press, 2005).
8 "God's love for each individual is totally personal and includes the mystery of this uniqueness that cannot be divulged to other human beings." Ratzinger, *Jesus of Nazareth*, 129.
9 *The Sound of Music* (Applause, 2010), Scene 8.
10 An Augustinian reading makes even more sense considering the film version's famous setting in Salzburg, Austria, and the Catholic culture in the background.
11 Perhaps Sister Mary Clarence means to call to mind one of the foremost composers of Black Catholic liturgical music, Father Clarence Rivers. See Emily Strand, "Sankofa: Reaching Back for Father Clarence Joseph Rivers," *American Catholic Studies* 135, no. 2 (Summer 2024), 91–110. For a rich study of the history of Black Catholic sisters, see Shannen Dee Williams, *Subversive Habits: Black Catholic Nuns in the Long African American Freedom Struggle* (Duke University Press, 2022).
12 See Tillich, *Theology of Culture*.
13 See Frank Burch Brown, *Good Taste, Bad Taste, Christian Taste: Aesthetics In Religious Life* (Oxford University Press, 2000).
14 Ian Bradley, *You've Got to Have a Dream: The Message of the Musical* (Westminster John Knox Press, 2005).
15 Johann Baptist Metz, *Faith in History and Society*, trans. J. Matthew Ashley (PublishDrive, 2007), 88.
16 Metz, *Faith in History and Society*, 89, emphasis original.
17 TD 1, 260, emphasis mine.
18 Artaud, *Theater and Its Double*.
19 Richard Schechner, *Between Theater and Anthropology* (University of Pennsylvania Press, 1985).
20 Mason, *The Performative Ground of Religion and Theatre*, 49.
21 TD 1, 260.
22 Boal, *Theatre of the Oppressed*.
23 See D. C. Schindler, "Notes Toward the Definition of Memory," *Communio: International Catholic Review* L, no. 2 (Summer 2023): 218–254. "Memory is not something

that lies simply in our heads, as it were; it is that in which we live, that is, it lies equally in what we do and in the world we make even as it makes us. Through memory we receive and allow ourselves to be formed by the great treasures that belong to our history and culture, which are particular reflections of eternal truths, all as a gift from God" (253).

24 Peggy Phelan, *Unmarked: the Politics of Performance* (Routledge, 1993), 146.
25 Philip Auslander, *Liveness: Performance in a Mediatized Culture* (Routledge, 1999).
26 José Esteban Muñoz, *Disidentifications: Queers of Color and the Performance of Politics* (University of Minnesota Press, 1999).
27 TD 2, 55.
28 Karen Kilby, *Balthasar: A (Very) Critical Introduction* (Eerdmans, 2012), rightly asks, "Is Balthasar himself, in his very construal of the whole of everything as a drama, not taking the role of theater critic—and perhaps also a theorist of drama—rather than an actor *within* the drama?" (65). Where von Balthasar seems to narrate the form of the drama of salvation history from beyond like a theological novelist, I argue throughout this book that theatrical theologians should self-consciously recognize the necessary context that comes from sitting in the house as an active coparticipant as a member of the audience.
29 Tennessee Williams, *The Glass Menagerie*, 1945, New Directions New Classics Edition (New Directions, 1949), 4.
30 Williams, *The Glass Menagerie*, 5.
31 See Bruce T. Morrill, *Anamnesis as Dangerous Memory: Political and Liturgical Theology in Dialogue* (Liturgical Press, 2000).
32 Alasdair MacIntyre makes this point well: "What I have called a history is an enacted dramatic narrative in which the characters are also the authors. The characters of course never start literally *ab initio*; they plunge *in medias res*, the beginnings of their story already made for them by what and who has gone before" (Alasdair MacIntyre, *After Virtue: A Study in Moral Theory* [University of Notre Dame Press, 1981], 215).
33 The allusion to Jung derives from Mary Zimmerman, *Metamorphoses* (Northwestern University Press, 2002).
34 Williams, *The Glass Menagerie*, x–xi.
35 Williams, *The Glass Menagerie*, 5.
36 Williams, *The Glass Menagerie*, 75.
37 Williams, *The Glass Menagerie*, 5.
38 Williams, *The Glass Menagerie*, 22.
39 Metz, *Faith in History and Society*, 90.
40 Williams, *The Glass Menagerie*, 31–32. Taking stock of theology, an answer to Tom's rhetorical question may well be "Jesus."
41 Williams, *The Glass Menagerie*, 65.
42 Williams, *The Glass Menagerie*, 45.
43 Williams, *The Glass Menagerie*, 110.
44 Williams, *The Glass Menagerie*, 77.
45 Williams, *The Glass Menagerie*, 124.
46 Williams, *The Glass Menagerie*, 47.
47 Metz, *Faith in History and Society*, 89.
48 Metz, *Faith in History and Society*, 91.
49 Metz, *Faith in History and Society*, 191.
50 Anaïs Mitchell, *Hadestown* (Concord Theatricals, 2021), 1–8.

NOTES

51 Mitchell, *Hadestown*, 58. The printed script ensures that the real-world names of the band's players are actually said: "Ladies and gentlemen, [*Trombonist*] on the trombone!" etc.
52 Maurice Blanchot, *The Space of Literature*, trans. Ann Smock (University of Nebraska Press, 1982).
53 Zimmerman returned to the Orpheus and Eurydice theme as the director for Matthew Aucoin's opera *Eurydice* (with a libretto by Sarah Ruhl after her play by the same name) at the Metropolitan Opera in 2021.
54 Mitchell, *Hadestown*, 24.
55 Mitchell, *Hadestown*, 47.
56 Mitchell, *Hadestown*, 98.
57 Mitchell, *Hadestown*, 52ff.
58 John Moriarty, *Turtle Was Gone a Long Time, Volume 1: Crossing the Kedron* (Lilliput, 1996), 64.
59 See "Wedding Song," Mitchell, *Hadestown*, 14ff.
60 The 2023 production of Ibsen's *A Doll's House* literalized this possibility of a "crack in the wall" of ideology when Nora literally exited from the stage through a loading door onto the Manhattan street outside.
61 Mitchell, *Hadestown*, 23.
62 Mitchell, *Hadestown*, 103.
63 Marvin Carlson, *The Haunted Stage: The Theatre as Memory Machine* (University of Michigan Press, 2003).
64 The term *devised theatre* can be divisive and confusing, especially for practitioners. I prefer this term as a generic catch-all for experimental collaborative theatre-making without a preexisting script because it nicely captures a semantic range that includes "dividing" (the work of theatre making can be split and shared among a group or the playwright can be understood as a "division" of the theatre-making process) as well as its more archaic sense of arranging, assigning, or setting in motion such as the phrase "devising a plan."
65 Friedrich Schleiermacher, *Hermeneutics and Criticism*, ed. Andrew Bowie (Cambridge, 1998).
66 For a concise history of *Godspell* from the perspective of theatre history, including its original Broadway run, see Bial, *Playing God*, 157–167.
67 Susan Sontag, "On Anton Artaud," in *Antonin Artaud: Selected Writings*, ed. Susan Sontag (University of California Press, 1976), xix.
68 Artaud, *Theater and Its Double*, 12.
69 Artaud, *Theater and Its Double*, 25.
70 Artaud, *Theater and Its Double*, 30.
71 Artaud, *Theater and Its Double*, 27.
72 Some audiences find *Godspell* to be too sacrilegious in its play with Christian holy scripture or call out its unreflecting replications of anti-Semitic tropes. At the same time, *Godspell* presents a consciously human and Jewish image of Jesus, who offers Hebrew prayers over bread and wine in its Last Supper scene.
73 See "Note" at the conclusion of 2012 edition of the *Godspell* libretto made available for productions by Music Theatre Intentional. *Godspell* continues to be a powerful source of community for those who perform the show.
74 Kevin Hart has rightfully noticed part of the problem: "All the same, we need to be clear that there is a difference between 'God is love' and 'Love is God'" (Kevin Hart, *Kingdoms of God* [Indiana University Press, 2014], 85). Primarily this plays out in the

need for God's love in order to fund human acts of loving: "We can love the neighbor not because we love God but because God loves us; it is a love that exceeds all that we can offer while in this world and not yet purged of sin" (Hart, *Kingdoms of God*, 87).
75 See *Gaudium et Spes*, 4, https://www.vatican.va/archive/hist_councils/ii_vatican_council/documents/vat-ii_const_19651207_gaudium-et-spes_en.html

IN-ONE: ON INSTRUMENTALIZING

1 An "in-one" refers to a short scene, often with a musical number, meant to be played in front of the main curtain to accommodate a complicated set change without resorting to a lengthy and boring blackout.
2 I am grateful for many conversations with Misty Anderson about this idea. See her forthcoming *God on Stage*.
3 See Tisa Wenger, *Religious Freedom: The Contested History of an American Ideal* (University of North Carolina Press, 2017).
4 Donalee Dox, *Reckoning with the Spirit in the Paradigm of Performance* (University of Michigan Press, 2016).
5 Anne M. Carpenter elegantly summarizes such an approach: "At more than one point, I will practice a method of 'reading-off' the theological form (*Gestalt*) of a work of literature at length, a reading of form that in some ways resembles literary-analytic strategies but that in a more technical if subterranean way mimics Hans Urs von Balthasar's method of theological reading, which is governed by a theological rather than a literary horizon." Anne M. Carpenter, *Nothing Gained Is Eternal* (Fortress, 2022), 81. My style is less subtle and my mimicry far less underground.
6 TD 1, 9.
7 See Bouchard, *Theater and Integrity*.
8 Carpenter, *Nothing Gained Is Eternal*, 149, on resourcing as representing Christ; 163 on whiteness.
9 Hermeneutic violence refers here to the willful imposition of an interpretation so to violate something of the object of interpretation's autonomy.
10 The phrase "transform into structure" belongs to the philosopher Hans-Georg Gadamer.

CHAPTER 4: TRADITION AND TRADITIONS

1 Maurice Blanchot, *The Writing of the Disaster*, trans. Ann Smock (University of Nebraska Press, 1995).
2 See Alisa Solomon, *Wonder of Wonders: A Cultural History of Fiddler on the Roof* (Metropolitan, 2013).
3 Yair Lipshitz, *Theatre and Judaism* (Red Globe, 2019), 19.
4 Henry Bial, *Acting Jewish: Negotiating Ethnicity on the American Stage and Screen* (University of Michigan Press, 2005).
5 Bial, *Acting Jewish*, 2.
6 Bial, *Acting Jewish*, 16.
7 Bial, *Acting Jewish*, 17.
8 Bial, *Acting Jewish*, 75.
9 Carlson, *The Haunted Stage*.

NOTES

10. Jesse Green, "A Yiddish Fiddler on the Roof? Sounds Crazy, Nu?," *New York Times*, July 17, 2018, https://www.nytimes.com/2018/07/17/theater/review-yiddish-fiddler-on-the-roof.html.
11. Bial, *Acting Jewish*, 85.
12. Wolf, *Beyond Broadway*, 231.
13. Hans-Georg Gadamer, *Truth and Method*, rev. ed., trans. Joel Weinsheimer and Donald G. Marshal (Continuum, 1989).
14. See Mark Knight, "*Wirkunggeschichte*, Reception History, Reception Theory," *Journal for the Study of the New Testament* 33, no. 2 (2010): 137–146, https://journals.sagepub.com/doi/pdf/10.1177/0142064X10385858.
15. Jürgen Habermas, *The Theory of Communicative Action*, 2 vols., trans. Thomas McCarthy (Beacon, 1985). See also Paul Ricoeur's discussion of the Gadamer-Habermas debate in "Hermeneutics and the Critique of Ideology," in *Hermeneutics and the Human Sciences*, ed. John B. Thompson (Cambridge University Press, 1981), 23–60.
16. Joseph Stein, Jerry Bock, and Sheldon Harnick, *Fiddler on the Roof* (Limelight, 1964), 153.
17. Dox, *Reckoning with the Spirit*, 60.
18. Mason, *The Performative Ground of Religion and Theatre*.
19. Both activities respond to the same "poetic impulse" that grounds creativity: "In theatre, ritual, storytelling, dance, theology, the hundred forms of performing, *poesis*, not *mimesis*, spreads through a group, whose actors mutually coordinate and mutually constitute each other as collaborators with existence's essential and ongoing undoneness" (Mason, *The Performative Ground of Religion and Theatre*, 156).
20. Mason, *The Performative Ground of Religion and Theatre*, 115, emphasis original.
21. Lipshitz, *Theatre and Judaism*, 20.
22. Stein et al., *Fiddler*, 21.
23. Contrast this with an *ad lib* from the Emcee in *Cabaret* once told to me by Larry D. Bouchard. At the top of "Money Makes the World Go Round," the Emcee could greet the balcony with a tongue-in-cheek "Hello, poor people!" Broadway, like all public and conspicuous consumption, remains aware of its market participations.
24. Stein et al., *Fiddler*, 104.
25. Stein et al., *Fiddler*, 101.
26. Stein et al., *Fiddler*, 135.
27. Stein et al., *Fiddler*, 135.
28. Karl Rahner, *Foundations of Christian Faith: An Introduction to the Idea of Christianity* (Seabury Press, 1978).
29. Such is the implication when "contextual theology" becomes the title of a particular subgenre of theology as opposed to uplifting when overlooked or marginalized contexts are given priority over the dominant contexts for theological knowledge production. The same can also be said for disciplinary procedures that relegate questions about God to the exclusive purview of theology or religious studies.
30. John Patrick Shanley, *Doubt, A Parable* (Theatre Communications Group, 2005) I, 5–6. I first developed the term *congregaudience* as a technical term in my practical work in liturgical drama alongside Kate Andre, Justin Crisp, and Justin Kosec. See Charles A. Gillespie, Justin Kosec, and Kate Stratton, "Treasure in Clay Jars: Liturgical Drama in Theory and Praxis," *Theatre Symposium Journal* 21 (2013): 90–103.
31. The gossip speech appears in *Doubt* VI, 35–37. The locker-room speech appears in *Doubt* III, 16–17.

32 *Fiddler on the Roof* opened on September 22, 1964.
33 Shanley, *Doubt* V, 30–31.
34 Shanley, *Doubt* III, 34.
35 Shanley, *Doubt* I, 5.
36 Hans Urs von Balthasar, *Razing the Bastions: On the Church in This Age* (Ignatius, 1993), 99.
37 Shanley, *Doubt* I, 6.
38 Shanley, "Preface," in *Doubt*, ix–x.
39 Shanley, "Preface," in *Doubt*, viii.
40 Shanley, *Doubt* I, 5.
41 "In the framework of Christian living and thinking, tradition can be nothing else than allowing oneself to be carried by the spiritual power of earlier generations, so that one may oneself, alive, come closer to the mystery. Thus one can adopt not only the correctness of findings and formulas, but also—unconditionally, and as the more important element in the truth—the immediate relationship to the event" (Balthasar, *Razing the Bastions*, 33).
42 Von Balthasar will consistently add Mariological dimensions to his ecclesiology. For example, "Access to the Father had already been opened when it was revealed that the Spirit who directs Jesus is also the Spirit who overshadows Mary—as the primal cell of the Church—and is breathed into the now-reconciled Church by the Passion. The self-surrendering attitude of the Son under the direction power of the Holy Spirit does not ultimately originate in itself but is ordained for a more comprehensive goal in the unity of the Spirit: the salvation of the world" (Hans Urs von Balthasar, "Spirit and Institution," in *Explorations in Theology, Volume IV: Spirit and Institution*, trans. Edward T. Oaks, SJ [Ignatius, 1994], 230).
43 *Doubt, A Parable* has at times been described as the first in Shanley's "Church and State" trilogy of plays about American hierarchy, alongside *Defiance* (2005) and *Storefront Church* (2012). On the structural issue of clericalism and abuse, see the report by Julie Hanlon Rubio and Paul J. Schutz, *Beyond 'Bad Apples': Understanding Clergy Perpetuated Sexual Abuse as a Structural Problem and Cultivating Strategies for Change*, https://www.scu.edu/ic/programs/bannan-forum/media--publications/beyond-bad-apples-/, accessed March 4, 2024.
44 Balthasar, *Razing the Bastions*, 33.
45 See Hart, *Kingdoms of God*.
46 I attended a talkback offered by Shanley for the 2024 revival, where he denied the play was primarily about priests or abuse in response to an audience question.
47 Shanley, *Doubt* VII, 39.
48 See Hans Urs von Balthasar, *Truth Is Symphonic: Aspects of Christian Pluralism* (Ignatius, 1987).
49 See, among many accounts, the *New York Times* front-page story by George Dugan, "U.S. Catholics Begin Reforms in the Mass," November 30, 1969), 1, 29 column 4.
50 Indeed, the Broadway revival made distinct design and staging choices from the original production and the print script—for example, Father Flynn wore green vestments for both sermons in the Roundabout revival in 2024—that subtly changed my understanding of the plot. My play at an experiment in historical-critical script/ural analysis makes documentary hypotheses based on the published source.
51 Shanley, *Doubt* I, 5.
52 Shanley, *Doubt* II, 14.

NOTES

53 Shanley, *Doubt* IV, 17.
54 See https://www.americanwx.com/bb/topic/707-nycs-first-and-last-freeze-dates/, accessed March 4, 2024. Pinpointing a night with strong wind—the sort that would cause a tree to fall in the garden and ultimately trip poor Sister Veronica, as referenced by Sister Aloysius on the phone to the groundskeeper in scene V (Shanley, *Doubt*, 25)—proves less clear. The best contender within the dates that make sense with the other pieces of evidence seems to be the evening of Monday, November 16; winds reached 26.5 miles per hour at 11 p.m. according to records available online at https://weatherspark.com/h/d/24500/1964/11/16/Historical-Weather-on-Monday-November-16-1964-in-The-Bronx-New-York-United-States#Figures-WindSpeedHeatMap.
55 For example, Shanley, *Doubt* V, 28.
56 "Intolerance" appears in *Doubt* V, 29; the costume direction appears in *Doubt*, scene vi, 36.
57 See the mass calendar available in *Catholic Advocate* 13, no. 47 (November 12, 1964), https://thecatholicnewsarchive.org/, accessed March 4, 2024.
58 Shanley, *Doubt* VII, 38.
59 Shanley, *Doubt* VII, 39.
60 The celebration of the Solemnity of Our Lord Jesus Christ, King of the Universe moved to the last Sunday of the year in the new liturgical calendar promulgated by Pope Paul VI to extend the work of the conciliar liturgical reform, cf. Paul VI's *moto proprio* on the liturgical year and the new Universal Roman Calendar, *Mysterii Paschalis*, February 14, 1969, https://www.vatican.va/content/paul-vi/en/motu_proprio/documents/hf_p-vi_motu-proprio_19690214_mysterii-paschalis.html, accessed March 4, 2024. Prior to 1969, the liturgical calendar placed the feast of Christ the King on the last Sunday in the month of October after its introduction by Pius XI in 1925, cf. the Encyclical of Pope Pius XI on the Feast of Christ the King, *Quas Primas*, December 11, 1925, https://www.vatican.va/content/pius-xi/en/encyclicals/documents/hf_p-xi_enc_11121925_quas-primas.html, accessed March 4, 2024.
61 Shanley, *Doubt* V, 30.
62 The weather becomes a symbolic driver in Shanley's film adaption. But it is still possible to square the events of the play with the historical weather data. The strongest winds recorded in the Bronx in November 1964 happened during the evening of Wednesday, November 25, as recorded at https://weatherspark.com/h/d/24500/1964/11/25/Historical-Weather-on-Wednesday-November-25-1964-in-The-Bronx-New-York-United-States#Figures-WindSpeedhttps://weatherspark.com/h/d/24500/1964/11/25/Historical-Weather-on-Wednesday-November-25-1964-in-The-Bronx-New-York-United-States#Figures-WindSpeed. This would require setting scene V on the morning of Thanksgiving and affect how the delivery of Sister Aloysius's line about protecting the bushes from the frost—"When it comes, it's too late"—would need to be delivered. She might play it with irony (because the frost had already happened) or so that it is taken to imply an overcorrection to horticultural incompetence (either on her own part for missing the frost or, as implied, that of the groundskeeper). All of which is to say that the freeze may not have been noticeable; Sister James does wonder, "Have we had a frost?" (Shanley, *Doubt* IV, 17).
63 Contrary to some popular misunderstandings, the Catholic dogma of the immaculate conception refers to the conception of *Mary* without original sin in the womb of her mother, traditionally called Saint Anne thanks to the aforementioned Gospel of James. The day set aside for reflection on the conception of Jesus would be the

Feast of the Annunciation, traditionally celebrated nine months before Christmas on March 25.
64 For a fuller history of the council, see John W. O'Malley, *What Happened at Vatican II?* (Belknap, 2008).
65 Like Shanley's movie version, the Roundabout revival did not include a second set of white and blue vestments but instead returned Flynn to the green and gold robes of the opening sermon for his gossip monologue. The film version of this sequence, interestingly, clashes all green vestments on Philip Seymore Hoffman with white and gold altar linens set up for an *ad orientem* celebration. Its extensive close-ups on Sisters Aloysius and James, but also the white altar boys who contrast with Donald Muller, clearly visible in the first scene, make sure toward whom the audience should presume Flynn is preaching.
66 Shanley, "Preface," in *Doubt*, ix.
67 Shanley, "Preface," in *Doubt*, ix.
68 See Richard W. Conklin, "Biographical Essay," https://hesburgh.nd.edu/, accessed April 12, 2025.
69 TD 1, 12.
70 Shanley, "Preface," in *Doubt*, viii.
71 My grounds for this claim are Augustinian. God creates and proclaims creation to be good. The problem of evil remains a problem *within the world*. I do not aim to offer an Augustinian theodicy but rather to suggest that the tradition following Augustine places the problem of evil within the Doctrine of Creation. Reason would be able to discern evil from good in the world without God revealing Godself, but God consistently reveals Godself to be good (cf. Thomas Aquinas in *ST* I.Q6). For Augustine, this tells us something about God and raises the stakes on the ontological status of evil as a privation of goodness: "For you evil does not exist at all, and not only for you but for your created universe, because there is nothing outside it which could break in and destroy the order which you have imposed upon it" (*Confessions*, xiii.19, Chadwick, 125). Augustinians throughout the tradition follow this point; Karl Barth, for example, places his reflections on Nothingness—*das Nichtige*—within the Doctrine of Creation. For Christian thought, evil does not reveal itself *or* God. Evil functions as a counter-revelation, as in the cross and the crucified peoples of the world, showing that which God opposes.
72 Shanley, *Doubt* IV, 24.
73 Shanley, *Doubt* IV, 20.
74 Shanley, *Doubt* IX, 57.
75 Shanley, *Doubt* IX, 58.
76 The stepping metaphor is instructive considering Augustine. No accidental change in physical distance by means of the step away from God determines a substantial change in metaphysical distance from the unchanging God, whom Augustine identifies to be "more inward than my most inward part and higher than the highest element within me" (*Confessions*, III.vi.11, Chadwick, 43). The realization that God can be "closer to me than I am to myself" (*interior intimo meo*) appears in the *Confessions* Book 3 context of Augustine's twinned discussions of theatre and rhetorical form and content. For this phrase as a hermeneutic key to Augustine's anthropology in the context of religious ethics, see Charles T. Mathewes, "Augustinian Anthropology: Interior intimo meo," *Journal of Religious Ethics* 27, no. 2 (1999): 195–221. Jean-Luc Marion, *In the Self's Place: The Approach of Saint Augustine* (Stanford University Press, 2012), too, finds

NOTES

this formulation to be the "principle that guides every itinerary toward oneself and toward God (for these is but one): 'Interior intimo meo, superior summo meo'" (260).
77 *Sacrosanctum Concilium* 7, https://www.vatican.va/archive/hist_councils/ii_vatican_council/documents/vat-ii_const_19631204_sacrosanctum-concilium_en.html.
78 *Gaudium et Spes* 1.

IN-ONE: ON BLASPHEMY

1 Johnson, *She Who Is*, 4.
2 Johnson, *She Who Is*, 4.
3 Johnson, *She Who Is*, 5.
4 Geoffrey Knapp, *Shakespeare's Tribe: Church, Nation, and Theater in Renaissance England* (University of Chicago Press, 2002) describes that elusive community of "theatre people."
5 Shanley's full dedication reads, "This play is dedicated to the many orders of Catholic nuns who have devoted their lives to serving others in hospitals, schools and retirement homes. Though they have been much maligned and ridiculed, who among us has been so generous?"
6 See Carol M. Cusack, *Invented Religions: Imagination, Fiction, Faith* (Routledge, 2010). Pastafarianism, a recognized religious nonprofit organization in the United States, points to measurable, correlational data in the world that could be used to justify belief in the Flying Spaghetti Monster. Official Pastafarian materials deny anything beyond the *appearance* of parody in their religious beliefs. Further, the website explicitly welcomes believers and atheists alike and argues, "This is NOT an atheists club" by distinguishing between opposition to religion per se and opposition to "crazy nonsense done in the name of religion." See https://www.spaghettimonster.org/about/, accessed September 13, 2021.
7 See www.flyingspaghetti.org.
8 Joseph P. Laycock, *Speak of the Devil: How the Satanic Temple Is Changing the Way We Talk About Religion* (Oxford University Press, 2017).
9 See Marcella Althaus-Reid, *Indecent Theology: Theological Perversions in Sex, Gender and Politics* (Routledge, 2000).
10 The number explains how "Hasa Diga Ebowai" translates literally into English as "fuck you, God."
11 See Max Perry Mueller, "A Cringe-worthy Depiction of Africa," *Harvard Divinity Bulletin* (Summer/Autumn 2012), https://bulletin.hds.harvard.edu/a-cringe-worthy-depiction-of-africa/, accessed January 18, 2024. For similar discussion of the shows problems in both religious knowledge and racist tropes, see Jared Farmer, "Why *The Book of Mormon* (the Musical) Is Awesomely Lame," *Religion Dispatches*, June 13, 2011, https://religiondispatches.org/why-ithe-book-of-mormoni-the-musical-is-awesomely-lame/, accessed January 18, 2024.
12 See Michael Paulson, "As Broadway Returns, Shows Rethink and Restage Depictions of Race," *New York Times*, October 23, 2021, https://www.nytimes.com/2021/10/23/theater/broadway-race-depictions.html. Similar micro-changes and cuts were made to *Hamilton* and *The Lion King*, but *The Book of Mormon* and its depiction of Africa received well-publicized criticism from Black actors while closed for the COVID-19 pandemic.
13 David Sterling Brown, *Shakespeare's White Others* (Cambridge University Press, 2023), 8. Brown goes on to propose a definition of whiteness as "a violent, incestuous,

interdependent power system; within this system, it is essential that white females birth, nurture, and celebrate the while males who own, oppress, and 'protect' them" (12).

14 For a theological engagement with Saartjie Baartman's story and the invention of race in a spectacle of the body through the pseudoscientific gaze, see M. Shawn Copeland, *Enfleshing Freedom* (Fortress, 2010), 9–12. For a theological interpretation of *Venus*, see Bouchard, *Theater and Integrity*, 200–206.

CHAPTER 5: ANGELS AND AMERICA AND APOCALYPSE

1 For a phenomenological reflection on this distinction between actuality and possibility, see Hart, *Kingdoms of God*, especially 141: "For a Christian the self-revelation of God in Jesus Christ cannot be a matter of eidetic possibility but must be claimed as an actuality. An actuality can overflow horizons; a possibility cannot saturate anything, and the most that a modification of the Kantian understanding, even one as robust as Marion's, can yield is revelation as an eidetic possibility."
2 See the first section of the theological triptych on theological aesthetics, *The Glory of the Lord*.
3 Advances in philosophy and quantum mechanics and science fiction all remind us that every world has its own time. Humans experience the world as a world through, with, and in time (cf. Heidegger). Carlo Rovelli explores the paradoxes of time at quantum scales in *The Order of Time* (Penguin, 2017); it makes little sense to ask "how long" it takes for an electron to travel a subatomic microdistance or the nonpassage of time for a photon traveling at the literal speed of light from the sun to burn my unprotected skin on the beach. We measure time from *our* world, but our world is not the only world. From *Star Trek*'s "stardate" system for a captain's log to the proper use of *world* for a non-Earth planetary system in *Star Wars* or *Dune* or *The Expanse*, worlds are always multiple. This is extremely important for the crossed horizons that link the "world of the play" on stage to the worlds of the lighting and sound designers in the back of the house, the audience, or the street outside.
4 See, among many texts, Warren Hoffman, *The Great White Way: Race and the Broadway Musical* (Rutgers, 2014).
5 Carpenter, *Nothing Gained Is Eternal*, 175.
6 The sentiment appears in multiple places in von Balthasar, most directly in *A Resume of My Thought* and TL 1, 17. This question is the theme of the second volume of *Theo-Logic*.
7 For a more thorough investigation of von Balthasar and the singularity of theatrical performance, see my article "Theodramatic Themes and Showtime in Nassim Soleimanpour's *White Rabbit Red Rabbit*," Religions 11, no. 10 (2020): 499, https://doi.org/10.3390/rel11100499.
8 God "has already taken the drama of existence which plays on the world stage and inserted it into his quite different 'play' which, nonetheless, he wishes to play on our stage. It is a case of the play within the play; our play 'plays' in his play" (TD 1, 20).
9 TD 5, 131ff.
10 TD 4, 19.
11 Von Balthasar also proposes a theological solution in the "certain veiling of his sight of the Father" of the Son's God-consciousness "right from the Incarnation" (TD 5, 125). "For the sake of obedience, [the Son] has renounced his divine foreknowledge

NOTES

and given it into the Father's keeping" (TD 5, 127). In dialogue with the visions of Adrienne von Speyr, von Balthasar develops his theory that "the Son's divine power and glory is *'laid up'* with the Father" in a way that not only secures the sacrificial and kenotic obedience of Son to the Father but also inextricably links the abyssal distance of Godforsakeness as a mode of kenotic relationality within God's triune life (TD 5, 257). See especially TD 5, 257–265.

12 TD 1, 18.
13 "The *good* which God does to us can only be experienced at the *truth* if we share in *performing* it (Jn 7:17; *:31f), we must 'do the truth in love' (*aletheuein en agape* [Eph 4:15]) not only in order to perceive the truth of the good but, equally, in order to embody it increasingly in the world" (TD 1, 20).
14 TD 4, 17.
15 "For Balthasar, there is a certain dynamic thread that links together truth with decision or action and that therefore links truth and freedom. [...] To be confronted with truth in time is not only to be confronted with a judgment of the intellect; it is also to be confronted with something that must be decided about: 'What you do not seize now is a lost opportunity'" (Carpenter, *Nothing Gained Is Eternal*, 125).
16 TD 5, 127.
17 TD 4, 92.
18 TD 4, 86.
19 Kushner, *Millennium Approaches (Angels in America)* (Theatre Communications Group, 2003), "Playwright's Notes," 11.
20 Kushner, *Millennium Approaches*, III.7, 125.
21 Kushner, *Millennium Approaches*, I.3, 24.
22 See Thomas A. Tweed, *Crossing and Dwelling: A Theory of Religion* (Harvard University Press, 2008).
23 Kushner, *Millennium Approaches*, I.5, 32.
24 See David Savran, "Ambivalence, Utopia, and a Queer Sort of Materialism: How 'Angels in America' Reconstructs the Nation," *Theatre Journal* 47, no. 2 (May 1995): 207–227. Savran ends his essay by arguing, "If *Angels in America* queers historical materialism (at least as Benjamin understand it), it does so by exposing the process by which the political (which ostensibly drives history) intersects with the personal and the sexual (which ostensibly are no more than footnotes to history. [...] More decisively than any other recent cultural text, *Angels* queers the America of Joseph Smith—and Ronald Reagan—by placing this oppressed class at the very center of American history, by showing it to be not just the depository of a special kind of knowledge, but by recognizing the central role that it has had in the construction of a national subject, polity, literature, and theatre" (227).
25 Walter Benjamin, "Theses on the Philosophy of History," in *Illuminations* ed. Hannah Arendt, trans. Harry Zohn (Schocken, 1969), 257–258.
26 Savan, "Ambivalence, Utopia, and a Queer Sort of Materialism," 211.
27 Kushner, *Millennium Approaches*, III.5, 118.
28 Kushner, *Millennium Approaches*, I.4, 27.
29 Walter Benjamin, "The Work of Art in the Age of Mechanical Reproduction," in *Illuminations*, ed. Hannah Arendt, trans. Harry Zohn (Schocken, 1969), 220.
30 Benjamin, "Work of Art," 221.
31 Benjamin places cinema in the context of a wider industry, but the ways in which cameras create the cult of celebrity ring continually true in the age of social media

influencers: "The film responds to the shriveling of the aura of with an artificial build-up of the 'personality' outside the studio. The cult of the movie star, fostered by the money of the film industry, preserves not the unique aura of the person but the 'spell of the personality,' the phony spell of a commodity" (Benjamin, "Work of Art," 231).

32 Benjamin, "Work of Art," 233.
33 Benjamin commented extensively on the theatre of Bertolt Brecht, whose work demands the work of judgment on the part of its audience. Many of Benjamin's worries about film in "The Work of Art" relate politically to film's capacity to pacify its audience: "The public is an examiner, but an absent-minded one" (241). Brecht's theatre sought the opposite in its rousing of a political consciousness through effects of strangeness. Most often, these effects function as presenting and making *known* the labor of theatre-making and its material conditions.
34 Benjamin, "Work of Art," 237.
35 Kushner, *Millennium Approaches*, I.2, 17ff.
36 *Millennium Approaches* opened at the Walter Kerr Theatre in April 1993 (where I saw both *Hadestown* and *Doubt*); *Cats* played the Winter Garden Theatre from 1982 to 2000.
37 This makes *Angels in America* well suited for film adaptation, as in the HBO version starring Meryl Streep and Al Pacino, but it also makes reading the script somewhat difficult for students. The intercutting effect works powerfully on stage, but the page lacks the spatial differentiation between lines and bodies.
38 Kushner, *Millennium Approaches*, I.7, 38.
39 Kushner, *Millennium Approaches*, I.7, 40.
40 Harper's argument implies what von Balthasar says about the self-identification of Jesus of Nazareth as one and the same as his heavenly Father: "Unless we say that Jesus of Nazareth is a deranged idiot or that he never uttered these words, we must admit that we are in the presence of an impenetrable mystery, which is none other than the mystery of the Trinity" (TD5, 492).
41 Kushner, *Millennium Approaches*, I.7, 40. Though I can find no evidence that Kushner imagined that Harper, a Mormon, would have read the Catholic Trappist Thomas Merton, there are deep resonances between this line of *Millennium Approaches* and Merton's reflections on his experience of a similar revelation about *all* people at the corner of Fourth and Walnut in Louisville: "Then it was as if I suddenly saw the secret beauty of their hearts, the depths of their hearts where neither sin nor desire nor self-knowledge can reach, the core of their reality, the person that each one is in God's eyes. If only they could all see themselves as they really *are*. [. . .] At the center of our being is a point of nothingness which is untouched by sin and by illusion, a point of pure truth . . . I have no program for this seeing. It is only given. But the gate of heaven is everywhere" (Thomas Merton, *Conjectures of a Guilty Bystander* [Doubleday, 1968], 158).
42 See TD 4.
43 Jonathan Larson, *Rent* (Applause, 2008). The uttered "amen" does not exist in the printed script nor in some recorded productions, but the line can be heard on the original cast recording of "Life Support."
44 TD 5, 492–493.
45 As in the "Apotheosis of Washington" fresco that adorns the Capitol dome or the Lincoln Memorial's iteration of a Greco-Roman temple.

NOTES

46 TD 5, 137.
47 Lin-Manuel Miranda and Jeremy McCarter, *Hamilton: The Revolution* (Little Brown, 2012), 53.
48 Miranda and McCarter, *Hamilton*, 254.
49 Larry D. Bouchard, "Religion and the Limits of Metatheatre in *Our Town* and *Sunday in the Park with George*," *Religions* 11, no. 2 (2020): 94.
50 Miranda and McCarter, *Hamilton*, 281.
51 TD 5, 32.
52 Benjamin's point about the close-up returns. The gasp may well have provoked so much conversation due to the mediation of the camera.

CHAPTER 6: STAGING SACRAMENTAL SPECTACLES

1 See Ricoeur, *Interpretation Theory*.
2 See Evan Henerson, "'The Word of Your Body' Is Reborn in Deaf West's *Spring Awakening*," *Playbill*, September 8, 2014, https://playbill.com/article/the-word-of-your-body-is-reborn-in-deaf-wests-spring-awakening-com-329874, accessed February 22, 2025. I follow the standardized practice of discussing Deafness (with a capital D) as a linguistic minority and culture. When I use "deaf" (lowercase d), I mean to signal a "nonhearing person."
3 Duncan Sheik and Steven Sater, *Spring Awakening* (Theatre Communications Group, 2007), 12.
4 Frank Wedekind, *Frühlings Erwachen*, in *Werke*, ed. Erhard Weindl (Artemis and Winkler Verlag, 1994), 473–548.
5 Theatre creates a unique opportunity to visualize interiority by doubling characters, as in Brian Friel's *Philadelphia, Here I Come!* and its difference between Public Gar and Private Gar. Key to Deaf West's model of inclusivity is how the Deafness operates on stage as public self-presentation *in addition* to the presentation of the play.
6 "According to Livingston (1997), deaf students should be taught in the same way as hearing students, and to accomplish this both ASL and English need to coexist in the classroom" (Marc Marschark et al., eds., *Bilingualism and Bilingual Deaf Education* [Oxford University Press, 2014], 7). "The assumption that transfer could occur between a sign language and a written/spoken language was called into question because the conditions in Cummins's interdependency hypothesis—shared foundational proficiencies [the two iceberg model, shared proficiencies under the water level, but manifest in two different languages]—could not be fulfilled. At the same time, however, various studies have indicated that sign language proficiency correlates with reading proficiency (e.g., Hermans, Knoors, Ormel, & Verhoeven, 2008; Prinz & Strong, 1998), Strong and Prinz, 1997), suggesting transfer even if Cummins's framework does not apply. Such findings notwithstanding, there are indications that spoken language proficiency correlates more highly than sign language with reading proficiency in bilingual deaf children (Niederberger, 2008) and that transfer between sign and written language may only occur after a certain threshold proficiency in sign language has been reached (Hermans, Ormel & Knoors, 2010; see also Holzinger & Fellinger)" (Knoors et al., *Bilingualism and Bilingual Deaf Education*, 11).
7 Alison Kafer, *Feminist, Queer, Crip* (Indiana University Press, 2013).
8 Sheik and Sater, *Spring Awakening*, 56ff.

9 MELCHIOR: O glaub mir, es gibt keine *Liebe*! – Alles Eigenutz, alles Egoismus! – Ich liebe dich so wenig, wie du mich liebst. –
   WENDLA: – – Nicht! – – – – – – – –Nicht, Melchior! – –
   MELCHIOR: – – – Wendla!
   WENDLA: O Melchior! – – – – – – – – nicht – nicht – – (Wedekind, *Werke*, 507, emphasis original).
10 Sheik and Sater, *Spring Awakening*, 81–82..
11 The problematic of von Balthasar's use of gendered and sexualized language remains a significant topic of debate in Balthasarian scholarship in no small part due to how symbols of gendered identity map onto his theology of kenosis and his understanding of trinitarian relations. An elegant summary of Balthasarian problems appears throughout Kilby, *Balthasar*. Jennifer Newsome Martin uncovers an origin story for von Balthasar's gendered symbols in his reliance on and development of Russian Sophiologies, especially Sergei Bulgakov's notion of *Urkenosis*. Jennifer Newsome Martin, "The 'Whence' and the 'Whither' of Balthasar's Gendered Theology: Rehabilitating Kenosis for Feminist Theology," *Modern Theology* 31, no. 2 (April 2015): 211–234, argues that taking stock of this wider genealogical context necessarily "softens certain lines of feminist critique" (213, see also 231–234). Many critics charge that von Balthasar's reliance on nuptial imagery and sexual metaphor in his theological analogies undermines the entirety of his theological project. See Tina Beattie's critiques in *New Catholic Feminism: Theology and Theory* (Routledge, 2006). On the theme of sexual consent in von Balthasar, see Elizabeth T. Vasko, "The Difference Gender Makes: Nuptiality, Analogy, and the Limits of Appropriating Hans Urs von Balthasar's Theology in the Context of Sexual Violence," *Journal of Religion* 94 (2014): 504–528. Von Balthasar's decision to link "passivity" with the symbolic feminine anchors many of the objections to his theology. Masculine and feminine become symbols of active-giving and passive-receiving, as if to receive is always to be acted on. For Linn Marie Tonstad, the negative implications for the understanding of gender and sexuality are "symptomatic: the fundamental problem is not merely that Balthasar uses terms with gendered connotations but that contrasts between activity and passivity should not be applied to the immanent trinity" (Linn Marie Tonstad, *God and Difference: The Trinity, Sexuality, and the Transformation of Finitude* [Routledge, 2016], 29). The passivity problem is also symptomatic of his mistaken theatrical theory. Kilby rightly asks, "Is Balthasar himself, in his very construal of the whole of everything as a drama, not taking the role of theater critic—and perhaps also a theorist of drama—rather than an actor *within* the drama?" (Kilby, *Balthasar*, 65). Where von Balthasar seems to narrate the form of the drama of salvation history from beyond like a theological novelist, I argue throughout this book that theatrical theologians should self-consciously recognize the necessary context that comes from sitting in the house as an active co-participant in the audience.
12 The Catechism of the Catholic Church (CCC 2856) cites St. Cyril of Jerusalem's argument that *amen* means *so be it*.
13 "Christians know above all else that the Church's *sacraments* directly communicate heavenly reality to them by brining to them the heavenly Lord, who comes to earth. [...] First and foremost Holy Mass is a union between heaven and earth" (TD 5, 134).
14 Implied, here, is a reference to the number "The Word of Your Body" from Act I.
15 Even if Exodus 19:19 is read to mean that God answered Moses's speech with thunder, there remains some perception of a call-and-response conversation.

NOTES

16 Hans Urs von Balthasar, *The Glory of the Lord*, 2nd ed. (Ignatius, 1992).
17 See Canon XI of the seventh session of the Council of Trent (Denzinger 1611).
18 I am grateful to Christina M. Gschwandtner for helping me to formulate this point about the centrality of religious context. On interpreting ritual, see her *Reading Religious Ritual with Ricoeur: Between Fragility and Hope* (Roman and Littlefield, 2021).
19 See Austen, *How to Do Things with Words*.
20 See Mason, *The Performative Ground of Religion and Theatre*.
21 The movement to ecumenism was also on von Balthasar's radar as he made the transition from writing his theological aesthetics to theological dramatic theory.
22 Catholic theology makes a further distinction between the seven sacraments instituted by the Christ, and that mediate grace regardless of the moral or ecclesial worthiness of the sacramental minister, and the many religious objects and ritual actions instituted by the church that Catholic theology understands as "sacramentals" to prepare the faithful to receive the grace of the sacraments. See CCC 1677.
23 Kevin Hart, *Poetry and Revelation: For a Phenomenology of Religious Poetry* (Bloomsbury Academic, 2017), xii.
24 I see a direct parallel between von Balthasar's understanding of the theatrical triad of author-actor-director in TD 1 and his trinitarian formulae in the theological volumes of *Theo-Drama*, but how closely the theatrical analogy tracks or determines his theology remains an open question. If there is an overdetermined analogy, I contend that his theology drives his understanding of theatre rather than the reverse.
25 Cf. TD 3, 220–228. "Between the divine and the created natures there is an essential abyss. It cannot be circumvented. The fact that the person of Jesus Christ bridges this abyss without harm to his unity should render us speechless in the presence of the mystery of his person" (TD 3, 220). This irreducible gulf will be unified by the incarnate God-human. "Now the question arises: How can such a union [between divine and human in Christology] be possible, given the 'abyss' between two different realities that have nothing in common? This can be made credible to some extent in the aspect of being (which is more abstract), but in the aspect of consciousness it becomes acutely difficult. [. . .] Jesus experiences his human consciousness entirely in terms of mission" (TD 3, 223–224). The principle by which von Balthasar finds credibility in Jesus as the concrete analogy of being is the dramatic transition from role to mission prepared from dramatic resources in TD 1. "We can even say that, in the cry of derelicition on the Cross, Jesus reveals how God is forsaken by sinners. [. . .] He is the revelation of man as he ought to be, as he is and he is once more to become (through Christ's action on man's behalf). However, this latter aspect takes place *concomitantly*: Jesus does not live in order to exhibit himself as the highest example of the human specifies but solely to fulfill the Father's will" (TD 3, 225, emphasis original).
26 See Copeland, *Enfleshing Freedom*, on the incarnation as enfleshing a "dynamic realization of personhood," 92.
27 On "permeable membranes" and performance, see Dox, *Reckoning with the Spirit*, 60.
28 Ghost lights traditionally illuminate the stage during times when it is not in use. See "Ghost Light" in James Fisher, *Historical Dictionary of American Theatre: Beginnings* (Rowman and Littlefield, 2015).
29 Blanchot, *The Space of Literature*, 21

30 TD 5, 269, quoting von Speyr.
31 Balthasar, *Theodramatik* V, 243.
32 Theologically, von Balthasar seems to be addressing a "full loneliness" for God the Father and for God the Son as a way to more deeply understand the mystery of the cross. My point, here, is to emphasize how theatre helpfully forestalls the language of loneliness migrating into the symbol of God as if God's triunity were an image of affective loneliness, an experience of lack. God does not need the world and so God would not experience loneliness as something missing from the mystery of God's eternal triune life.
33 The point is properly banal, though often forgotten. Nobody is materially the same as another body. Categorizations such as gender operate like interpretive genres. See Mary Gerhart, *Genre Choices, Gender Questions* (University of Oklahoma Press, 1993). In theologies inflected through sacraments, only the body of Christ can be found identically, really, and fully if mysteriously in the materially distinct bodies of any fragment of the eucharistic sacrament. All humans may indeed share in *one* body: that is, the Christ's. In baptism, St. Paul suggests that generic markers that separate bodies no longer hold once one has put on the Christ like a new costume and role; see, for example, Galatians 3:27–28: "For all you who were baptized into Christ have clothed yourselves with Christ. There is neither Jew nor Greek; there is neither slave nor free person, there is not male and female; for you are all one in Christ Jesus."
34 TD 5, 521.
35 Denzinger 806. It appears with a discussion of the injunction from Jesus (here called *Veritas*, "the Truth") in Matthew 5:45: "You must be perfect as your heavenly Father is perfect."
36 Difference in von Balthasar is constitutive of analogy. Analogies require difference in order to function; it is dissimilarity that grounds analogy in the first place. I do not mean to endorse a position of radical alterity as if analogies prove or expand from difference because individuation constitutes being. Rather, I hold a fundamentally relational ontology wherein interrelation (something that requires differentiation) remains prior to individuation. Analogies make sense by illustrating and foregrounding similarities that persist *despite* irreducible difference. An approach to "irreducible difference" can be found throughout D. C. Schindler, *Hans Urs von Balthasar and the Dramatic Structure of Truth* (Fordham, 2004) in the context of a description of consciousness (e.g., 36).

CHAPTER 7: VARIATIONS ON A THEME

1 *Gaudium et Spes* 1, 4.
2 "The eternal Son of God, in his utter transcendence, chose to love each of us with a human heart. His human emotions became the sacrament of that infinite and endless love. His heart, then, is not merely a symbol for some disembodied spiritual truth. In gazing upon the Lord's heart, we contemplate a physical reality, his human flesh, which enables him to possess genuine human emotions and feelings, like ourselves, albeit fully transformed by his divine love" (Francis, *Dilexit Nos*, 60).
3 TD 2, 151.
4 See the two "apologias" to "my theological colleagues" and "men of letters" that open *Theo-Drama* (TD 1, 9).
5 My phrasing here means to recall the language of the Catholic liturgy. My thanks to Callie Tabor for pointing this out.

NOTES

6 I allude, here, to the agreed rules of the Actors Equity Association, the union for live theatrical actors in the United States. So-called Equity rules are often invoked by amateur and semiprofessional theatre companies as a baseline for workplace safety and professional conduct.
7 See von Balthasar's distinction between theological aesthetics and aesthetic theology (GL 1, 37).
8 See James Henry Harris, *Beyond the Tyranny of the Text: Preaching in Front of the Bible to Create a New World* (Fortress, 2019).
9 The phrase "scene of composition" belongs to Larry D. Bouchard.
10 Such work often produces great theological insight. For an exemplary case, see Brent Little, *Acts of Faith and Imagination: Theological Patterns in Catholic Fiction* (Catholic University of America Press, 2023).
11 Dorothee Solle, *Suffering* (Fortress, 1975), 75.
12 Solle, *Suffering*, 74.
13 See Claire Maria Chambers, *Performance Studies and Negative Epistemology: Performance Apophatics* (Palgrave Macmillan, 2017).
14 Many of the plays and moments I planned to discuss could not fit. Further, I realized throughout writing that another book would be required to include more detailed reflections on William Shakespeare, Eugene O'Neill, Stephen Sondheim, August Wilson, and Tennessee Williams. *God on Broadway* lays methodological foundations for that future work.

ACKNOWLEDGMENTS: CURTAIN CALL

1 See Victor Turner, *The Forest of Symbols: Aspects of Ndembu Ritual* (Cornell University Press, 1970) and *Dramas, Fields, and Metaphors: Symbolic Action in Human Society* (Cornell University Press, 1974).

Index

Note: References following "n" refer to notes.

A
absolute mortality, 135
Acting Jewish: Negotiating Identity on the American Stage and Screen (Bial), 91
An Act of God show, 15–17
Actors Equity Association, 216n6
aesthetic theology, 61
    God and Beauty in, 58–59
    von Balthasar's warnings about, 58, 80
Albee, Edward, 24
Alighieri, Dante, 10
allegories, 106, 108
Amazing Grace show, 15
American Sign Language (ASL), 152, 153
American Theatre-Industrial Complex, 23
American vaudeville theatre, 1
analogy of being (*analogia entis*), 162, 214n25
Anderson, Misty, 83
and word, ideas of, 12
angels
    American fascination with, 127
    Hamilton show, 143–45
    in *Millennium Approaches* show, 136–39
    in *Perestroika* show, 135, 141
    in *RENT* show, 140–42
    revealing God's time, 128–29
Angels in America show, 7, 128, 134–36, 138, 211n37
Angelus Novus painting (Klee), 136
anti-theatrical bias, 25, 35
apocalyptic/apocalypse, 127, 130
    and eternity, 147
    imagery, 132–33
    revelations, 129, 139
    visionary prophets, 136
    vision in *RENT* show, 142–43
    visions in *Millennium Approaches* show, 136
    Y2K, 136
apophatic theology, 171, 174
Aronson-Lehavi, Sharon, 13
Artaud, Antonin, 51, 63, 77, 199n31
    "The Theater and the Plague" essay, 77–81
    "theatre of cruelty" theory, 63, 77, 81
art, concept of, 200n4
ASL. *See* American Sign Language
attention to spectacle
    and active participation, 54
    cost of, 53–54
    in creative sense, 50–51
    diversion of audience, 54–55
    passive attention of sleep, 54
    as route to prayer, 51–52, 55
    spectacle of human condition, 52–53
Auerbach, Erich, 31–32
Augustine of Hippo, 29, 167, 207n71
    Auerbach's views about rhetorical effect, 31–32
    concerns about actors' passions, 31
    Confessions, 30, 31, 169–70, 207n76
    criticism about Roman performances, 30–31
    influence in Broadway spectacles, 169
    Sermon 272, 33
    trinitarian theological speculation, 35
"aura" 137

INDEX

Austin, J. L., 198n24
autos sacramentales, 8

B
Baartman, Saartjie, 209n14
Barker, Benjamin, 39–40
Barth, Karl, 41
"Beethoven Paradigm," 5
Being and Time (Heidegger), 130
Benjamin, Walter, 136, 210n31, 211n33
    "aura" 137
    "chain of events," 139
    Jetztzeit, 138
    "Theses on the Philosophy of History," 136–37
    "The Work of Art in the Age of Mechanical Reproduction," 137–38
Berkshire Theatre Group in Pittsfield, 75. See also *Godspell* musical
Berlin, Irving, 19–20, 21
Beyond Broadway: The Pleasure and Promise of Musical Theatre Across America (Wolf), 13
Bial, Henry, 7, 91, 93
Black Mass, 121
Blanchot, Maurice, 163
blasphemy, 118
    accusation on *Doubt, A Parable*, 119
    The Book of Mormon show, 7, 15, 16, 118, 119, 122–25
    as disclosures of God, 122
    nonbeliever's blasphemy, 120
    Park's *Venus* show, 125
    and Satanists/Satanism, 120–21
Bloody Bloody Andrew Jackson musical, 143
Bock, Jerry, 90
The Book of Mormon show, 7, 15, 16, 28, 119
    plot of, 124–25
    religious ideology, 122–23
    symbol of God on Broadway, 118
    works inspired by, 123
Bouchard, Larry D., 8, 191n4
Brecht, Bertolt, 79, 86, 211n33
Broadway magic, 25
Broadway theatre, 1, 14–17. See also dangerous memory of God; safe memories of God
    anthems for show business, 19

audiences, 3–4
    and commercial theology, 23–25, 36–37
    LuPone paradigm, 5–7
    preshow announcements, 4–5
    shows about ideas about God, 7
    standards and practices, 14
    theatrical culture, 1–2
    traits of, 174–75
    Wolf's argument, 13–14
Brown, David Sterling, 124–25
Buffalo Bill, 21
Bulgakov, Sergei, 213n13
"burden of liveness," 64
Burr, Aaron, 144
Butler, Octavia E., 113

C
Cabaret show, 27, 195n15
Calvin, John, 10
Carlson, Marvin, 92
Carpenter, Anne M., 46, 86, 131, 203n5
Catholic theology, 214n22
Cats show, 58, 59, 61
cave of illusions, 26–27
caves of intellectual imprisonment, 27
Christian(s)/Christianity, 131. See also theological/theology
    aesthetics, 61
    care for others, 42
    commercial interests, 35
    discipleship, 9
    disclose Godself, 43
    Edenic fall, 114
    incarnation, belief in, 168
    performance anxiety, 33–34
    revelation of God, 40, 41
    sacraments of, 47–48
    triune God, belief in, 41, 197n17
City of God (Augustine of Hippo), 29, 30, 32–33
civil theology, 30
"Climb Ev'ry Mountain," 59–60
Cobb, Keith Hamilton, 23
Cohn, Roy, 138
collaborative creation, 74–75
collective effervescence, 48, 54, 81
The Color Purple show, 15, 16
commercial theology of Broadway, 23–25

INDEX

Confessions (Augustine of Hippo), 30, 31, 169–70, 207n76
congregaudience, 102, 109, 204n30
contextual theology, 204n29
Craigo-Snell, Shannon, 8
creatio continua (continuous creation), 34
The Crucible show (Miller), 15, 16
Cunningham, Elder, 119, 123

D
danger and taboo theory, 5–6
dangerous memory of God. *See also* safe memories of God
   "burden of liveness," 64
   in Christian theology, 61–62
   cross-cultural complexity between religion and theatre, 63
   Godspell musical, 75–82
   Mitchell's *Hadestown* album, 69–73
   role of drama, 63–64
   theatrical performance, 64–65
   and theatrical revival, 73–75
   Williams's *The Glass Menagerie*, 65–69
da Vinci, Leonardo, 140
Deaf community, 153
Deaf West Theatre Company, 151. *See also Spring Awakening* musical revival
   doubling of characters, 152–54, 156, 162
   model aims for theatrical credibility, 152
   spirituality of sexual complexity, 162
   surplus meaning, 153
Dear Evan Hansen show, 15, 170–71
   apophatic theology in, 171, 174
   "The Connor Project," 172
   epistolary narrative self, 171–72
   titular pronoun works, 173–74
   "You are not alone," 172–73, 174
   "You Will Be Found," 172
Death of a Salesman (Miller), 52–53
Dei Verbum, 41
devised theatre, 74, 202n64
Disgraced show, 7
Divine Comedy (Dante), 10
documentary theatre, 108
The Door McAllen community in Texas, 85

Doubt, A Parable (film), 109
Doubt, A Parable play, 89, 102, 155, 205n43. *See also Fiddler on the Roof* music; Sister Aloysius (character)
   benedictions, 113–17
   charge of blasphemy, 119
   connection between spirit and institution, 104
   evidence from interviews and research, 108
   focusing sexual abuse crisis in Roman Catholic Church, 107–8
   historical moment, importance of, 109–10
   parables, importance of, 108
   preaching on theme of gossip, 110–11
   questions on credibility of institutions and leaders, 103, 104–5
   religious dimension, 112
   "second act", 98, 99, 124, 129
   Shanley's theatrical response, 101–2
Douglas, Mary, 5
Dox, Donalee, 86, 95–96
Durkheim, Émile, 48, 54, 81

E
Edwards, Nicholas, 76
Eine Kindertragodie (Wedekind), 153
eisegetical process, 84
Eliot, T. S., 58, 200n3
Ellacuría, Ignacio, 42
eternity, 146–47

F
faithfulness, 100
fakery, 25, 96, 193n25
The Family Reunion (play), 200n3
Fiddler on the Roof (film), 93
Fiddler on the Roof show, 15, 16, 85–86, 89, 116, 117. *See also Doubt, A Parable* play
   audience response, 99–100
   Bial's analysis of traditions, 91–92
   characterization, 92–93
   Lipshitz's statement, 90–91
   meanings and memories of, 93–94
   negotiations of tradition, 94–95
   porous nostalgia, 94, 95–97
   public and private prayers, 97–99

INDEX

Fiddler on the Roof show (*continued*)
   religious tradition of, 97
   theological suggestions, 100–101
   "Tradition" song, 90, 98–100
fire, spectacle of, 49–50
flash photography, 5
Flores, Nichole M., 53
forgiveness, 42, 145, 155
fragment-work, 15
Francis (Pope), 134
Francis of Assisi, 10
Friel, Brian, 153
Frühlings Erwachen show (Wedekind), 152

G
Gadamer, Hans-Georg, 94
   hermeneutic theory, 197n22
   "history of influence" (*Wirkungsgeschichte*), 94
   "transformation into structure," 203n10
Galileo show, 7
Gem of the Ocean show, 7
The Glass Menagerie show (Williams), 65–69
God–Broadway relationship, 14–17
   ideas of *and* word, 12
   ideas of *on* word, 12–13, 14
God, concept of, 12. *See also* revelation of God; show business of God; symbol of God functions; temporality of God
   love for world, 132, 200n8
   performances on world stage, 14
   in theology, 84, 128
Godspell musical, 1, 11, 28, 75–76, 202n72
   Artaud's "The Theater and the Plague" essay, 77–79
   controversies over, 79–81
   reception history, 168
   references and equipment requirements, 76–77
   song about proclaiming God's life, 81–82
   surplus meaning, 151–52
Goehr, Lydia, 5
Goizueta, Roberto S., 8
The Greatest Showman (film), 55

Great White Way. *See* Broadway theatre
Guys and Dolls show, 7
Gypsy show (2009), 5

H
Hadestown show (Mitchell), 69–73
Hamilton, Alexander, 143–45
Hamilton, Eliza, 128, 145–49
Hamilton show (Miranda), 15, 85, 128, 143. *See also Millennium Approaches* show (Kushner); *RENT* show
   Angelica's "It's Quiet Uptown" narration, 145
   Eliza's gasp, 145–49
   theatrical temporal dilemma, 143–44
Hammerstein, Oscar II, 19, 24, 59, 61, 130
Hand to God show, 15, 16
Hansberry, Lorraine, 24
Harris, James Henry, 136, 171
   theology of revelation, 139
Hart, Trevor, 9
"Hasa Diga Eebowai" song, 123–24
Hedwig and the Angry Inch show, 7
Heidegger, Martin, 130
hermeneutic(s), 197n22
   of interpretation theory, 43–44
   of tradition, 94
   violence, 203n9
Hesburgh, Theodore M., 113
Holy Spirit, 35, 104, 120, 142
Holy Trinity, 9, 12, 35, 41, 164, 168
The Humans show, 15

I
"I Believe" song, 151, 155–57, 159
ideological process, 84
Immaculate Conception, 111, 206n63
incarnation, 129, 133
   dramatic performance of, 163
   logic of, 162
infinite God, 118, 132
Institutes of Christian Religion (Calvin), 10
instrumentalization of theatre, 84, 113
   modes of, 87
   negative risks minimization, 87–88
   order of authorial operations, 84–85
   religionists, problem for, 85–86
   theatre lovers, problem for, 85

theological task of resourcing, 86–87
interestedness, 44
Into the Woods (Sondheim), 175

J
Javerbaum, David, 17
JB show, 7
Jennings, Willie James, 15
Jesus Christ Superstar show, 7, 11
Jewison, Norman, 93
John Chrysostom, 28
Johnson, Elizabeth, 118–19
Jones, Bill T., 152

K
Kafer, Alison, 154
Kern, Jerome, 130
Klee, Paul, 136
Kushner, Tony, 43, 128, 134. *See also* *Millennium Approaches* show (Kushner)
   about absolute mortality, 135
   dramatic role of spectacular revelations, 136
   Perestroika play, 135, 141

L
La Bohème (Puccini), 140
The Laramie Project, 108, 135
Larson, Jonathan, 140
The Last Days of Judas Iscariot play, 7
Last Supper (da Vinci), 140
Latin Rite Catholics, 33
Lawrence, John, 144
Laycock, Joseph, 120
Les Misérables show, 15, 16, 175, 199n38
Levenson, Steven, 170
Leyerle, Blake, 28
liberated temporality, 141
liberation theology, 8
Lipshitz, Yair, 90
liveness
   as analogy for dangerous memory of God, 69
   burden of, 64
   performance connection to, 64
   and theatrical revival, 73
Loman, Willy, 199n36

Lopez, Robert, 123
LuPone paradigm, 5–7, 54, 63

M
Manifestation, 36, 97, 129
   of god, 47
   of theatre, 27
Marion, Jean-Luc, 46–47, 207n76, 209n1
Marriage of Figaro song (Mozart), 145
Mason, David V., 6, 63, 96
McCarraher, Eugene, 24
"Memory" song (Webber), 57–58
Menken, Alan, 59
Merman, Ethel, 23
Merrily We Roll Along song, 23
Merton, Thomas, 211n41
metanoia, 173
Metz, Johann Baptist, 61–62, 66, 68
Millennium Approaches show (Kushner), 128, 134, 139, 211n41. *See also* *Hamilton* show (Miranda); *RENT* show
   absolute mortality, 135
   Benjamin's theory of history, 136–38
   focus on theology's problem of expectations, 135
   revelations in, 135
Miller, Arthur, 16, 24, 52
Milli, Flo, 90
Miranda, Lin-Manuel, 143, 145, 147, 148
Mitchell, Anaïs, 69
Molina, Alfred, 93
Mormonism, 122–23
Muñoz, José Esteban, 64
Murphy, Connor, 173

N
natural theology, 129–30
Nazi symbolism, 195n15
neologism, 12
nostalgia, 84. *See also* porous nostalgia

O
Oakley, Annie, 21, 22
Obama, Barack, 143
Oklahoma! song, 1, 19, 24, 154
O'Neill, Eugene, 24
"On the Spectacles" (Tertullian), 27

221

INDEX

On the Trinity (*De Trinitate*) (Augustine), 35
on word, ideas of, 12–13, 14
The Order of Time (Rovelli), 209n3

P
Parable of the Sower (Butler), 113
parables, 106, 108, 113. *See also Doubt, A Parable* play
   emotions and moral choices, 106–7
   hyper-particular dramaturgy, 112
   inarticulacy of theological-symbolic meaning, 106, 107
   meta-parable, 114–15
   Mitchell's *Hadestown* show, 69–73, 70, 71
   parabolic storytelling, 105–6
   porous nostalgia, 112
   self-interpretation, senses of, 105
"paradigm of performance (Dox)," 86
Parks, Suzan-Lori, 125
Pasek, Benj, 170
Pastafarianism, 120, 208n6
Paul, Justin, 170
peoplehood, 100
Perestroika play (Kushner), 135, 141
The Performance of Religion (Sautter), 6
performative(s), 48, 121, 198n24
   belonging, 96
   ground, 63
   utterance, 198n24
The Performative Ground of Religion and Theatre (Mason), 96
Performing Religion on the Secular Stage (Aronson-Lehavi), 13
Phaedrus myth, 26, 194n10
Phantom of the Opera show, 3
Phelan, Peggy, 64
Philadelphia, Here I Come! (Friel), 153–54
Plato
   cave of illusions, 26
   challenge to artistic choice, 26
   problems with imitation, 25, 26
   theory of forms, 25–26
poesis, 63, 97, 192n10, 204n19
porous nostalgia, 112, 130
   in *Fiddler on the Roof*, 93, 94–97, 100
   parables creating conditions for, 107

Prince, Hal, 196n1
Prolegomena (von Balthasar), 8, 11, 167
Puccini, Giacomo, 140
pyrotechnics, 49

Q
Quash, Ben, 8
Quinto, Zachary, 67

R
Razing the Bastions (von Balthasar), 102
Reagan, Ronald, 136, 210n24
RENT show, 128, 139–40. *See also Hamilton* show (Miranda); *Millennium Approaches* show (Kushner)
   apocalyptic visions, 142–43
   Christian interpretations of Angel character, 140–42
revelation of God, 40, 55, 114, 127, 129–30, 139, 175
   Harper's theology of, 139
   hermeneutics of interpretation theory, 43–44
   humans experiencing, 41
   phenomenological attention to theatrical phenomena, 46–47
   practical and social dimension, 42
   and sacraments, 47–48
   Schleiermacher's theories, 44–45
   show business as analogy for, 23, 24–25
   through spectacle, 42–43
   and spectacles of fire, 49–50
   and theatrical phenomenon, 48–49
   theological interpretations, 43
   tiem of, 127–29
   von Balthasar's argument, 45–46
revelations of evil, 114–15
revivifying, 73
Ricoeur, Paul, 44, 151, 171
Robbins, Jerome, 95
Robeson, Paul, 130
Rodgers, Richard, 19, 24, 59, 61
Roundabout Theatre Company, 103
Rovelli, Carlo, 209n3

S
sacramental/sacraments, 47–48, 151, 166
   imagination, 159

INDEX

theatrical, 157–61, 166
Sacrosanctum Concilium, 54, 116
safe memories of God, 57, 83, 84. *See also* dangerous memory of God on Broadway
  Cats show, 58, 59, 61
  direct citations, 59–60
  and memories of beauty, 58–59
  Sister Act show, 59, 60–61
  Sound of Music show, 59, 61
  Webber's "Memory" song, 57–58
Saint Augustine. *See* Augustine of Hippo
Satanists/Satanism, 120–21
Sautter, Cia, 6
Savan, David, 137
Schleiermacher, Friedrich, 44–45
Schneider, Rebecca, 12
Schuyler, Angelica, 128, 143–45
Shakespeare's White Others (Brown), 124–25
Shakespeare, William, 74
Shanley, Sean Patrick, 101–3, 114. *See also Doubt, A Parable* play
  memories of Catholic schooling, 108
  parabolic approach, 107
  questioning credibility of institutions, 103
  work of Catholic theology, 105
Sheik, Duncan, 152
Shoham, Hizky, 96–97
Show Boat show, 130
show business of God, 19–20, 34, 55
  attracting customers, 21–22
  commercialization, 35–37
  performances, 22–23
  theatre role in, 20–21
Sister Act show, 59, 60–61
Sister Aloysius (character), 102, 108, 109, 117. *See also Doubt, A Parable* play
  accusations of Father Flynn, 110–11, 115
  discussion of script's costume choices, 110
  doubtful benediction, 115–17
  steps away from God, 115, 119
Slater, Glenn, 59
Slater, Steven, 152
Smith, Joseph, 210n24

Sondheim, Stephen, 23, 39, 175
"The Song of Purple Summer," 163
Sontag, Susan, 27, 77
Soo, Phillipa, 148–49
The Sound of Music show, 7, 59, 61
spectacles, 9, 131, 133, 169. *See also* attention to spectacle
  Augustine's criticism, 29–33, 35
  concentrating culture of, 35
  of fire, 49–50
  of human condition, 52–53
  inviting vice and distraction, 28
  Plato's criticism, 25–26
  problem of, 46–47
  of symbol of God, 40
  Tertullian's criticism, 27–28, 35
  theatrical phenomenon as, 48–49
Spring Awakening musical revival (Slater and Sheik)
  actors of, 154
  analogia entis, 162
  ASL performance, 152, 153, 154
  bodies of actors in presence of audiences, 162
  changes in 2006 musical version, 155–56
  communion, 165
  creed, 156
  gestures of stylized choreography, 154
  "I Believe" song, 151, 155, 156, 157
  plot of, 153
  silence of audience, 163, 164–65
  "The Song of Purple Summer," 163
  theatrical sacraments, 157–61, 166
  theology and sexuality, 156–57
  theory of analogy, 165
stage business, 22
Stanislavsky, Konstantin, 105
States, Bert O., 52
Stewart, Zachary, 17
St. John XXIII (Pope), 102, 112
Stroker, Ali, 154
"supertime" (von Balthasar's notion), 67, 146, 147
surplus meaning, 151–52, 153, 155, 164–65
Sweeney Todd musical (Sondheim), 39–40
symbol of God functions, 118
  Johnson's concept of, 118–19

223

INDEX

symbol of God functions (*continued*)
    nonbeliever's blasphemy, 120
    questions about theological efficacy, 121
    transcendental reference to God, 120
symbol of God on Broadway, 4, 7, 13–16, 37, 40, 89, 106, 114
    in *Doubt, A Parable* play, 109
    in *Fiddler on the Roof* show, 101
    tools and attitudes to interpret, 17

T
"technocratic paradigm," 134
Tectonic Theatre Project, 108
temporality of God, 130
    action of tradition, 131
    confrontation between fate and freedom (von Balthasar), 133
    question of divine temporality, 133–34
temporality, theatrical, 131–32
    existence within performance history, 127, 129
Tertullian, 27
    coining *trinitas*, 35
    objections to Roman shows, 27–28
"The Theater and the Plague" essay (Artaud), 77–78
The Theater and Its Double essay collection (Artaud), 77, 199n31
Theatre and History (Schneider), 12
"theatre of cruelty" theory, 63, 77
theatrical drama, 63, 148
    dramatic resources, 7
    role in enlivens history, 147
    self-interpretation, senses of, 105
theatrical theology, 7, 11
    theodramatic analogy and, 8–9
    writings and story of St. Paul, 9–10
theatron, 9–10, 20
theatrum mundi theme, 19, 167, 193n26
Theo-Drama (von Balthasar), 7, 12, 147, 193n29
    about hermeneutics in, 44
    Prolegomena to, 8, 11, 167
    question of divine temporality, 133–34
    review of history of European theatre, 8
    surplus meaning of worldly performance, 164–65
    The Action, 134

theodramatic(s), 11, 127, 132, 148, 155, 162–163, 168
    theatrical theology and, 8–9
Theodramatik, 11, 12, 193n28, 197n15, 215n31 See *Theo-Drama* (von Balthasar)
theological/theology, 2–3, 6, 30, 59, 61–62, 84, 132, 169, 171
    addressing problem of spectacles, 46
    commercial, 23–25, 36–37
    dramatic theory, 11, 64–65, 114
    engagement and reflection, 24
    extra-ecclesial, 122
    as interestedness, 44
    as hermeneutics, interpretation of God, 43–46
    about mass culture, 57
    struggling with meanings, 106
    Vander Lugt and Hart's argument on, 8–9
theophany, 47, 50, 157
"There's No Business Like Show Business" song, 19–20, 21
"Theses on the Philosophy of History" (Benjamin), 136–37
traditions of Broadway, 89, 131
    Doubt, A Parable play, 89, 101–17
    ecclesial, 89–90
    Fiddler on the Roof song, 89, 90–101
    hermeneutics of, 94
"transform into structure," 203n10
trinitas, 35

U
Urkenosis, 213n13

V
Vander Lugt, Wesley, 9
Vanhoozer, Kevin, 8
van Hove, Ivo, 16
Venus play (Parks), 125
von Balthasar, Hans Urs, 2, 7, 35, 59, 127, 155, 165, 167–68. See also *Theo-Drama* (von Balthasar)
    adding mariological dimensions to ecclesiology, 205n42
    addressing "full loneliness," 215n32

about analogy of being, 162
christological trinitarian pattern, 104
constitutive of analogy, 215n36
critique of inevitable progress, 134
about dangerous memory of God, 62
discussions of drama, 133, 191n1
"dramatic resources" for systematic theology, 7–8
about dramatic theology, 101
about eternity, 146–47
gendered language, 213n11
about human experience of alienation, 102
identification of meta-parable, 114–15
insistent on God's loneliness, 164
about Judaism, 135
Prolegomena, 8, 11, 167
Razing the Bastions, 102
The Action, 134
theological dramatic theory, 64–65
about theological interpretation of God, 45–46
about theology as hermeneutics, 44
understanding Christ, 141–42

W
Walatka, Todd, 8
Washington, George, 144, 148
Webber, Andrew Lloyd, 57–58
Wedekind, Frank, 152, 153
Weil, Simone, 51
Wilder, Thornton, 24
Wild West show, 21, 22
Williams, Tennessee, 24, 65–66
Wilson, August, 23
Wolf, Stacy, 13, 93
Wooden O, 62
"The Work of Art in the Age of Mechanical Reproduction" (Benjamin), 137

Z
Ziegfeld, Florenz, 130

www.ingramcontent.com/pod-product-compliance
Ingram Content Group UK Ltd.
Pitfield, Milton Keynes, MK11 3LW, UK
UKHW042144140126
466995UK00005B/289